Praise for *Sky Watch*

"Anyone who loves horses will love *Sky Watch*, which tells the tale of one of the greatest American Saddlebreds of all time. Through meticulous research and beautiful, down-to-earth prose, Hudelson places me ringside, letting me relive the drama and excitement of the 1980s show horse world exactly as it happened. All horse enthusiasts have their own Sky Watch, a horse who inspires them for decades to come. This book is their story, too."—William Marple, American Saddlebred historian

"In the tradition of great human-animal nonfiction such as Helen Macdonald's *H is for Hawk* and Lyanda Lynn Haupt's *Mozart's Starling*, Hudelson seamlessly weaves her own story alongside the historical account of a famed animal, sharing both the coming-of-age tale of Sky Watch, a champion Saddlebred horse, and Hudelson's own coming-of-age story as a horsewoman and a mother. A beautiful showing of love and passion between humans and non-humans, Hudelson embraces generations of both horses and horse-women. . . . A must-read for anyone who loves animals, but especially for those who are wading into parenthood or who have wanted to pursue a passion that feels like a fantasy."—E.B. Bartels, author of *Good Grief: On Loving Pets, Here and Hereafter*

"Emma Hudelson's *Sky Watch* is a beautiful braided memoir deftly weaving the dramatic story of Saddlebred horses' biggest star, Sky Watch; the history of horsemanship; and Hudelson's own life with horses. I loved being immersed in this world and was moved by the obsession, adventure, and the biggest delight of all—how we care for one another, allowing what's brightest about those we love, both human and animal, to shine."—Tessa Fontaine, author of *The Electric Woman: A Memoir in Death-Defying Acts*

"A love story with many deep levels—from the research into champion Sky Watch and the breed of the American Saddlebred, to the love of young girls and horses, to the love of mothers and daughters—Emma Hudelson's book is well-researched, thoughtful, engaging, smart, and lively. As a horse lover and a reader, I adored it. If you love animals, don't miss this gem."—Annie Hartnett, author of *Rabbit Cake* and *Unlikely Animals*

"What is more compelling than a remarkable horse making history? In this engaging first-person narrative, Emma Hudelson weaves the rise of show horse Sky Watch with a portrait of the magical, mysterious world of American Saddlebred horses and her own powerful story with the breed. Beautiful horses and masterful showmanship abound, but ultimately this is a story about love—in all its forms."—Kristen Iversen, author of *Full Body Burden: Growing Up in the Nuclear Shadow of Rocky Flats* and *Molly Brown: Unraveling the Myth*

"The story of Sky Watch is irresistible. It has drama, surprise, intrigue, and a cast of compelling figures, none more remarkable than our four-legged hero. Hudelson is the perfect guide—knowledgeable and determined, adept with narrative and deeply engaged. Her passion for both Sky Watch and the American Saddlebred is clear, contagious, and propulsive. I loved learning about this horse and this world."—Chris Bachelder, coauthor of *Dayswork* and author of *The Throwback Special*

"Hudelson tells a big, complex story about our families, our culture, and a powerful and intelligent species-other, and she tells it beautifully: the weave of personal memoir and historical reconstruction, the multidimensional characterization of both humans and horses, the skillful pacing and searching and empathic narrative persona all make *Sky Watch* wonderfully informative and a pleasure to read."—Andrew Levy, author of *Huck Finn's America: Mark Twain and the Era That Shaped His Masterpiece* and *Brain Wider Than the Sky: A Migraine Diary*

"In *Sky Watch*, Hudelson takes us to a place outside of time as she paints a portrait of a legendary horse, a story filled with setbacks, victories, and a great rivalry, and then deftly weaves in her own love of the Saddlebred and its beauty, a love passed down from her mother and offered now to the next generation."—Susan Neville, author of *The Town of Whispering Dolls* and *Sailing the Inland Sea: On Writing, Literature, and Land*

"*Sky Watch* shares not only the story of this champion Saddlebred and his great career in the ring, but also one woman's contemplation of the role horses have played and will continue to play as she enters a new phase in her life. From the first page to the final one, *Sky Watch* is an utterly fascinating look at a classic equine world that will leave you rushing to learn more about Saddle-breds while also running to hug your favorite equine friend."—Jennifer Kelly, author of *The Foxes of Belair: Gallant Fox, Omaha, and the Quest for the Triple Crown*

"In Hudelson's personal, lyrical, and ultimately brave explanation of how a great horse like Sky Watch became a magical and redemptive force in her own life, she makes him that for the rest of us as well. This book will be enjoyed and cherished by anyone whose life has been changed for the better through their love of a horse."—Mary Perdue, author of *Landaluce: The Story of Seattle Slew's First Champion*

Sky Watch

Sky Watch

Chasing an American Saddlebred Story

EMMA HUDELSON

UNIVERSITY PRESS OF KENTUCKY

Copyright © 2024 by The University Press of Kentucky

Scholarly publisher for the Commonwealth,
serving Bellarmine University, Berea College, Centre
College of Kentucky, Eastern Kentucky University,
The Filson Historical Society, Georgetown College,
Kentucky Historical Society, Kentucky State University,
Morehead State University, Murray State University,
Northern Kentucky University, Spalding University,
Transylvania University, University of Kentucky,
University of Louisville, University of Pikeville, and
Western Kentucky University.
All rights reserved.

Editorial and Sales Offices: The University Press of Kentucky
663 South Limestone Street, Lexington, Kentucky 40508-4008
www.kentuckypress.com

Cataloging-in-Publication data is available from the Library of Congress.

ISBN 978-0-8131-9910-8 (hardcover)
ISBN 978-0-8131-9911-5 (pdf)
ISBN 978-0-8131-9912-2 (epub)

This book is printed on acid-free paper meeting
the requirements of the American National Standard
for Permanence in Paper for Printed Library Materials.

∞

Manufactured in the United States of America.

Member of the Association
of University Presses

For the American Saddlebred.
For Fern.

When we reach the horse that is perfect in symmetry, style, quality, and disposition, he will be a saddle horse and no questions will be asked.
—John H. Wallace, *The Horse of America in His Derivation, History, and Development*

Contents

A Note on Abbreviations

An American Saddlebred that has gained enough points at shows licensed by the United States Equestrian Federation earns the abbreviation CH (Champion) as a permanent prefix to his or her name. Points are earned by winning or taking second place in championship, stake, and qualifying classes in which at least four or six horses have competed, depending on the class. The abbreviations WGC (World's Grand Champion), WCC (World's Champion of Champions), WC (World's Champion), RWGC (Reserve World's Grand Champion), RWCC (Reserve World's Champion of Champions), and RWC (Reserve World's Champion) indicate titles won at the World's Championship Horse Show rather than permanent name changes but are generally appended to horses' names in print. The same is true for the abbreviation BHF, which indicates a mare who is in the Broodmare Hall of Fame. For readability, the text of this book uses all horses' original names without prefix or titles. However, it's important to honor those horses who have earned their Champion status or a World's Championship Horse Show title or are recognized in the Broodmare Hall of Fame. See the following list of horses that appear in this book, with their full names and appended titles:

CH Beloved Belinda (WCC, WC, RWCC, RWC)
CH Callaway's Mr. Republican (WCC, WC, RWGC, RWC)
CH Candle Dance (RWC, BHF)
Captain Denmark (WC, RWGC, RWC)
CH CCV Casey's Final Countdown (WGC, RWC)
Darlene's Dilly (WC)
CH Finisterre's Gift of Love (WGC, WC, RWGC, RWC)
Flight Time (WC)
CH French Commander (RWGC, RWC)
CH French Wine (RWGC, RWC)
CH Giddy-Up-Go (WC, RWGC, RWC)
CH Imperator (WGC, WCC, WC, RWGC, RWCC, RWC)
CH Lady Carrigan (WGC, WC)
Mirror Mirror (WC, RWCC)
CH Memories' Citation (WGC, WC, RWGC)
CH My-My (WGC, WC)
CH Naranda (WCC, WC, RWC)
CH New York, New York (WC, RWCC)
CH Nutorious (WCC, WC, RWCC, RWC)
CH Our Golden Duchess (WGC, WCC, WC, RWGC)
CH The Phoenix SM (WCC, WC, RWGC, RWC)
Rare Treasure (RWC)
CH Rhythm 'n Jazz (WC, RWC)
The Rose (WC)
CH Sky Watch (WGC, WCC, WC)
Spider Red (WC)
CH Stutz Bearcat (WCC, WC, RWCC, RWC)
CH The Talk of the Town (RWC)
CH Valley Venture (WC, RWCC, RWC)
CH Well Chosen (WCC, WC, RWC)
CH Wing Commander (WGC, WC, RWGC)
CH Yorktown (WGC, WC)

Author's Note

This book became possible through the generosity and kindness of the Saddlebred community. Thank you to all who shared photos, videos, news clippings, and memories of this great horse. Because so much of Saddlebred history unfolds in barn aisles, home arenas, and warm-up rings, places where cameras and reporters can't be found, many of the scenes in this book are constructed as composites of what little sits in the archives, memories shared with me, and my own experiences with the American Saddlebred. I've done my best to indicate where the exact record ends and my own compiling begins. Please note that I've created some composite scenes and supporting characters. Storytelling is part of Saddlebred culture, so my intention is to bring these unrecorded places, people, and events into the written record as best I can. These stories deserve to be told. The Saddlebred magic belongs to us all.

Prologue

The bugle sounded, and the white gates opened. Not heaven, but as close as an American Saddlebred can get: the Five-Gaited World's Grand Championship at the Kentucky State Fair. In 1982, the winner would take home $7,500, but in a sport filled with horses the price of houses, prize money didn't matter. Reputations stood at stake. A new contender named Sky Watch, just five years old, challenged Imperator, the two-time world's champion.

Sky Watch burst into Freedom Hall and trotted down the rail. On his back sat twenty-nine-year-old Mitchell Clark, the only one who could channel the horse's energy into fireworks instead of an atom bomb. Mitch had the arms of a basketball player and the trunk of a quarterback buttoned into his dress shirt. He wore a formal riding habit, navy, with a red tie tucked into his vest, but no suit could dress up his farm-boy face. As he rode, all focus, his mouth dropped open. The horse Mitch piloted only stood 15.2 hands high—five feet at the withers, smallish for a Saddlebred—but he moved like a Roman candle. At Sky Watch's entry, the audience of fifteen thousand thundered. The stallion snorted, already so full of himself he could burst. He'd never heard so much noise—until Imperator hit the gate. When the reigning champ entered the ring, the decibels crested. Fans packed the stands shoulder to shoulder, but the crowd grew so loud, no one could hear the person next to him.

Some horses jump. Some race. Others rope. American Saddlebreds show. They always have. In nineteenth-century America, farmers would gather in the town square on court days, the antecedent to today's county fair but minus the Ferris wheel and deep-fried Twinkies. Socializing turned to bragging—whose saddle horse could rack faster, whose buggy horse could trot bigger—and bragging turned into a spontaneous horse show. At the turn of the twentieth century, every county, state, and national fair included show rings full of American Saddle Horses, as Saddlebreds were known then. By

1

the 1950s, newspapers covered Saddlebred shows the way they cover baseball games today.

On top of Sky Watch, Mitch Clark had to feel all that history pulsing through the reins, as well as his own personal history. Young as he was, he rode in the shadow of his grandfather Garland Bradshaw, the man hailed as one of the greatest Saddlebred trainers in history. That year, in 1982, both Sky Watch and Mitch had a lot to prove. The stallion high-stepped past the first judge as if a victory pass were inevitable. But it wasn't. No winner would be announced for another thirty-five minutes. Sky Watch's first real Louisville test had only just begun.

Sky Watch has been dead for decades, but in my mind, he's still trotting high. All too often, I sit at my laptop and ignore the ding of incoming emails to watch his old show videos. Just thinking about sitting on a horse that special sends sparks through my spine. No one is offering me a ride on a stallion contending for a World's Championship title, but it sure looks like fun. More than fun. Transformative. Enlightening. Equine nirvana. Saddlebred heaven.

With a mother who had trotted more victory passes than she could count and a preference for cleaning stalls over cleaning my room, I started riding Saddlebreds before I could write my name. As they grow up and leave home for college or work, most young riders leave horses behind. For me, it was different. Binge drinking and boys robbed me of horses, as did the depression that settled over me like a never-ending hangover.

At twenty-three, I quit drinking, started meditating, and found a good therapist. Ten years later, I was married, working as a writer and teacher, and hadn't had a too-depressed-to-get-out-of-bed day in years. That stability made horses possible again. My new mare—Mine! My own!—was pretty and sweet, but she moved nothing like Sky Watch. Even though she was training with one of the best trainers in the state, we would never compete with the six-figure horses on the green shavings in Louisville.

Realistically, though, only a few people have the type of bank account to back half-million-dollar horses, and the industry can't rely on wealth alone. In fact, the Saddlebred industry is in decline. The breeding numbers have been taking a nosedive for decades. At most shows, the grandstands are empty, with only the horse show moms there to cheer on the winners. For a breed designed to entertain a crowd, what does it mean when the crowd disappears?

Women like me—upper-middle class, midcareer—might be the future for Saddlebreds. More than 80 percent of Saddlebred competitors are female, and only a few are the trust-fund type. The rest of us tell our trainers to find a budget horse—something young and untried or something that needs remedial training. We buy secondhand suits. We spend our vacation funds on horse shows instead of beach resorts. The women who take private jets to the showgrounds might buy horses that beat ours more often than not, but we're here to give those rich girls a run for their money. We might get out-bought, but we try not to get outridden.

No one could outride Mitch. At home, my laptop balanced on my knees, I watched Mitch and Sky Watch trot through the gate. My favorite part. With a trot like that, no one could guess when Sky Watch started training; he was so wild he had to be herded into his stall like a cow. No one knew that he battled injury every year, the force of his own body just as much his adversary as Imperator was. On my screen, he muscled into the ring to try and take the title from the two-time world's champion. Win or lose, the spectacle of Sky Watch drew my attention like a magnet.

Something else needed my attention, though. I hit pause, tabbing away from the video and returning to the open tab for my doctor's website. In just a few clicks, the appointment confirmation appeared. A prepregnancy health check. At thirty-four, I was a little old to be what horse breeders would call a "maiden mare": one who hadn't yet given birth.

Once I told my doctor about my pregnancy plans, would she tell me to stop riding? Better not to think about it—better to click back to the video, rewind, and press play. The organ music swelled. The announcer's microphone crackled. "And now Sky Watch, presented by Mitchell Clark . . ." The crowd's responding roar drowned him out. As Sky Watch blazed down the rail, my shoulders straightened and my skin tightened, my chest rising with horse-sized love.

Part I

1977–1980

1

Seeing Sky Watch

One morning, instead of asking me how I'd slept, my husband, Ben, handed me a cup of coffee and said, "I think we should have a baby."

I sat down and took a sip. I was due at the barn in an hour, but my mare could wait. She wasn't Sky Watch, who would have been stamping in his stall if another horse headed to the arena before him. Bee—listed as My Queen Bee in the American Saddlebred Registry—shared little with the legendary stallion, only a great-great-great-great-grandfather, the blood diluted to transparency. Comparing her to him was like trying to find the ancestral grape in both purple Fanta and wine. Still, she was mine.

Ben rubbed his palm over his buzzed head. He would grow his dark hair out for years, until it hit ponytail length, and then shave it all off. As an IT manager, he had to stay professional, but underneath his checked button-downs lurked Iron Maiden T-shirts. As a writer, I could get away with a lot more, which explained the tattoos blooming across my shoulders, the gauged ears, and the unstyled brown hair clipped into a mass on the back of my head. If the secondhand shops that supplied my clothes could characterize my style, they'd call it "downtown hippie cowgirl." Pencil skirt, peasant top, cowboy boots. Big wooden earrings. No makeup.

"Okay," I said, taking it in. "Okay. I'm on board, but I'm a little surprised."

For years, Ben and I had waffled about breeding. When we first got married, me twenty-seven, him thirty-three, we both were against it. So against it that Ben underwent a vasectomy. It was reversible, we told ourselves. Then, a couple of years later, with my thirties looming, my thinking softened. Maybe a kid would be fun. Most of my friends had already had one. Some were expecting their second. At that point, when I talked to Ben about kids, he said he'd be into it if I was. That's a great way to decide to pick up Thai food for dinner instead of Indian but not to bring a new life into the world.

We decided to table the discussion. For four more years. Until now, apparently.

"What brought this on?" I asked.

Ben launched into an explanation about legacy, about wanting to pass something on. I nodded along, only half listening. The other half of my brain wondered about the safety of riding pregnant. It had been just a month since I'd bought Bee, my first horse in over fifteen years. Nestling my saddle on her back and climbing on had felt like coming home. To a nonrider, horses looked like a hobby. But riding wasn't knitting or Frisbee golf. Horses enlarged my heart in ways that didn't make sense to a nonrider.

"We'll be smart about our timing," Ben said, pulling me back into the present. "There's no rush."

"I'm thirty-four," I said. "There's a little bit of a rush."

"Nah." Ben waved a hand. "You're in fantastic shape. We don't drink or smoke. We eat a lot of kale. We could wait until you turned forty, and we'd be fine."

"Let's not wait that long," I said. "What were you thinking?"

"I could get the vasectomy reversed this year. We could start trying next summer."

Next summer, I calculated. That would give me one full show season, a chance to show my new horse before the pregnancy. "I like that," I told Ben, scooting next to him on the couch so I could lean into his chest. "Let's do it."

A year and a half before that conversation, Ben had gifted me with a starter set of three riding lessons at a local Saddlebred barn.

"This is what I want for my birthday," I'd said, pointing at a website with a banner at the top: "New Rider Special! Three Lessons for $100."

Ben scratched his beard. "What happens when the three lessons are done?"

I maintained eye contact. "We'll see."

"This is going to be your new thing, isn't it?"

"Maybe." I unclipped my frizzy brown hair and held it in a low ponytail at the nape of my neck. Almost enough for a show bun. "I'm not planning on competing or anything. Yet."

Ben smiled. "Yet," he repeated.

"And it's not new. I rode horses when I was a kid. I showed in the World's Championship with my first horse, Glamour Boy. Then we bought Keeper as a colt, and he went on to be a champion. It was my life. Barn every weekend. Horse shows all summer."

"I know. You've told me. I've seen the pictures." Ben had seen me oscillate between obsessions. First, running. Then, yoga. Now, it was time for me to get back to my roots.

"Didn't you wear a bowler hat?" he asked. It was a derby, but close enough. I nodded. "And the horses are always standing like this?" Ben hiked up one leg and held the opposite arm up, elbow and wrist bent, hand at eye level.

"They're not standing." I laughed. "Those are action shots. They're trotting. Look. If you get the first three lessons and I like it, I'll take it from there," I reassured him. "I've already checked my budget. I can swing it."

"You know you'll like it." Ben's eyebrows rose.

"I know," I said. "Think of it as me making amends to myself." As a teenager, I chose drinks and drugs over high-stepping horses. Major depressive disorder followed. Or maybe it came first, and I was, as my therapist said, self-medicating. It's hard to tell. Either way, by the time I had graduated from college—a year late, thanks to my extracurricular barstool activities—I'd sworn off the booze, found a therapist, and met Ben. But it was too late. Horses had slipped out of my life. It might have been for the best. My brain needed to heal before I was ready to sit on a horse again. Riding takes a level of confidence that, for a long time, I couldn't muster.

Ben squeezed my shoulder and headed for the front door, where he tightened the laces on his running shoes. He understood. In high school, he'd been a cross-country star, but his own stint with partying left him teamless by college. Ever since, he'd been trying to make friends with running again, battling a cycle of training and injury, injury and training.

Within months of my first lesson, my mom agreed to ship me my old show suits from adolescence, which, thanks to my need to burn off anxious energy with exercise, still fit. She'd cared enough to keep them zipped into garment bags with cubes of cedar to ward off the moths. Of course she had. She'd been a horsewoman too, and every horsewoman, even when without a horse, is ready to swing into the saddle and hit the ring.

For a full show season, borrowed horses carried me into classes where we placed dead last, didn't earn a ribbon at all, or were excused from the ring for bad behavior. These were unfinished mounts or problem horses, trainer-owned or with owners who were ready to sell. My instructor at the time—all the gods love her—put more faith in me than she should have. She thought I could improve those horses' show records. I didn't. Apparently, judges don't like it when your horse leaps over puddles, stands on his hind legs in the lineup, or canters like a wildebeest.

Eventually, that instructor and I parted ways in a goodbye that felt more like a breakup than a business decision. Horses have that effect. The relationships built at the barn will run deeper than money if you let them. Still, that "New Rider Special" got me back into the ring, giving me the gift of Saddlebreds, of snugging a derby onto my head and pushing my horse into a park trot. It's a gift I'll be forever grateful for.

The ribbons, or lack thereof, didn't matter to me. I was so happy to be showing Saddlebreds again that I would have entered on a low-backed lesson horse if it meant suiting up and trotting through the in-gate. All season long, I'd marveled at how much the crowds in the stands had dwindled. In all my old show photos, people filled the bleachers and arena seats, their eyes on my horse. Now, only a handful of spectators clapped for the winner. Half stared at their phones instead of the action in front of them. The horses trotted higher than ever, but no audience cheered them on.

When my 2019 *Journal of the American Saddlebred* arrived, reporting on breeding numbers and serving as the annual "state of the breed," I quaked. In the fifteen years since my last horse show, the number of new foals registered every year had dropped by 50 percent. At this rate, the breed could fade away. What had happened? I didn't know, but by digging into the history at the American Saddlebred Museum, maybe I could learn. If making amends to myself meant showing Saddlebreds, the breed needed to stay alive.

Based at the Kentucky Horse Park in Lexington, in a building not much bigger than my house, the American Saddlebred Museum holds hundreds of years of history. When I visited, it included glass cases holding eighteenth-century bits, Civil War–era saddlebags, and turn-of-the-century horseshoes, all celebrating Saddlebreds. For twelve dollars, patrons could peruse the exhibits, admire the full-size horse-and-buggy model, swipe and click through a digital gallery of more than a century's worth of world champions, and even climb on a signature Lane Fox saddle in front of a green screen to see themselves projected on a horse making a victory pass in Freedom Hall. The museum has since been renovated, with a new history wing done in spa-worthy exposed beams, but during my trip, it looked much as it had fifteen years before, when I visited as a teenager.

In a mini theater in one corner of the museum, an informational video looped, the type done in voice-over while a montage of images and videos flash onto the screen. In it, Sky Watch trotted onto the screen in one of the high-tension moments of his career: a duel with Imperator, both horses racing down the rail in an encore performance that would determine the winner of the World's Grand Championship. As the on-screen audience roared, Sky Watch rounded a turn to pass Imperator, his eyes focused, his red coat nearly black with sweat, his long front legs reaching up and out, up and out. Flying doesn't describe it. Sky Watch soared.

Chills shot through me. Tears prickled my eyes. What heart. Sky Watch seemed to know he was competing for the equivalent of a crown, and he gave his all, churning his legs high even as his nostrils flared with effort. *This is it*, I thought. *This is why Saddlebreds matter.* Such spectacle, such performance. My right hand found its way to my chest, as if someone had started the national anthem. I couldn't wait to get home and hop on a Saddlebred. Maybe even—and here, my breath caught—buy one. Yes. No more borrowed horses. Time to go shopping. A horse like Sky Watch might never be in my budget, but surely, I could find something to trot through the in-gate. A show horse of my own. That video footage reminded me what a privilege it was to sit on a Saddlebred and show. Seeing Sky Watch pulsed Saddlebred magic through me.

In thirty seconds, the moment ended. As the credits rolled and the closing music tinkled, instead of standing up and moving on to another part of the museum, I waited for the film to loop again. And again. By the fourth viewing, another visitor had entered the theater. Unwilling to share Sky Watch with a stranger, I tiptoed out, still lit from within.

Sky Watch is the only horse who makes everyone who's ever seen him, whether in person or, like me, just on a video, go all starry-eyed. Even jaded trainers drop their voices when they mention him. It's not just his string of wins. There are other greats with better show records. Sky Watch's grandfather, Wing Commander, won more than any other horse. In his most famous photo, from the October 1954 issue of *Life* magazine, he's standing next to a wall of his blue and championship ribbons. In the summers of 1946 through 1964, Wing shipped to a new show every weekend, earning 237 first-place ribbons. In his entire career, he only lost twice. Once he retired from showing, his breeding-shed contributions changed the Saddlebred forever. His legacy includes 367 foals and six World's Grand Championships, a show ring record only matched by another great, the mare My-My, who died of liver failure at eleven years old, her career not yet over. A tragedy. Not a pretty mare, My-My made up for her homeliness with pure athleticism. In a photo from the July 10, 1968, *Lexington Herald*, another mare, Anacacho Chapel Belle, attempts to pass My-My at the rack, so close that the two riders could bump stirrups. My-My's attention doesn't waver, her head staying arrow straight while the other mare twists and comes off her feet. My-My's a legend, worthy of the entire wing dedicated to her in the remodeled American Saddlebred Museum.

Wing was a campaigner. My-My was a freight train. Sky Watch, though, was otherworldly. For a breed whose job is to perform, he represents the epitome of performance. Even when non-horse people see footage of him, their mouths gape. "Now, that's a horse," they say. They get it. That feeling, like floating, of watching Sky Watch zip across the screen. No other horse causes the same tingle and rise. I should have known Sky Watch was the key. Understanding Sky Watch meant understanding my compulsion to ride, show, and even own an American Saddlebred—even though I hadn't taken a victory pass since the terror of Y2K turned out to be a nonevent, even though the cost of training might strain my bank account, even though a World's Championship title might never be within reach.

On my way home from the museum, I tracked down a YouTube video of the clip from Sky Watch and Imperator's duel and sent it to my mom, risking highway texting and driving to connect with the one person who might understand the horse-induced fireworks bursting in me. "Have you seen this? It's unbelievable. This is a Saddlebred!" She responded, "Wow! So cool. What a horse." I knew she'd get it. What a horse, indeed. Sky Watch was magical.

Seeing Sky Watch that day changed me in an unexplainable way. He'd always been in my orbit, because anyone who's sat astride a Saddlebred knows who he is, but he'd been more celebrity than trotting, breathing being. And oh, how he trotted! Back at home, I typed Sky Watch's name into Google and hit search. Videos, photos, Wikipedia, newspapers. Check, check, check. Give me everything. Then, in another tab, another search: "American Saddlebreds for sale." Had I known then that my jodhpurs would soon be replaced by maternity pants, maybe my search history would have looked different.

On a warm June night in 1977, Sky Watch's dam circled in her stall. Aries Golden Gift, a mare with the bright chestnut coat her name promised, wrinkled her eyelids and pawed at the straw bedding. With a groan, she low-ered her heavy self—front knees first, then hocks, and then a quarter roll to land on her side. Contractions shuddered through her body.

Three years earlier, the mare had given birth to her first, a colt. He lived through the fragile first hours of a foal's life, the tender months of nosing his mother's teats, and the years of training, when horses learn what humans expect in return for the grain, hay, and clean bedding. Then, she birthed another. A filly. That one looked special, but a hip injury prevented her from ever entering training. Either way, Aries Golden Gift had proved herself as a broodmare. Just like her dam, her grandam, and her entire damline, she understood the next steps. She knew what the pain meant, knew the larger pain to come. The sleeping colt in her belly now would be her third, and her owner, Della Large, had high expectations for him.

Della lived in high-society Chicago and got her start in Saddlebreds in the late 1940s and 1950s, when she could be found wearing a riding suit looking not all that different from the one Mitch Clark would wear in 1982 when Sky Watch first challenged Imperator, or the one I would wear twenty years later as a junior exhibitor. In one of my favorite photos of Della, she's mounted on a five-gaited horse with a blaze tapering from his upper lip to his forehead. In another, she's posed in a dark dress in a marble lobby. With a solid frame, arched eyebrows, and dark lipstick, Della looked as if she meant business, whether dressed for the show ring or wrapped in white mink for a fashion show.

Being the wife of a communications mogul meant that Della didn't need to work. She got to devote her life to what she loved most, and Della loved the American Saddlebred. Around a horse, the woman who stood like a steamship melted into a cooing girl. Her eyes grew starry. Her jawline eased. She laughed a little more easily. Even though her riding habits probably cost more than my wedding gown, she could relax in them. At the fashion shows, garden parties, and fundraiser luncheons she presided over, Della had to remain in control. Maybe riding gave her the chance to give up some power. There's only so much control a person can have on a horse. She grew up in the era of the sidesaddle, but Della had enough tomboy in her to embrace riding astride. In all the photos of Della on a horse, she's in riding pants, grinning, with one leg on either side. Naturally, the horse is always a Saddlebred.

Saddlebreds are best known for competing in the saddle seat discipline, which is different from other equestrian events. A saddle seat class isn't like a hunter class, in which each horse-rider team enters the ring alone and attempts a series of jumps, racing against the clock. It's not a race, with a dozen horses running together to the finish line. It's not like a polo match on grass, where two teams face off and hammer balls up and down a field. It's not a rodeo, where the equines navigate obstacles like barrels or work a herd of cattle. It's not dressage, with a single horse and rider performing a series of choreographed steps in a silent arena.

Saddle seat classes involve multiple horse-human teams in the show ring at once, performing the different gaits—walk, trot, canter, and, in five-gaited classes, the slow gait and rack—at the same time. The shows are divided into classes according to the different gaits and the different ages and types of horse and rider. Three-gaited. Five-gaited. Pleasure. Amateur. Open. Junior exhibitor. All the work is done to the patter of an announcer, the tinkling of an organ, and the cheers of an audience. It's a performance. Entertainment. Saddle seat shows are all about spectacle. The blue ribbon goes to the best entertainer in the ring. Every horse can trot, but not every horse's trot is worth watching. Unless it's a Saddlebred in performance training.

Horses competing in saddle seat are judged on form, brilliance, beauty, and athleticism. Prima ballerinas, but they're dancing in the dirt, en masse, so there's a touch of demolition derby about the whole thing. Unless it's an equitation class, the riding can get wild, with the riders growling, yelling, and bouncing on the horses' backs, doing whatever it takes to get the highest steps, the most power, and the tightest headset. In the most exciting classes, the horses get wild too, just short of losing control at every step. In those classes, the spectators get just as wild, shouting and clapping for their favorites. Riding Saddlebreds is challenging. Riders must maintain strong cores, light hands, and excellent balance. It's not easy to keep a storm from turning into a tornado.

While the horses perform for the crowd, the judge or judges stand in the center to rank the horses and decide whether they've earned a blue ribbon and a victory pass, a brown eighth-place ribbon, or something in between. The winning horse will be both athletic and graceful, stepping high and maintaining an elevated headset with neck arched and nose collected in. Most importantly, he'll look happy, ears up and eyes alert. Saddlebreds love the performance. Under the arena lights, surrounded by a cheering crowd, they flourish. Their whole bodies bloom.

In 1956, Della wanted a horse like that. After seeing legendary trainer Tom Moore win at Chicago's South Shore with Valley View Queen, she couldn't find her checkbook fast enough. Valley View Queen might not have been her first horse, but she was one of Della's first champions. Della already knew she loved the thrill of the show—hearing the organ and announcer, cheering for the horses, smelling the tanbark, dodging a clod of dirt as the winner trotted her victory pass. She liked Valley View Queen, liked seeing her win, and she wanted more like her. Then more. And more. Eventually, owning blue-ribbon winners wasn't enough. She wanted to breed them and unlock the magic formula that produces winners. Between the 1950s and the 1980s, dozens of broodmares passed through Della Large's hands. Not all produced their own offspring, but many did, and many of those babies went on to greatness in the show ring.

By 1977, when her mare Aries Golden Gift felt those contractions, the name Della Large meant more than the wife of a telephone tycoon. She had earned a reputation as a businesswoman in her own right, owning and breeding American Saddlebreds. Good ones, good enough to earn her a breeder's highest honor—the American Saddlebred Horse and Breeders Association Breeders Award—in 1985. When I googled "Judson Large," the search brought up pictures of his wife Della, not the tycoon himself.

Everyone who knew Della seemed to love her. Brendan Heintz, a Saddlebred historian, credits her with making a greater contribution to the breed than anyone else. He might be right. Hundreds, even thousands, of horses can be traced back to Della, whether through direct ownership or through breeding lineage. With no shortage of funds, she shipped her well-bred horses to the top trainers of her day, boosting their careers and making some a household name in the Saddlebred industry. Tom Moore. Earl Teater. Garland Bradshaw.

Della loved every one of her horses. Although she sent them to faraway farms and hired help to do the feeding, cleaning, and training, she liked being involved with her babies. Later in life, a car accident kept her housebound at her Chicago Gold Coast high-rise, but even then, she'd spend hours on the phone with people like Brendan Heintz. Or Jim Walls, the great equine artist. Or Mary-Ann Teater, now Mary-Ann Pardieck, once the wife of the late, great Saddlebred breeder Lou Teater. In Kentucky, the Saddlebred's home state, the Teaters ran the best breeding operation in the breed's history—the one that produced Sky Watch.

Even dressed in fur, Della let her horses snuggle her, the act captured in a black-and-white photo of her favorite stud, Genius Bourbon King, reaching over a fence to press his long face against her, his eyes closed tight with joy. Della's arms wrap around his head, her gaze steady on him, her smile kind. Saddlebred fans still remember her walking a favorite filly on back trails north of Chicago or promoting the breed at a formal event at the Ambassador Hotel by bringing a living, breathing, snorting Saddlebred to stand at the awning. There, the horse and Della stood at the entryway, and, to two guests' delight, the long-necked equine drank a Coke straight from the bottle they offered. In that photo, Della's caught midsentence, mouth open. She's holding her horse's lead shank loosely, apparently unworried about Coke or horse slobber staining her long white coat.

I never met Della Large, but she feels like kin, maybe because she reminds me of my grandmother Fern Denton, who was well enough off to keep me in horses and show suits for my early junior exhibitor career. We called her Dearie. She loved horses, but from a distance. Even though she never swung a leg over one, she didn't miss a single class in my mom's girlhood show career, and she'd fly out from Texas to watch my shows, sitting ringside in a linen pantsuit, clapping and whispering "Good job" every time I rode past.

Dearie was the type of woman who didn't leave the house without lipstick and hose. She didn't own jeans. If she wore pants, she donned pleated slacks. Button-up blouses, tailored skirts, and cardigans filled her closet. She kept her jewelry in a locked box. For most, dressing for the barn means wearing an old T-shirt and jeans. For Dearie, it meant dark slacks and a striped oxford shirt, with black penny loafers on her feet. Before entering her leather-seated Lincoln to drive home from a day at the stables, she'd knock the dust from her shoes, never trailing it back into the car as I always did—and still do today.

In Della and Dearie's era, Saddlebreds loomed large, as they had for over a century. The first official horse show unfolded in 1816. One hundred and one years after that, the first Five-Gaited World's Grand Championship in Louisville—the same class Mitch and Sky Watch entered in 1982. In 1917, World's Championship was a misleading title, since early twentieth-century American Saddlebreds lived almost exclusively in the United States. They've since trotted into Canada, New Zealand, and Europe, and, incredibly, they've become one of the most popular breeds in South Africa. In Della's post–World War II America, though, the American Saddlebred still represented the legacy of being the first breed developed in the United States. The horse America made. Saddlebred horse shows became weekend entertainment, as common as a baseball game—with a classy twist. Perfect for women with a penchant for competition, a love of animals, and a few extra dollars in their bank accounts.

In the second half of the twentieth century, these women popped up on the rail and in the saddle at shows all over the country. At Houston's Pin Oak Charity Horse Show, the blond Joan Robinson Hill won championships with her gray gaited mare, Beloved Belinda. My mom, who grew up showing in Texas, remembers the team with a beam and a chuckle. "No one showed grays back then!" Joan liked to ride her victory passes with the reins in one hand—a brag-worthy tradition usually only observed by men. Joan's riding career ended early, in a tragic scandal that resulted in one book and one made-for-TV movie. Her plastic surgeon husband—marriage number three for Joan—murdered her and then, a few years later, was murdered himself.

At Madison Square Garden, Saddlebreds racked in front of audiences big enough to fill that legendary arena. There, Joanne Link trotted a victory pass in the amateur three-gaited championship, her top hat pushed back to show off the curled bangs of her pageboy cut. Afterward, her tux exchanged for a white sweatshirt, she sponged the sweat from her horse's pink nose herself. No groom in sight. In the photo capturing the moment, the white-blazed Saddlebred glances sideways at the camera while Joanne's attention remains trained on her horse, her chin tilted up, her eyes looking down at his muzzle.

In Lexington, Kentucky, Saddlebreds lined up under the lights of the Red Mile. In 1961, the lineup included the sharp-eared walk-trot horse Bold Bandit and his upright rider Anne Durham, now Anne Judd, who looked especially elegant caught in the camera's flash in the winner's circle. Anne Judd, who began showing at the age of four, went on to showing, training, and judging fame, establishing equestrian programs internationally. All these women—Joan, Joanne, Anne, Della—were excellent riders, but in those days, none could have imagined themselves in the saddle for the big one, the gaited stake at Louisville.

Back then, women who owned horses of Sky Watch's caliber didn't ride them. They let their trainers, the paid professionals, handle that. At the Chicago Horse Show, Della's American Saddlebreds trotted to the winner's circle while she watched from the grandstand, clapping her gloved hands. While

Dearie didn't command the same level of wealth and status as Della, I could imagine the two of them being friends, applauding side by side for the horse who performed best, maybe even letting a curse word slip from their lips. "Tom Moore can ride the hell out of a horse, can't he?"

The state of Saddlebreds today might dismay Della and Dearie. While there are more shows than ever, no one except other exhibitors and, if those exhibitors are lucky, their family and friends cheer from the stands. At show after show, the big coliseums are empty, their rows of arena chairs left folded up. In a space that can seat thousands, maybe only fifty seats are filled. The folks who do show up make noise, thank goodness, yipping and yelling "Yeah, boy," the traditional Saddlebred call of praise. Their enthusiasm makes the audience seem larger than it is. The lack of attendance isn't because of the cost. At most shows, admission is free, but the grand old stadiums the horses trot into are empty. The American Saddlebred show horse world looks vacant, not fashionable. This future for the industry seemed improbable in the 1970s, when Della considered which stud to breed her beloved mares to next.

Saddlebred bloodlines can be dizzying, but not to Della. She studied them. She followed her trainers' and breeders' suggestions, but she knew pedigrees, too. Della's favorite stallion, Genius Bourbon King, fathered Aries Golden Gift, and Della was counting on those genes to breed true. Genius Bourbon King changed the look of Saddlebreds forever, stamping his line with a sculpted face and fine throatlatch. Della matched those movie-star looks with power, courtesy of Flight Time, the five-gaited son of the great Wing Commander. Flight Time followed in his daddy's footsteps to take a World's Championship at Louisville. In the show ring and in the breeding shed, Wing garnered more fame than any Saddlebred before him. In his twenty-nine-year life span, Wing Commander fathered more than 350 foals. He stayed busy, and he probably liked his job.

It takes eleven months for a foal to come to term, so in the year leading up to June 14, 1977, Aries Golden Gift spent her energy growing fifty-four vertebrae, twenty feet of intestines, and four hard little hooves. With one last, massive effort, she would get to see the hundred-pound product of all that invisible work. Taking deep gulps of air, the laboring mama pushed. Her eyes rolled, the equine sign of fear. Usually, a frightened horse only wants to run, but Aries Golden Gift knew she needed to stay put. She knew the next steps. The amniotic sac dropped, a bubble bulging beneath her tail. She rolled from side to chest to side again, her vast belly contracting and expanding. A sharp pain hit, and two hooves appeared, smaller than fists. Foals emerge feet first, plunging through the birth canal with their front legs positioned like a diver's arms.

With one last push, Aries Golden Gift squeezed the colt's shoulders out. The rest came quickly, a dark blob wrapped in a white sac. Easy, compared to the first birth. Mama finished the job her baby's hooves had started: she tore the sac open and licked it away from the foal's head, clearing amniotic fluid from his nostrils. Sky Watch took his first breaths. His mama nickered from deep in her chest, ears perked forward, eager to meet the newest member of the herd.

Today, broodmares can be monitored with a transmitter implant. The magnetic device, no bigger than a pinkie knuckle, is stitched into the vulva. When labor begins, the birth canal opens, and the magnets separate, activating an alert via cell phone. No birth goes unattended. Some breeders keep motion-detector cameras on their broodmares twenty-four hours a day, seven days a week.

When Sky Watch came into the world, no such tech existed. Instead, a night watchman monitored all the mares. Since mares tend to give birth overnight and the delivery process can be quick, some births occur unwitnessed, but Lou Teater wouldn't have missed Sky Watch's birth. After answering the night watchman's phone call, he would have jumped in the car and rushed down to the foaling barn, an old tobacco barn converted to stalls. With as busy as the Teaters were in 1977, it probably wasn't his first trip of the night.

Lou Teater, who managed the breeding farm that produced Sky Watch, died in 1994, but his wife, Mary-Ann, assures me he would have been present. That year, they had too many births for her to remember, so the details of Sky Watch's birth have been lost. "All I can say," Mary-Ann said, "is that he was an unremarkable colt." Weak and wobbly, like all newborns. No blaze or stockings to make him memorable. Just one white hind foot, on the left. Sky Watch didn't jump to his feet and rack around the stall, but he didn't struggle either. A nice colt, sure, but as boring as they come. Nothing to distinguish him from the dozens of other births at the Teaters' farm that year. "Since I don't remember Lou saying anything about his birth," Mary-Ann said, "it must have been unremarkable too."

The best I can do is picture how one of the finest Saddlebreds in history came into the world. If Aries Golden Gift had been in trouble, Lou would have been right there to help, but most births are "unremarkable," happening unassisted. After all, horses have been giving birth without the help of humans for thousands of years. After viewing hours of equine parturition videos, the miracle never fading, I felt ready to birth a colt myself. With the new plan to expand my family, I had good reason to watch birthing videos, no matter the species.

I imagine that, hearing his mama's call, the still-sleepy newborn tried to lift his head. Instead of lifting, it bobbled. Weak and slick as an otter, Sky Watch didn't look like a winner. He didn't even look like a horse. Half-drowned greyhound, maybe. In the womb, dams give their foals a constant dose of naturally occurring neurosteroids to keep them quiet and sleeping for their eleven-month gestation. Those darling little hooves could do a lot of damage if the baby were to start trotting in utero, so foals have to stay sleepy until they hit the straw. The birth canal's squeeze wakes them up, stimulating their own neural nets, but for a while, they look a hint hungover.

After forty-five minutes or so of head bobbing and wobbling, the future champion tried to make it to his feet. He spidered a front leg out and paused before trying the other one. With both knees bent, he rose, inch by inch, his hindquarters working to unfold. The front legs splayed, and down he slid. Mama gave him a gentle nudge with her muzzle and an encouraging nicker. If she could push a hundred-pound being out of her body, the least he could do was stand. Sky Watch tried again, each of his legs seeming to have more joints than it needed, each movement uncoordinated and off balance. When he finally straightened all four legs, he swayed like a miniature skyscraper, but he knew right where to go. Standing up for the first time is hungry work.

2

Twice a Day

A year had passed since my pilgrimage to the American Saddlebred Museum, the origin of my obsession with Sky Watch and my plan to buy a horse. At this point, pregnancy wasn't on my radar yet. As my friends gave birth and disappeared into the cocoon of early motherhood, I felt twinges of longing but ignored them. Who needed babies when there were Saddlebreds to show? Some of them were for sale—some, even, within my price range, which was only slightly above the blue book value on my Jetta. Before any serious horse searching began, I presented Ben with a PowerPoint, complete with charts and graphs analyzing the cost-benefit analysis.

"Owning a horse is more expensive than therapy," I conceded, making an understatement, "but it will do more for me than any therapy session ever could." Another understatement. At the barn, my shoulders dropped. My brow unfurrowed. Standing in a stall, cradling a hoof, and excavating the dirt and manure from its underside, the stresses of life in the twenty-first century dissipated. No tweets. No DMs. No email. Out in farmland, my cell phone barely got a signal. When there was a trip to the barn beckoning at the end of the week, the pressure of deadlines and word counts didn't seem so pressing. Since I'd started riding again, my mental health had reached a high point unseen since childhood—since the last time horses had been part of my weekly routine. A decade of therapy had helped too, but something about being around horses solidified me.

At the end of my presentation, Ben sighed. "How can I say no?"

I hugged him close. "Thank you."

For months, I lurked on Facebook groups. Saddlebreds for Sale. Saddlebreds Under $50k. Saddlebreds Under $20k. Then, finally, one I could afford: Saddlebreds Under $10k. Here, the ads looked something like these:

"Fifteen-year-old pleasure gelding for sale through no fault of his own. Owner going to college. Sound and easy keeper. Could be a great first show horse. Lots of blue ribbons still in his future! $9,000 or best offer."

"Four-year-old gelding for sale. Trainer-owned, so he's been on the back burner for a while but shows lots of promise. Green-broke to ride but has been turned out all year to make room for client horses. All reasonable offers considered!"

"Three-year-old mare, asking $6,500 but willing to negotiate. Started under saddle and shown successfully. Could go in any direction: show horse, lesson horse, or broodmare. Breeder-owned, so need to make room for more with foaling season coming up. Located in Missouri, but come try her at the All American Horse Classic in Indianapolis."

That last one sounded promising—and she was headed to my hometown. In the videos her owner posted, the mare carried her head high on a long neck. With a deep liver chestnut coat, she looked almost black. She didn't have anything like Sky Watch's motion, but nothing in my price range would. I could try her out and, if it all worked out, stick her in training. My Queen Bee. She even had a good name. I texted my mom the videos of her from the Facebook group.

"What do you think of her?" I asked my mom over the phone.

"She's cute!" she said. "I like her headset." I heard water running in the background and knew she was watering flowers as we talked. My mom was the type of gardener who clipped yellowed leaves immediately and repotted as soon as a plant became root-bound. Her home looked like a botanical garden furnished with a blend of antiques and midcentury modern pieces. One day, maybe my house would look that way. "Not much motion," she said, "but maybe that's okay."

"I could always show her for a season or two and then, once she's good and broke, lease her out as a lesson horse," I reasoned. "She's pretty, and she's in my price range. It might be fun."

"Definitely!" my mom agreed. "It's so exciting that you're back into Saddlebreds and thinking of getting one of your own."

"Isn't it?" I said. "You should get one too!"

"Wouldn't that be fun?"

"Lots of Saddlebreds for sale right now. It's the post-Louisville gold rush. Trust me, I've been looking." My mom could write a check for a horse from a Facebook group a step or two above the one I'd been poking around.

I rode My Queen Bee in the same show arena where I'd shown countless times as a kid. Her then owner, a Missouri beauty queen who raised Saddlebreds between modeling gigs, stood in the middle, her glossy brown hair impervious to the humidity that had frizzed mine. Next to her stooped her aging mentor, who came from a legendary family of trainers best known for teaching their charges elaborate tricks. He had removed his portable oxygen concentrator for the event, pulling the cannula from where it perched above a drooping mustache. A beauty queen and a circus trainer. The show horse business attracts all types.

My Queen Bee flicked her ears forward and moved off down the rail, her head high.

The trainer called to me: "Go ahead and trot her whenever you're ready, honey."

We trotted, my hips rising in and out of the saddle in time with My Queen Bee's outside front leg. With a bump of my pinkies, she raised her head, and when we hit the far turn, I worked the bottom rein with my middle fingers, asking her to flex her neck. As we headed for the straightaway, my thighs squeezed her up and into the bridle. In the near turn, more bumping, more flexing, then a push to the bit, and away we went. Lap one. My Queen Bee couldn't lift her legs much, but still, as I looked at that neck arching in front me, the long mane bouncing up with every step, a smile crept onto my face. This could be *my* horse.

All too soon, the trainer called out, "That's good. Let her walk."

With my hips deep in the saddle, we walked. I took the reins in one hand and stroked the mare's neck. Soft and warm as bread. By the end of the ride, her hide had dampened with sweat, her scent rich and thick, almost edible, the aroma better than any antidepressant.

To get a sense of her stall manners, I asked if I could put My Queen Bee away and rub her dry. The steps felt automatic, as regular as a heartbeat. *Enter the stall. Circle the horse to the left and face forward. Unbuckle the girth. Slide it out of the martingale loop. Lift the saddle from her back. Remove the bridle; slip the halter over her head. Attach the crossties dangling from the stall to the halter, tethering the horse in place in front of the electric fan so its breeze can dry the sweat from her sides. Rub her flanks with a towel, ruffling the hair against the grain and then smoothing it back down.* Through it all, My Queen Bee stood quietly, happy to be fussed over. The work calmed me. As I patted her neck, the mare side-eyed me, then widened her jaw and clamped down on one crosstie, her top lip wiggling.

"You're goofy," I told her, gazing into the pool of her eye. She let go and gazed back.

Before I left her stall, I knew she'd leave the show on a trailer headed not back to Missouri but to an Indiana barn. It's inadvisable to bring a checkbook when trying a horse for the first time. Better to wait a day or two before making an offer. Mine sat in my glove box, full of checks just waiting to be signed.

Poor Ben. He hadn't counted on marrying a horse girl, on accepting that a big chunk of my income would go to board and training, a new suit, and a new saddle. To him, horses were part of my past, a door that had closed before we'd met. All this—the dirty boots by the door, the Saddlebred magazines stacked on my desk, my weekends away at horse shows sleeping in crummy hotels instead of at home with him—surprised him. To me, though, horses weren't new. They were in my blood.

In the 1960s, while everyone else learned the twist, my mom mastered every equitation pattern in the American Horse Shows Association rule book. She shined as a junior exhibitor in the saddle seat show circuit in the Southeast, riding serpentines in hushed arenas while spectators held their applause and their breath until she finished. My mom liked the feeling of grit under her fingernails and sweat on her back but could, with a touch of mascara and the right pair of earrings, turn into elegance itself. I craved both the grit and the elegance. Still do. Dozens of other horsewomen I know learned their love of all things equine through their maternal line. There's a lineage here, an ancestry.

A horse's bloodlines list daddy above dam. *Sultan's Santana, by Supreme Sultan, out of Grand View's Majorette. Supreme Sultan, by Valley View Supreme, out of Melody O'Lee.* "By" the sire and "out of" the dam, as if the stallion did all the work and the mare just served as container. If I wrote it out, my pedigree would follow the damline. That lineage includes my mom and also her mother, Dearie, the well-off grandmother who reminds me of Della Large.

One summer, Dearie bought me lessons at a local saddle seat barn. She drove me there herself, my mom up front with her, me in the back seat reading *Stormy, Misty's Foal* for the fifth time. The barn looked and smelled like every barn I've been in since. Rows of metal-barred wooden box stalls filled with horses. A sawdust aisleway. Green, fenced pastures beyond. A tack room hung with saddles, bridles, and harnesses. Barn cats snaking around my legs. Permeating all of it, the earthy tang of manure, the rich scent of leather, and, most of all, the musk of horse.

It took no more than one trot around the arena for me to plummet into love with Westmoreland, the old gelding I was riding in a sunny outdoor arena shaded by old-growth oaks. Some horses jumped at shadows, but Westmoreland trotted along without a bobble. He was big but gentle, an aged chestnut with a white stripe down his face who, even after more than a decade of showing, could still high-step like the Saddlebred he was. At my last lesson, I lingered at his stall, unwilling to say goodbye.

Candee, the shag-haired trainer, turned to my mom with an idea. "The two of them would make a great show team. She's eight, right? She'd be a knockout in the eight-and-under at the Texas State Fair."

Then Dearie sealed the deal. "And when is that, exactly?"

The timing was perfect. The fair would take place just before the fall semester started. My mom taught ballet at Butler University, passing on the skills that she'd used to launch herself into an international performing career right out of high school. That career took her away from horses, for what she'd assumed would be forever. When she returned to the United States, she finished her education, collecting degrees until she finished her master of fine arts in performance. Along the way, she birthed and raised my two big brothers, who have never had any interest in horses but who are good sports about visiting the barn when they're in town. Then, seven years after the second brother was born, a pleasant surprise. Me. A baby girl who, according to my toddler pictures, reached over the fence to pat every horse she saw. I eventually became my mom's ticket back into the horse world—this time, as spectator instead of exhibitor, although she did show a couple of horses in the mid-1990s.

In the weeks between my last lesson in Texas and the 1994 fair, my mom and Dearie outfitted me in a tiny three-piece navy-blue suit and derby. Not many girls fly into their first horse show, but I boarded a plane back to Dallas, a magenta Caboodle packed with hair spray and cast-off Clinique samples nestled in the luggage my mom stowed in the overhead bin. Even in the eight-and-under division, girls were expected to wear makeup—tastefully applied, of course. My mom understood performance and costume. A decade as a soloist in companies like Amsterdam's Scapino Ballet had taught her the meaning of audience and artistry, and horsewomanship on a Saddlebred involved as much spectacle as *Swan Lake*.

The state fair blurred by: A cowboy statue bigger than a house, his arm waving an unending "Howdy." A midway sizzling on black Dallas asphalt.

An enormous indoor arena with too many rows of seats to count. My mom, wearing loose-cut cotton shorts, a square linen top, and Jackie O.–style sunglasses, marched me past the noisy roller coasters but paused to buy me a lemon shake-up and elephant ear—getting nothing for herself. She still maintained a dancer's diet, her only indulgence an afternoon snack of Diet Coke with a package of peanut butter crackers. Dearie, in her slacks and blouse, headed straight for the arena to find a seat near the rail.

I won that class, making my first-ever victory pass, but the ribbon isn't important. Westmoreland's muscles had worked in time with mine, his body responding to the signals Candee had taught my own body to use. Through the whole class—trotting into the ring to an organist's rendition of "New York, New York," guiding my horse around the other little girls, walking, reversing, trotting again, and, finally, posing in the lineup—my smile was genuine. I had, as horse lovers say, "caught the horse bug," that mysterious compulsion to be around horses at any cost. Once I became an adult, the horse bug, stirred from dormancy, spurred the request for the New Rider Special, my pilgrimage to the American Saddlebred Museum, and finally, the purchase of my own horse.

The horse bug changed Sky Watch from a historical figure into an obsession. I spent hours lurking on Facebook pages dedicated to Saddlebred history, reading comments written by people decades older than me, the type who understood the benefits of orthotics and progressive lenses but could still list all twenty-three living trainers who had won World's Grand Championship honors. After the internet gave me everything it could, I started collecting old magazines from the 1980s, marking the pages where Sky Watch appeared in black-and-white action photos, his muscles like a topographic map of the bluegrass hills where he was born. The magazines offered a glimpse into the show rings of the past, but I needed to know what had happened in the places professional photographers didn't visit. In the stalls and warm-up rings. Along the barn aisle and at the home arena. To understand the magic of Sky Watch, I needed to talk to the man who, in those old photographs, rode Sky Watch to victory.

I needed Mitch Clark. A barn friend gave me his wife's number, and one evening, my heart pounding, I dialed it. She fetched Mitch, and he agreed to let me visit. Soon. The following week. Better now than later, I thought; the three-hour drive to Danville, Kentucky, might not feel so good with morning sickness. That, of course, was if everything went according to plan: Vasectomy reversal in the summer. Pregnant by this time next year, all the gods willing. As cautious as Ben was, he probably wouldn't let me leave the state after my first trimester.

Dearie's copy of Emily Post's 1928 *Etiquette* didn't cover what to bring when meeting a legendary horse trainer. Wine? What if he doesn't drink? Coffee? How does he take it? Cupcakes? He's a man in his sixties, not a twelve-year-old girl. Standing in line at a coffee shop near Lexington, Kentucky, in early March 2020 (just before the world imploded with the COVID-19 pandemic), I settled on muffins. Probably, no one would eat the muffins, but I had lived in Virginia for a decade, long enough to know that in the South, it's better to show up with food no one will eat than to show up empty-handed.

For someone like me, a lifelong Saddlebred lover but a nobody in the Saddlebred world, meeting Mitch Clark was like meeting Beyoncé. Sure, my old horse Keeper of the Stars had become a world's champion, a horse Saddlebred enthusiasts still remember, but that all happened after he'd been sold. My name never really attached to him. I had the honor of being the first young girl to ride him, but in classes with me, he was still too much horse. We rarely delivered a clean ride. There was always a mistake: Coming off his feet. Breaking out of the trot. Flubbing a canter depart. Only after we'd sold Keeper—for five times what we'd bought him for—did he make good on his promise and become a world's champion while I pretended not to care that someone else was taking my horse further than I ever did.

Should I mention Keeper to Mitch? He might know him. Some trainers did. No, I decided. Better to let myself stand on my own merits, whatever those are. My mission wasn't to make myself look good. It was to learn the story of Sky Watch, a horse who, even though I'd never seen him perform in person, gave me goose bumps—a horse who represented everything this breed stands for: Independence. Determination. Athleticism.

As I approached from the highway, the barn loomed, surrounded by wooden pasture fencing and a stone gateway bearing the property's name: Mitchell Clark Stables. At the iron gate, a kind-voiced woman buzzed me through. Was that Vicky, Mitch's wife? Too nervous to ask, I thanked her, shouting into the intercom like an octogenarian on a cell phone. The gate whirred shut behind me. What should I call Mitch? Mr. Clark? Mitchell? Sir? In all our phone conversations, I'd kept my politeness ramped up, assuming that sixty-something-year-old Kentuckians like talking to a well-mannered woman. He'd agreed to let me visit, so it must have worked.

Mitch strode forward to meet me as soon as I entered the barn. He threw his long arms wide, his smile creasing his cheeks. "Welcome!" he said, shaking my hand as if we were old friends. His hands dwarfed mine, and mine aren't small. "Now, what was your name again, honey?"

We'd spoken on the phone three times already, but I reminded him. "Emma Hudelson, sir. Your facility is beautiful." I meant it. The concrete-floored hallway boasted doors to storage and an upstairs office on one side and a wash rack on the other. Beyond it, a cavernous arena. Two rows of stalls lined up in the middle of the arena, their sliding doors facing each other. White, windowed walls let in tall rectangles of light in which dust motes floated. The air smelled of fresh dirt, hay, and horse. Leather and manure. Liniment and Murphy's Oil Soap. Barn magic. No matter the barn, the perfume stayed the same. "Thank you for letting me visit today."

In jeans, chaps, and a flannel shirt, with white hair pulled back into a ponytail no longer than my thumb, Mitch didn't look special. He looked like someone you'd run into buying the value-sized bag of dog food at Walmart. His face was kinder than I'd expected, with a wide, friendly nose and soft eyes. Even in his sixties, the man was still in good shape. The only signs of age were deep laugh lines, skin weathered by decades of outdoor work, and white hair. Other than that, he looked like the Mitch I knew from the videos and photos I'd pored over, the ones from the early 1980s, when his hair was still brown and cut close to his head.

"Now, I'm not ignoring you, dear, but I've got to check on a tractor issue. Just hang tight, and I'll be right with you."

"Of course." I looked around and then remembered the sack of muffins. "I brought y'all some muffins. Thought you and your guys might be hungry by midmorning." When I ventured south, my long-gone Virginia drawl always sneaked in.

"That was kind of you. They'll find a good home." Mitch gestured toward a tiny kitchen between the stalls. "You can just set those there. I'll be right back."

Then Mitchell Edward Clark left me to stand in the aisleway alone, surrounded by his horses. The trust among horse people is amazing. How did he know I wasn't dumb enough to do something like step into one of his colts' stalls? Or open one up and let a filly slip through? Or steal a saddle or two?

As it turned out, I wasn't really alone. Assistant trainer Anthio Marcos stood next to a cross-tied chestnut three-year-old wearing a bridle under his halter. He introduced himself while squirting liquid from a bottle into the horse's mouth.

"It's glycerin and peppermint." The horse tongued up the mixture, his eyes focused. When Anthio pulled it away, he stretched his neck toward it, continuing to chomp and lick, reaching like a baby for his bottle. "They love it." Anthio patted the colt on the neck.

"I can see that."

Anthio looked like a young, lean-faced Antonio Banderas, with prominent eyebrows, slicked-back hair, and soulful eyes. He'd been working with Mitch for two years as an assistant trainer. His days started at seven and ended at five, and his job seemed to mostly include grooming horses and holding them while his boss climbed on them, but he glowed. Every other sentence contained a superlative. "I'm super fortunate to be here. It's the best. It's been the greatest learning experience, for sure."

Mitch returned, talking loudly into his cell phone about hydraulics and oil. As he hung up and mounted, he turned to me. "I promise I'll be right with you. Just gotta ride this colt. Then we'll get some lunch and talk."

I followed him out of the narrow aisle, eager to see him ride. Mitch clucked the colt into a bouncy walk, moving him diagonally down one side of the arena, the hind feet crossing over with each step. He sat loose in the saddle, his limbs hanging, his hands light on the reins. As he urged the youngster into a trot, his elbows pulled back. He didn't post a step, didn't rise and fall in time with the trot as all riders learn to do in the first lesson, an instructor chanting, "Up, down! Up, down!" with every step. Instead, Mitch let his body weight drive the horse forward, pushing him into the bridle so he'd engage his hind end, bring his head up and back, and tuck his chin in. When he returned with the chestnut colt, Anthio had another one waiting for him. Then another. For Mitch, "be right with you" is relative. I didn't mind the wait. I'd hang out in a barn aisle all day to watch a master like Mitch at work.

Across the street at Cheddar's, Mitch greeted everyone, from the feather-mustached host to the gaggle of servers at the bar. "Hi, son. How you been?" He tipped an imaginary hat. "Hey, sweetheart, where's your section? Did you miss me? I know you did." He grinned while he talked, and his voice filled the room. Mitch accepted the menus a young, dark-haired waitress handed over. "Thank you, dear. I'll try my best to find something good on here, but it won't be easy." He winked, still smiling. She dimpled and sashayed away. Then he turned back to me and, still smiling, explained. "I eat here all the time, but I always give them shit."

Then, he began to talk about Sky Watch, and I shut my mouth and let him go. The true story turned out to be better than the legend, better than what the photos and videos had promised.

A colt's first year passes in a haze of milk and grass, the warm sun and the warm flanks of his dam equally welcome. On the 237 acres of Teater and Sons, Aries Golden Gift would have taught Sky Watch all about herd politics. With nips to the withers, she taught him not to follow other horses too closely and not to kick his paddock mates unless they deserved it. Head down to the ground meant submission. Head up meant superiority, and that's where Aries Golden Gift liked it. After all, she was a superior mare, sharp-eared and long-legged, used to being admired, as she is in the only photo I've found of her, where her trainer, Marty Mueller, accepts a blue ribbon while parking the mare in the winner's circle, her head high, her nostrils flared, as if shocked at the audacity of the man behind the camera's flash.

When the time came, Sky Watch was weaned, and he keened for his mama with all the other weanlings. Within a day, the babies quieted, and the mares breathed relief. Those baby teeth were sharp—and teaching those babies to be proper horses took energy. Now Aries Golden Gift could roll in her stall without worrying about knocking her colt out with a stray hoof. She strolled around her pasture with the other broodmares, with a sedateness befitting their status as matriarchs. Most of them were pregnant again already, having been bred not long after their last babies were born.

For the next six months, Sky Watch cavorted with the other colts, crow-hopping and galloping over the Kentucky hills. He learned about wearing a halter (sort of) and loading onto a trailer—not really, but enough that a man, maybe Lou Teater himself, could slam the door shut behind him and pull away with a reasonable expectation that the colt would be in one piece when they arrived as his destination. If the Teater boys had had any idea of just how special that colt would become, of his future as the horse who, along with his rival, would define a decade, they never would have let him off the farm.

When the trailer pulled up to Ridgefields Farm in the fall of 1978, no one there knew what to expect from the three youngsters shifting inside. A twenty-five-year-old Mitch Clark followed his grandfather, Hall of Fame trainer Garland Bradshaw, out of the green-roofed barn and into the driveway where the truck idled.

Garland had gone into semiretirement after selling his stock in a dispersal sale the fall before. A handful of horses stayed on the farm, and he insisted on working the best horses himself, charging over $330 a month for board and training—equal to about $1,200 today. Garland saved the low-born souls, the ones destined to run the auction ring, for his grandson. Many of the great trainers still alive today trace their own training back to Garland, calling Ridgefields Farm "Garland Bradshaw University." While Garland taught many, no one got quite the same education as Mitch.

Since starting under his grandfather as a kid in grade school, Mitch had always worked these bottom-of-the-barrel horses. Every six months, Garland hauled Mitch's half-dozen grunts to Tattersall's, where they'd be auctioned off. Some moved on to the show ring. Others became trail horses or pasture pets. The ones who didn't sell, well, they faced a different fate, one that priced them by the pound, with a buyer who couldn't care less about bloodlines. To be in the horse business means knowing this but trying to forget it.

For over a decade, Mitch's string of horses had turned over twice a year. When the trailer hauling his charges pulled away each fall and spring, he didn't mourn. He knew better than to get attached. By the time Sky Watch landed with him, Mitch had trained more horses than he could count.

In the booth at Cheddar's, more than four decades since Sky Watch's arrival at Ridgefields, Mitch accepted his potpie from our waitress. "I made all my mistakes on those no-count horses." He leaned in. "You have to make 'em somewhere. No one my age could have been on as many of them as I had. I'd been training, at least part-time, since before high school."

The farm Garland and Mitch worked had been dedicated to Saddlebreds since 1947. Located just south of Danville, a small town that's now encroaching on the farm's green acres, the land looked like an advertisement for Kentucky. Green hills surrounded the white-brick house, with six spring-fed ponds pocking the two hundred acres of fields. Two barns stood on the property, replacing the ones destroyed by fires, an all-too-common disaster in the equestrian world. The first, in June 1964, had killed more than thirty horses and nearly killed Garland's desire to continue his vocation. The second, two decades later, had threatened Sky Watch.

Weeks before the trailer holding Sky Watch arrived, one of the Teater boys telephoned Garland. Only the best came under Garland's care. Lady Carrigan. Easter Present. Della Large's Scarlet Flame, who died in the 1964 fire. Della had a new prospect to send Garland's way: a long yearling by Flight Time, out of Aries Golden Gift. Since this colt hadn't even been clipped to a lead rope yet, Garland earmarked him for Mitch. He was approaching the far side of his seventies. Let the youngster handle the wild ones.

The men let down the trailer's ramp. While the other two horses unloaded calmly enough that no one remembers them, Sky Watch jumped out, clearing the ramp. As a yearling, Sky Watch was already a deep russet, thick necked as a Morgan. Mitch had to herd the colt into his stall as you would a cow. He wouldn't have been out of line to ask if there'd been a mix-up. Could this freight train be the wrong horse? He barely looked like a Saddlebred.

Since horses didn't yet pay his bills, Mitch sold stereos. High-end stereos, but still. The grandson of a legendary horse trainer didn't manage champions himself. He slung Sonys. In the mornings, he rose before the sun to clean stalls, then feed and work his horses. With a wife, Cyndy, at home to support, he had no choice. The two barely saw each other, but Mitch promised her it wouldn't be like that forever.

"I had to provide." Mitch spread his hands, palms up, his potpie mostly uneaten.

"Wow," I said. "I'll bet she hated your schedule." I fingered the cell phone in my pocket, wondering what time it was but hesitant to pull it out and break the spell. We must have been sitting for more than an hour, and there were horses still to work at the barn. Mitch, though, had just gotten started.

He puffed out his cheeks and stirred his pie. "You bet she did. So really, the timing of Sky Watch was perfect."

Until the day Sky Watch arrived, Mitch hadn't worked many horses from paying clients, which are the bread and butter of a horse trainer's business. He worked the farm-owned horses, the ones who had been on the back burner. Most of Mitch's string wound up in Tattersall's sale ring, bringing in a couple of thousand dollars if Mitch was lucky. Other than Darlene's Dilly, who'd taken the two-year-old gaited stake in Louisville, Mitch hadn't worked anything with real talent. Not yet. Much of what makes Saddlebreds special is genetic. Big lung capacity gives them stamina. A broad chest provides strength. Rounded hindquarters propel them forward. A long neck, set high on the withers, lets them hold their head up without the help of artificial aids like overcheck bridles. A narrow throatlatch allows for their chess-piece head-set, chin tucked, jaw angled in. But not all genes breed true. The horses Mitch worked were less than blessed, genetically speaking.

Sky Watch had solid breeding, but his conformation as a yearling didn't show it yet. He was also man-shy. Reach for a man-shy horse's head, and he'll crane it in the air, eyes all saucers. Take one step toward him, and he'll jump five feet away. Only time and patience teach a colt to understand his handlers. It takes hours spent in the stall, rubbing him all over with your hands, feeling the muscles soften, then rubbing him with the lead rope to show him that it isn't, after all, a snake.

"He'd barely had a halter on him," Mitch said, blowing on a piece of pot-pie before forking it to his mouth. "I mean, dadgum." Mitch is the type of man who can say *dadgum* unironically and get away with it. "You couldn't lead him."

After teaching him the basics, Mitch started Sky Watch in long lines, like all unbroken colts. In long lining, the trainer holds the ends of thirty-foot lines and drives the horse from the ground, with the trainer walking behind him or asking the horse to circle widely around him. Long lining allows direct communication with a horse's mouth, a first education in steering and softening.

As Mitch tells it, over the next few weeks, Granddaddy Garland observed while Mitch and Sky Watch battled in the high-ceilinged arena. Unlike many young ones in training, the red colt rarely spooked or shied. He didn't react to things like the prey animal he was, skittering at the sound of Garland unwrapping his stick of gum. Instead, he oozed power. If he did spook, jumping five feet sideways, he did it with purpose, not fear. Garland folded his arms and laughed, then walked away, sliding the barn door shut behind him. Lucky for him, Sky Watch wasn't his problem. Young Mitchell was doing just fine with him. He didn't need to step in. Not yet.

With an iron mouth and the energy of a toddler on a diet of Pixy Stix, Sky Watch wore Mitch out. Worse, he couldn't trot over a corncob. For a breed that should high-step like a majorette, that was not a good sign. Months had passed. They were into January now, meaning that Sky Watch had turned two, at least according to the registry (all Saddlebreds gain a year on

January 1, regardless of their actual birth date). Mitch knew Della needed an update, and though he knew how to sell stereos, he didn't know how to sell the news about Sky Watch. I can imagine Mitch and Garland standing in the barn aisle, the two men facing each other, both broad through the shoulders, one gray haired and spectacled, the other smooth faced.

"She won't listen to me, but she'll listen to you."

Garland tilted his head back. "I'll take care of her. You take care of that colt."

Della had a dream for Sky Watch. She imagined him in the two-year-old fine harness class at Louisville, pulling a four-wheeled buggy over the green shavings. Fine harness horses are elegant and refined. Because their bodies aren't hidden by a saddle, their conformation is on display, so they'd better be as beautiful as they are high-stepping. None of those descriptors matched two-year-old Sky Watch, but Garland said they owed it to Mrs. Large to try to get him hitched to a cart. The first day Mitch tried to hitch him, Sky Watch's tail swished in warning. "Come on, boy," Mitch murmured. "We've got to do this sometime. Mrs. Large wants you in harness." He sighed. "God help us all."

While Garland guided the cart's shafts toward the loops dangling on either side of the harness, Mitch kept a hand on Sky Watch's chest. As if a hand could hold back a three-hundred-volt shock. Without warning, Sky Watch launched himself skyward, and the harness snapped. Mitch had to let go of the bridle and grab the lines while the horse jumped down the straight-away. He hauled back on the bit and eventually brought the colt back under control.

The next day, the same thing. Another jumping performance good enough for the Grand National. Another broken harness. Then another. On the fourth day, before Mitch could even try to hook the cart, he saw his grandfather striding toward him with purpose. Garland eyed Sky Watch, who buzzed in his stall like a teenage boy spoiling for a fight. He sidestepped left and right, jerking his head and narrowing his eyes.

Garland looked the horse up and down. "I do believe you're going to have to ride this colt."

"Mrs. Large wants him in harness." Mitch followed his grandfather's gaze over the horse. "What am I supposed to do?"

"Son, he's broken three of our four harnesses, and those three aren't fixed yet. The history of the past three attempts tells me he's probably going to break this one too. If he keeps it up, no horse in this barn is going to be driving anytime soon, and I can't afford for that to happen. We have good horses here who need to work. You're getting beaten up out there. You need to ride this one." The king had spoken. Garland wanted the young man to make a name for himself on his own, but this time, he'd had no choice but to step in. And Mitch had no choice but to listen.

Mitch let all the air out of his chest. "Let's get a saddle on the son of a buck, then." He didn't let himself think about how he'd climb up there. With a colt like Sky Watch, there wouldn't be time for the usual steps of starting a horse under saddle—lying belly down on the horse's back and letting him adjust to the weight; standing in the left stirrup, hand on the withers, to give the right leg a few test swings—before slipping onto the colt's back. No, Mitch would have to hop on, hold on, and hope for the best.

With the reins gathered in his hands, Mitch launched off his right leg just as Sky Watch tore away. He was up. As if Mitch hadn't spent hours with Sky Watch in long lines, softening him to the bridle, the colt locked his jaw as he tore around the indoor arena. Garland slid the door shut, cutting off any possible escape route. Many horses buck or rear the first time they feel weight on their back, but Sky Watch seethed forward, not up.

"Whup, trot, boy. You can do it." Mitch bounced the snaffle bit back, and the forward lunges settled into a jolting trot. Rather than post the trot, rising up and down in time with the horse's movement, Mitch sat it, just as he would later do on the day I visited. On a horse moving like Sky Watch, this is about as comfortable as gunning a Jeep through a lumberjacked forest. Maybe male riders should wear a cup when they start colts under saddle.

At the restaurant, I didn't ask Mitch if he'd protected his package for this first ride, but my mind stayed with him in that old arena. I pictured what it would feel like to mount all that power and channel it into something productive. "How long did it take for Sky Watch to settle in and learn all of his gaits?"

"He didn't." Mitch huffed.

After weeks of watching Mitch and Sky Watch fight each other up and down the arena, Garland stepped in again. "Why don't you try to rack that one?" He folded a piece of chewing gum into his jaw. "Might take the edge off."

Teaching a Saddlebred to rack is a process. Even though the breed is predisposed to the four-beat gait, they have to learn it, just as a girl with ballerina genes has to learn to dance *en pointe*. She can't step into those boxy pink shoes, pop up on her toes, and execute a set of fouettés right away.

Mitch taught Sky Watch to rack using the same methods he would use forty years later for the chestnut colt who liked Anthio's peppermint cocktail so much. First, he had the shoeing changed: barefoot and trimmed up front, shoes behind. The next day, the farrier's job done, Mitch took over. He mounted, the dawn birds all a-chirp, the arena footing moist and mulchy fragrant. As usual, Sky Watch took off, all power. One lap, two laps, and then Mitch had had enough. He pulled Sky Watch down to an animated walk, the colt's tail swishing like a broom behind him. Then, Mitch asked for the rack. He urged Sky Watch to walk faster. To keep the horse from breaking into a trot, he sat back in the saddle and widened his hands. Sky Watch pivoted one ear back, and then another. Mitch tipped the colt's head from side to side as he walked, timing it just right so the horse would start to reach under him with his hind feet.

Sky Watch boomed forward, but not at a rack. Mitch pulled him back down and tried again. And again. Plenty of propulsion and power, that was for sure, but not at the gait he wanted. He could feel the horse's frustration building beneath him, so he stopped. The barn swallows swooped in and out of the rafters. Out of the corner of his eye, Mitch saw Garland leaning against the doorway of the arena. Mitch breathed in and out, trying to relax his body so his horse would relax. Sky Watch continued to push himself forward, straining against Mitch's hold and escaping it more often than not. Garland shook his head, pocketed his hands, and walked away.

Finally, Mitch consented to letting the horse trot, trying to end on some sort of good note. He peered around Sky Watch's neck, trying to see if, at least, the baby stallion was starting to use his legs at all. He wasn't, but Mitch brought him to a stop anyway and patted him twice on the neck before dismounting. He could spend all morning on the colt, but he had four more to work before exchanging chaps for slacks and selling overpriced stereos to people who had no idea their salesman spent his mornings wrestling with a rank two-year-old.

After six weeks of rides that looked and felt as rough as those, Mitch knew something had to change. He stood in front of Sky Watch's stall, arms crossed, and watched him. He'd already worked him, but even after a ride that would have tired any other horse, Sky Watch danced in his stall like a clogger. "You want to go again?" As if the horse understood, he stopped. "Fine. We can do that."

When Mitch had finished with the last horse in his string that day, he returned to Sky Watch's stall, where the colt stood with alert ears, as if waiting for him. "Okay, colt. Twice a day it is." Sky Watch didn't exactly rack that day, but the second time-out felt more like a ride and less like a fight. From then on, Mitch worked him twice a day. Just like some students need advanced classes to stay focused, Sky Watch needed to work harder, and more often, to learn to enjoy his job.

When the waitress brought the check to the Cheddar's booth, I already had my hand on my wallet, but Mitch beat me to it.

"I don't think so. This one's on me."

"It's the least I can do," I protested. "You have to let me buy lunch."

Mitch grinned and stuck his chin out. "Oh, no, I don't." He counted out a few bills and stacked them. "It's my pleasure. Truly."

"Next time, it's my treat," I said. But really, would there be a next time? How many more trips to Kentucky would I be able to make once my belly started to swell? Or with a baby in tow? *Plenty*, I thought, imagining standing in Mitch's barn with an infant strapped to my chest, her big eyes following the colt he'd be racking down the aisle. In all my fantasies about motherhood, the baby had always been a girl. Someone needed to inherit the maternal legacy of horses.

As Mitch and I exited the restaurant, he described his usual workday with Sky Watch. "Since I had to leave at noon to sell stereos, I'd get to the barn early to feed and knock the stalls, then ride him. Right before I left, I'd ride him again. By the second ride of the day, he was still strong but a little more willing."

He smiled, his eyes crinkling. "And he was racking."

3

Sparkle and Sweat

Sky Watch's first horse show wasn't going to be the two-year-old fine harness stake at Louisville. Instead, it would be the two-year-old five-gaited stake, a class that demands top athleticism from very young horses. It's hard on a two-year-old to perform all five gaits with a rider on board under the pressure of a crowd-filled arena, but it's a fun class to watch—for the type of people who like to watch the Indy 500 just for the wrecks. With over one hundred thousand injuries related to horseback riding a year, it isn't hard to find those types at a horse show. That was especially true in the 1980s. The decade that simultaneously brought in back-combed bangs, parachute pants, and the double-breasted power suit was anything but risk averse.

In any era, going to a horse show feels like a trip to the farm, but with a party twist. There's the tang of livestock urine soaked into sawdust and, on top of that, the Aqua Net used on both horse and human manes. The ring, which might also take turns being a basketball stadium or ice-skating rink, is footed with tanbark instead of ice or floorboards, but potted ferns and chrysanthemums brighten the judges' stand in the center. Mulched paths lead from the stables to the ring, and horses mince along them, keyed up and snorting, their hides satin, their riders dressed in three-piece suits.

When I was a kid, while my peers vacationed in lake houses or flew to Florida beaches, my mom steered us to fairgrounds all over the Midwest and South. My specialty, like hers, was equitation. In equitation, the rider, not the horse, is under scrutiny. The horse needs to look sharp and behave himself, but the rider is the one the judges watch. Her job is to make the difficult task of riding a Saddlebred look easy, to make invisible the thousands of constant adjustments it takes to balance five feet above the ground on a fast-moving being.

At the 1996 All American Horse Classic in the Pepsi Coliseum at the Indiana State Fairgrounds, the age-ten-and-under equitation pattern seemed easy. *Using the rail to your right, trot on the right diagonal to the arena's three-quarter point and continue to trot a half circle. Halt. Complete a figure eight at the trot. Halt. Pivot to the left. On the left diagonal, trot the rail to the lineup.* Throughout the entire class—trotting into the arena with six other girls, smoothing down to a walk, reversing for the second-direction trot, then walking, then heeding the call to the lineup—the pattern instructions turned circles in my head, which had started to hurt. My mom always bobby-pinned my wispy brown hair tight enough to give me a headache. If she didn't feel scalp scrape as she drove the pins in, she wasn't doing her job. I resisted the temptation to hold the reins in one hand and reach for my bun to loosen it. Silently, I asked my horse for patience, but I needed it more than he did. *Just a few more minutes, Glamour Boy. Almost there.*

An hour before my class, my mom and I circled the arena, walking the pattern I'd have to do. Once. Twice. Three times. Dodging around the competition, who were all doing the same thing. My mom made sure my suit pants were rolled up so they wouldn't get smudged, but she didn't seem to notice the dirt sifting in her Danskos.

"Once more, Em?"

"No, Mom. I've got it. Can we go now?" I hated patterns like I hated fractions.

"Why don't you do it once without me." It wasn't a question.

"Fine." I turned around and stomped through the lines and circles but pivoted the wrong way after the figure eight. "Don't help me!" I called to my mom. "I'll do it."

I kept my gaze down as I walked, circled, and pivoted. Without guidance, and without my horse underneath me, the pivot tricked me again.

"Em, Glamour Boy can't do this without you." He and I made a good-looking pair, him brushed to a high shine, me in a dove-gray suit, white vest, and pink tie. As long as I pointed Glamour Boy in the right direction, I could just think the word: *Trot.* But no matter how well he listened, to telegraph the pattern to him, I would have to understand it myself.

"I know."

"Let's try again together. We've got time. But first, close your eyes and picture it. Hands up, like you're holding reins. Pretend you're in the saddle."

All that preparation didn't ease my nerves as I waited my turn in the lineup. Then, the announcer's voice rang out. "Number 313, you're on deck." That was me. We were in the running. I inched my fingers forward on the reins and rebalanced my feet in my stirrups. I squeezed my thighs in, just barely, and Glamour Boy trotted out. The reins felt electric in my hands, which needed to stay quiet, soft enough to hold an eggshell yet able to contact Glamour Boy's mouth. Half circle, halt, figure eight, halt. Now the pivot—*landed it!*—and the trot all the way back to the lineup.

Without dropping my hands, I scratched Glamour Boy's neck with an index finger while we waited for the rest of the girls to finish their pattern. The judges could always be watching, so my body held its equitation position. Even after the patterns, during the deliberation period, while the organist picked out a syrup-slow "Georgia on My Mind," my hands stayed together and my heels down, calves flared out. Even when a fly landed on my face and crawled his own figure eights around my freckles, I kept still. Even as the announcer called out first place, while my gut rose and then sank, and then second (more sinking), I didn't move. Then, finally (*pleasepleaseplease*), my name for third.

My mom met me at the gate, and I handed her my ribbon. She patted Glamour Boy on the shoulder and beamed. "You did it! I knew you could."

We hadn't won, but Glamour Boy and I had performed, and we'd performed well. We'd entered a tradition more than a century old, entertaining a crowd with a show of horse-human partnership and a test of skill. At the time, I didn't feel the weight of all that legacy, but it pulsed around me and through me, the power of the damline that had brought Glamour Boy to me and me to Glamour Boy.

The perfectionism of equitation could be grueling, but the real meaning of the sparkle and sweat stood in the partnership between ten-year-old girl and thousand-pound creature. Dearie funded more than entry fees and tailored suits, and my mom taught me more than how to count strides and pivot. This privilege is something I don't take for granted. These women invested in my confidence, grit, humility, and ability to win or lose with grace. With Glamour Boy, I learned more than leg positioning. I learned to take care of a being much larger than me. I learned to communicate with a soul who couldn't speak in words. My experience isn't unique. Just ask my mom. Or Della. Or that Missouri beauty queen who sold me My Queen Bee.

At ten, I didn't think about any of that. The horse-human bond didn't require reflection. It existed in the moment, surrounding me like air, ever present and automatic as a heartbeat.

With my mom at Glamour Boy's head, I dropped the reins, leaned over, and hugged my horse, absorbing his warmth.

For Mitch and Sky Watch, the 1979 two-year-old five-gaited stake and its World's Championship title glimmered, just a few months away. As we drove back to his barn, Mitch told me to brake. "I want to show you something." He pointed to the road sign across the street from his gates. Skywatch Drive.

"That's so cool!" I said. "Danville named a road after him?"

"Yes, ma'am. I was honored."

"He deserves it. When did he really start getting good? When did you know you had a potential champion?"

Mitch fixed his eyes on me. "When he learned to rack, everything changed. He started picking his legs up a little more, and then one day, boom!" Mitch fisted his hands and mimed it, churning his elbows up by his ears and reaching out and down, like a swimmer doing the crawl through a pool of piranhas. "He did that floaty shit with his trot."

"No horse trots like he did."

"No, ma'am. Especially not back then, in the seventies." Mitch pointed us back toward his barn. "Just pull out here. There you go." Mitch directed me in the same voice he used with his colts. He must've sensed my nerves. I hadn't planned on chauffeuring Mitch in my Jetta. Otherwise, I would have vacuumed. "We couldn't breed the kind of motion into them that we can today. The folks at Louisville didn't know what hit them."

The grueling schedule of Louisville's World's Championship Horse Show, with morning, afternoon, and evening sessions, requires trainers and grooms to work horses late at night. Some trainers are still holding the ends of long lines well past midnight, but no matter how late they're awake, the horses still need their 6:00 a.m. breakfast. Equines thrive on routine, and horse shows already disrupt their routines enough. The humans sacrifice their own routines to make things as easy on the horses as possible. They're the stars, and a show is stressful enough.

Earlier that week, Mitch worked Sky Watch in front of his grandfather. As he trotted by, Redd Crabtree, another famous trainer, joined Garland at the rail. The pair managed to look crisp in their usual khakis and short-sleeved button-up shirts, in spite of the humidity that clung after the rains earlier in the week. Mitch smiled to himself and then refocused on Sky Watch, who didn't tolerate any waver in his rider's attention. Mitch let gravity pull his body down in the saddle and maintained steady pressure from hip to calf to remind the colt he was fully present. The pair bounce-walked up the rail, bending left and right. Sky Watch relaxed and mouthed the bit, working his jaw and flexing his neck. As Mitch felt the contact through the reins, he asked his young horse for a trot with a single click of his tongue. Right away, Sky Watch churned forward, reaching out high and strong with his front legs.

As he zipped past the pair of trainers, Mitch saw Garland elbowing Redd in the ribs and pointing at Sky Watch. Mitch decided to show off a bit, so he took Sky Watch deep into the arena's far turn, giving the colt a chance to feel the footing beneath him, and then angled out to make an off-rail pass. Sky Watch brightened in the face of this new trajectory because unlike most two-year-olds, he didn't need the rail for security. He marched across the ring like he owned it.

When they hit the far end of the ring, Mitch asked Sky Watch to pick up the slow gait. One, two, three, four, with each foot seeming to hang suspended in the air for a millisecond longer than it should. Mitch let his hips slide in the saddle, and he used leg pressure to cross Sky Watch straight through the middle of the ring, clucking to ask for more speed as they hit the opposite rail. The two-year-old showed no sign of tiring. His head didn't lower; his chin didn't jut; his ears swiveled up and forward. If anything, the colt's engine gained more horsepower with every circuit of the ring. Garland's cheeks wrinkled into a grin, and he elbowed the younger trainer again. Redd popped his mouth closed and crossed his arms. Mitch had a special colt, but more importantly, he could ride the hair off him.

Mitch knew that the two-year-old class at Louisville was his chance. The young man wanted to step out of his grandfather's shadow and prove himself as a trainer in his own right. More than anything, he wanted to stop selling stereos. Mitch loved Saddlebreds, not Sonys, and the cramped indoor quarters of the electronics shop made him squirm. The open expanse of Ridge-fields Farm, the white-painted wood of its barns and buildings, the rolling hills they sat on, and the black, gray, and chestnut-coated creatures who trotted the fence line, tossing their heads and whinnying to greet him—those put a smile on his face. Coaxial cables and capacitors couldn't transmit the electricity of an American Saddlebred.

In 1979, twenty-one two-year-olds were entered in the five-gaited stake. The arena at Freedom Hall can handle a class that big, but for a group of babies who are off the farm for the first time, that's a massive class. Two-year-olds are gambles. Like teenage humans, their bodies and minds are changing daily, sometimes hourly. Their legs might be too long or too short. Their necks might be stunted or thin. Their hind ends might trail behind them when they trot. Some of them seem promising on paper but move like duds. Others are confident at home, real powerhouses, but turn into Jell-O at a show. A colt who shows well in his two-year-old year might grow awkwardly in his three-year-old year and lose whatever talent he had. Some two-year-olds aren't ready, physically or mentally, for the rigors of training and showing. For this reason, many think two-year-olds shouldn't be shown at all, and definitely not under saddle in a gaited class. Others seem to be born athletes, but their fuse burns a hair too hot, and they burn themselves up before they get the chance to light up the room.

Sky Watch tended more toward the latter. Now that he, as Mitch said, "had a mouth on him," he was ready to go off like a rocket. Mitch had the difficult job of keeping him in the stratosphere. As he tacked his horse up before the class, he tried to breathe as easily as if this were just another weekday workout, but Sky Watch could tell the difference. He jigged in the crossties. He craned his neck and snapped his teeth when Mitch tightened his girth. This was no ordinary day. Sky Watch didn't usually get his hooves sanded and painted with black shoe polish for rides at the farm. At home, Mitch didn't braid a red ribbon into his forelock and mane. Mitch didn't put a brace in his tail either, a controversial part of the Saddlebred breed standards.

Some Saddlebreds have their tails released in a minor surgical procedure performed by a vet. Two small muscles on either side of the tail receive a tiny nick. The tail is then placed in a tail set—a supportive cup that straps to the horse via a custom-fit harness. Like a bra, but for horses' tails. As the cuts heal, the muscles lengthen. When my surgeon repaired a cartilage tear in my hip, he performed a similar procedure on my psoas. "Like filleting a hot dog," he explained. I grimaced at his simile. He continued: "It'll open up the muscle and give you more range of motion. Don't worry. You'll heal quick." He was right. After a week or two, I'd forgotten all about my filleted hot dog hip, which makes me feel a little better when I see Saddlebreds with released tails today. My own trainer skips the procedure whenever possible, choosing instead to stretch the tail gradually over time, but he'll ask a vet to release them if they're especially tight or if he thinks it'll help them move more freely.

Releasing a horse's tail makes it spout from the horse's rump in a graceful curve that mirrors the rise of the neck from the withers. Trainers swear this procedure frees up the horses' back muscles and helps them engage their hind ends, but it's also cosmetic, and it's as hated in the animal-welfare community as cutting Doberman puppies' ears into pointy triangles.

Internet horse forums are full of equestrians spitting venom about the cruelty of tail alteration of any kind. In a fashion left over from nineteenth-century British carriage horses, Hackney horses and ponies have their tails docked, removing the lower part of the bone and most of the hair, giving their butts a sassy bob cut Posh Spice would envy. Some Quarter Horses designated for Western pleasure classes receive nerve blocks to keep the tail hanging low, straight, and still. "Leave them natural!" the keyboard advocates cry. "This is *abuse*. Anyone who says they love their horses but *mutilates* them like this is *evil*."

June Wemlinger was a groom in the 1970s and 1980s and worked with some of the top Saddlebred trainers in the country. Jack Nevitt. Redd Crabtree. Bob Vessel. Debbie Foley, one of the first female trainers, who looks like a steelworker and rides like a cowboy. June died suddenly in April 2023, and the Saddlebred community mourned her loss via Facebook. Until her death, June kept rescued and retired Saddlebreds at home. She liked giving them a safe place to live out their last years. June thought the Saddlebred tail shenanigans hurt the breed's image.

"People see that, and they don't know what to think," she said to me in a phone interview. "Even if it's not that bad for the horses, it sure looks bad, and we need all the help we can get to protect the breed. I wish USEF would just ban it." USEF—the United States Equestrian Federation—is the governing body for equestrian sports in the US. They set the bar for all things horse show, so their influence is mighty. June wasn't wrong. If the breed is facing declining numbers and declining fans in the stands, then why not eliminate something that turns people away from the breed?

Tradition is a mighty power, though, and tradition says that Saddlebreds need to be shown with braced tails in certain classes. A Saddlebred with its tail over its back does make a stunning picture. Think Ariana Grande's high ponytail, but on a horse's butt. In the days before a show, Saddlebreds wear their tail sets to put their tail in position and limber it up. A half hour before a horse heads into his class, a trainer or groom will massage and stretch the base of the tail, then tie it in place to a brace. If a tail set is like a bra, a tail brace is like a push-up bra, holding the tail up and helping it bend over in a graceful curve. The brace doesn't look comfortable, but most horses don't seem to be bothered by it. Once the tail is in place, the trainer might add fullness by attaching a switch or two, which is like an equine weave. These switches are made of real horsehair and can cost more than I paid for My Queen Bee.

To add the final touch to a Saddlebred's tail, grooms used to apply ginger salve to the horse's rectum to help them flag their tails even higher. This is technically illegal now, but most show horse barns keep the brown ointment in their storage trunks. A gingered anus probably feels as spicy as it sounds, but trainers claim that it isn't that bad, which makes me wonder if they've tried it themselves.

Not all Saddlebreds are shown with braced tails—pleasure classes, the ones designated for the less-showy horses like Bee, don't allow it. Pretty as they are, I wouldn't mind seeing the tail alterations disappear entirely. They're not as evil as they seem, but anything requiring this much explanation is more trouble than it's worth. One thing I know: I wouldn't have wanted to be the one to brace Sky Watch for the first time.

Sky Watch was all ears and legs as he hit Freedom Hall for the first time in 1979. Mitch hadn't noticed them yet, but more trainers leaned against the ringside rail than he had expected. Word travels fast in the Saddlebred world, and Redd Crabtree had seen his workout earlier in the week. The community was ready to see if Garland's grandson really had something or not, and as soon as they saw Sky Watch, they couldn't take their eyes off him.

Already, the baby stud had, as Indiana-based horse show manager Claire Panke Broemel said, "a masculine power."

"I never saw the other horses in the class," she said. "He was a coltish, lankier version of the great, mature horse you see on all the videos. When Mitch rode him into the arena, his head was in Mitch's lap—he wore the bridle like a five-year-old. And he trotted so high and square, you wondered if he would be able to rack. He could, and he did. Not as fast as he could trot, but as fast as he needed to."

With a herd of other two-year-olds to navigate around, that speed took a master like Mitch to handle. Two-year-old horses are unpredictable, especially in a noisy, bright, unfamiliar setting like Freedom Hall. On each trip around the arena, they see something new. With wide eyes, they toss their heads and step sideways when they're supposed to move forward. They throw in a buck or miniature rear. They come off their feet and break out of their gaits. No one, not even the judges at Louisville, faults babies for acting like babies in two-year-old classes, but a confident one will stand out.

In the open division, which means that professional trainers like Mitch can be at the helm of their horses, performance, not manners, is paramount. The horses are shown at the edge of control, threatening to explode at every step. In one open five-gaited class, I watched a light chestnut gelding jump so close to the judge, he nearly knocked down the decorative ferns in center ring. I turned to my friend Linda and groaned. "That's too bad. He's the best horse in the class."

Linda owns more Saddlebreds than she has fingers. A powerhouse in the insurance field, she's an award-winning entrepreneur with a business that's handled more than $1 billion in claims. Some people buy Corvettes or take up tennis at midlife. Instead, Linda found Saddlebreds, and she dove right in with the same girl-boss energy she brings to everything she does. Now, she breeds them too, making horses her side hustle.

"Oh, honey, that won't matter," she said. She stirred her drink, something pink and fruity looking, not what I'd expect from a CEO who commanded in a male-dominated landscape. I would've pegged Linda for a whiskey woman, but the surprise was delightful.

"Want to try some?" She jutted her chin toward her drink. "There's plenty in the cooler!" Then, she self-corrected. "That's right. You don't drink. Perfect." Linda laughed. "This barn needs a designated driver. Anyway, that horse is going to win it. I'd put money on it. This is an open class." A horse who's giving a thrilling performance will be forgiven an explosion or two. It's expected. The classes for younger horses receive even more leeway on manners.

In a two-year-old class, the judges reward performance, but they're also looking for brilliance and conformation. In those classes, judges are like college basketball scouts at a junior varsity game. Scouts know that the athletes they're watching haven't fully matured, but they can see the potential in the youngster with focused eyes and long, well-muscled legs. Even if he flubs it, if he's got the guts to barrel down center court and take a three-point shot with two other kids trying to block him, they know he's one to keep an eye on.

Calling a wild man like Sky Watch well-behaved is a stretch, but by all accounts, he behaved, outshowing the other two-year-olds as if they weren't even there. They trotted. Sky Watch floated. For weeks, Mitch had been working the colt off the rail, trying to get him used to taking his gaits without the security of a wall next to him. He had to. Sky Watch dictated the duo's lines down the rail. Mitch could ask him to take a certain trajectory, but if Sky Watch didn't like it, it wasn't worth arguing. So Mitch had to teach the colt to handle off-rail work. Two-year-olds usually stick to the rail. The openness of the center of the arena is too cavernous. With their 360-degree vision, the young ones can see too much. The rail gives them safety and security. But Sky Watch didn't need it.

With each lap around the arena, Sky Watch's trot grew more explosive. If God ever put a trot on a horse, it went to Sky Watch. A trot like that will pop most riders' hips up and out of the saddle, but Mitch could sit it without even posting, keeping his upper body balanced and bouncing along with it. However, many horses with a big trot can't rack. They're built for the one-two punch of the diagonal gait, two feet leaving the ground at the same time in opposing pairs. As Sky Watch kept trotting, some audience members nudged one another. "Sure, he can trot like a freak. But can he rack?" So far, they were impressed, but Sky Watch would have to perform well in all five gaits to truly make a name for himself. Saddlebred people are snobs. Many have too much money and too much time, and they love to judge one another.

When the announcer called the slow gait, Mitch sat deep, lifted and widened his hands, and rocked his horse back. Sky Watch telegraphed excitement back to his rider, his mouth solid yet soft on the bridle: *I thought you'd never ask.* What no one could see was the constant conversation between Mitch's body and the horse. He kept the colt moving forward, but no one could tell that he couldn't stick Sky Watch right where he wanted him. Really, it was a compromise. Mitch asked. The horse declined. Mitch accepted and redirected. The audience couldn't tell, but Sky Watch never wound up exactly where Mitch wanted him to be.

As he passed the other colts in the class, Sky Watch eyed them and stepped higher. A natural show horse, he knew what competition meant, and it was clear he didn't think much of his competition. He blew past them as if they were standing still, and they weren't even racking yet. Mitch had yet to discover his horse's full speed in the fourth and fifth gait, but he didn't need it. He could beat them going slow. It was almost as if he were the only horse in the class. Everyone who saw him said so. They used the terms *freak*, *star*, and *best*. Now-retired training great Bob Ruxer stood on the sidelines that day and will never forget it. "You could feel the earth shake when Sky Watch went by . . . After it was over, it was hard to remember who was second."

In the photographer's flash, Sky Watch stands with ears forward, all lank and legs, his neck lathered with sweat. The colt had just had an experience. His first time in the show ring. Now, he knew what all those hours of practice at home, all those two-workout days, were for. In the photograph, all the trainers lined up along the rail have their eyes trained on Sky Watch. The crowd in the stands too. Even the three award presenters, holding the end-table-sized silver trays that serve for trophies, gaze at the horse instead of the photographer, H. Leon "Sarge" Sargent. The only person in the photo not staring at the young powerhouse is Mitch, who gazes at the camera, his mouth dropped open as if caught mid-"whoa," his heels firm in the stirrup irons. The two-year-old gaited stake isn't usually the class that gets everyone talking, but that day, the entire fairgrounds buzzed with Sky Watch's name.

The next night, a five-year-old gelding named Imperator wowed the crowd in the horse show's biggest, most important class, the one that every trainer dreams of from the moment she pulls on her boots in the morning until she takes them off again at night: the Five-Gaited World's Grand Championship, where only the best of the best compete. In it are the top contenders of the mare, stallion, and gelding five-gaited classes that had taken place that week.

That Saturday night, Imperator took a reserve ribbon that some say could have been a victory pass. A liver chestnut with a white star on his forehead and a white snip edging from his right nostril like a flame, Imperator looked more like a painter's idea of the ideal Saddlebred than a real-life horse. Don Harris, one of the great showmen of the twentieth century, trained and exhibited him. "Make some noise," Don would encourage onlookers as he trotted the chocolate-brown gelding by. "He likes it." Don was right. Under the arena lights, Imperator bloomed.

Don stood long-legged and wiry, with calves that could wrap around a horse's barrel if he needed them to. He would hold his hat to his chest—the saddle seat equivalent of a magician's post-trick bow—when he knew he was making an especially good pass. His posture on horseback is still famous today. This year, when I visited Karin Folkers, my old trainer from my junior exhibitor days, she stuck me on an older gaited gelding. "I want you to slow gait him like Don Harris," she instructed. She meant I should tilt my pelvis under me, shift my weight back, lift my hands up to shoulder level, and stick my elbows out like wings. Don's positioning worked for me and that gelding, and it worked in 1979 too. When Imperator entered an arena, the attention flew to him. His expression, all focus and white-rimmed eyes, magnetized. *Look at me*, he seemed to say, *and I'll make it worth your while.*

When Don exited the arena with Imperator that year, he probably wasn't thinking about Sky Watch as the contender to beat. The red colt still had a few years in the baby classes—the three-year-old stake, the junior stake—before he'd be ready to face off against the big boys and girls. Surely, Don had heard the buzz, but he knew he had a grand horse, so he didn't worry about the youngster. He couldn't have known that he'd spend most of the 1980s facing Imperator off against Sky Watch, the two trading tricolor ribbons for the span of the decade.

In October 1979, Michele Macfarlane called her mother after a visit to Mitch Clark's. Petite and soft-voiced, Michele had let Mitch show her his nicest horses all day without giving much indication of which she wanted to buy. Born into the Scripps newspaper empire—practically American royalty—but raised as a California rancher's daughter, Michele and her mother had the bank account to buy out all of Mitch's stock if she were so inclined. In sensible slacks and blouse, Michele looked more like a schoolteacher than an heiress or a cowgirl, but her skill on horseback matched the depth of her wealth. Even though she could work show horses herself, she showed as an amateur. Amateur status isn't determined by skill but by paid vocation. As soon as an amateur accepts compensation for working with horses, whether training, teaching lessons, or grooming, she's not an amateur anymore. Michele didn't need to accept compensation for anything.

Today, the American Saddlebred world is dominated by the amateur. Most classes on any given show bill are designated for amateurs or junior exhibitors, but it hasn't always been that way. Horse shows used to be an exhibition sport, just like horse racing. The owners possessed the horses, but they left the riding to the professionals. No Kentucky Derby–winning owner ever climbs on his own horse. He'd be ridiculed if he tried. Saddlebreds used to be the same. The trainers did both the training and the exhibition. To borrow mystery author Rita Mae Brown's simile, it's as if the football coach got out there and played quarterback too. By the late 1970s, amateur classes had taken hold, but trainers still rode the top horses. No one else had the chops to handle mounts of that caliber—or so everyone supposed.

After visiting the top trainers in Kentucky and seeing what they had to offer, Michele knew she was ready to buy. October was the perfect time to buy a new horse. Show season was almost over, so trainers had more than four months to work their horses and get them prepped for the next year's spring shows. Back in the hotel that night, Michele dialed her mother in California. October in Kentucky can still be humid, nothing like the dry heat at her San Diego ranch, so I can picture Michele sitting near the air conditioner and enjoying its chill as she pressed the phone to her ear. She didn't even need to consider the long-distance charges she'd incur. Horses the price of houses were at stake.

"I like them both," she said, referring to Sky Watch and Buck Rogers, a deep chestnut harness horse from another nearby farm who also went on to World's Grand Champion titles. "Which horse should I buy?"

On the other end of the phone, for Ellen "Brownie" Scripps Davis, it would have been midafternoon. Why not buy a pair of world's champions before dinner? Brownie told her daughter to buy both. Della Large agreed to the $50,000 offer, and Sky Watch's fate was sealed. He'd leave the bluegrass of Kentucky for the eucalyptus trees of Southern California.

Soon afterward, Mitch wrapped Sky Watch's legs in soft bandages to prepare him for the long trip west. As usual, the stud colt couldn't stand still, but Mitch had gotten plenty of practice in working on him as a moving target. While the commission check from the sale eased the loss, he still felt a knot in his throat. He knew he was saying goodbye to the best horse he'd ever have the privilege of sitting on.

4

Difficult Horses

On an early spring Saturday, I closed myself into the bedroom to make a phone call of my own. A month after meeting Mitch, I looked up Michele Macfarlane in the American Saddlebred Horse and Breeders Association's member directory. It took a week and most of a day to work up the courage to call the woman who'd become a role model to all female saddle seat riders. In Indiana, it was just past lunchtime. Late morning in California. The morning barn chores should be wrapping up, the day shifting into the rhythm of working horses. I expected only to reach her voice mail, but to my delight, a breathy "Hello" came through the speaker after just two rings.

"Oh, hi! I'm looking for Michele Macfarlane. Is she available?"

"This is Michele." Her voice was higher than I expected, brighter.

"Oh my gosh! Wow. Okay." Eventually, I stopped stumbling over my words. "I'm interested in Sky Watch and want to learn more about him. I'm too young to have seen him show, but he's . . ." Here, words failed me. ". . . very important to the breed. No other horse can compare."

"Well, thank you. That was a long time ago, you know. Have you talked to Mitchell? He knows the horse best."

"Yes. He's been great. But I'd love to hear your perspective too." I paced along the bed while I talked.

I prepared to ask my first question: Is it Sky Watch or Skywatch? In the advertisements and on the street sign in Danville, he's Skywatch. In the registry, he's Sky Watch. That's the name Della Large gave him after seeing it on the Weather Channel, according to Mary-Ann Teater. It hearkened back to Flight Time, which echoed Wing Commander. Della enjoyed naming her babies. Is there a reason Michele advertised him as Skywatch instead? People in the horse world take names seriously. Before I could spit any of that out, Michele stopped me.

"Maybe," she said, "what would help would be if you wrote some questions down for me and emailed them? Then I could have time to think about my answers before I respond. My memory isn't what it used to be."

When I hung up, I held Michele's email address and her personal cell phone number. She suggested I text her if I needed to reach her. "Michele and I are on texting terms now," I crowed to Ben, waving the Post-it note like a victory flag.

Ben stuck his head into my office. "I see that. Good for you, sweetie. Nice work." He looked out over the backyard, all scrub grass and dirt, a far cry from the manicured San Diego landscaping of Michele's Scripps Miramar Ranch. Ben wore lawn-mowing shoes, the final working iteration of his worn-out running shoes, which were lined up along a wall in our garage. The rotation went like this: running shoes, dog-walking shoes, lawn-mowing shoes, garbage. "I need to get back out there before it rains."

Ben's indifference didn't bother me. Michele Macfarlane, *the* Michele Macfarlane, was going to give me insight on Sky Watch. Everyone, from my horse trainer to strangers on the internet, had warned me about how shy she was, how hesitant to talk about herself. Somehow, though, I'd gotten through to her. My name might have meant nothing to a Saddlebred mogul like her, but she'd agreed to help me. Maybe she liked the sound of my voice. Maybe she was flattered by my interest. Or maybe—here, I quaked, unwilling to go down this mental path—she would ditch me, leaving my questions unanswered. The next day, I typed and retyped a set of questions for Michele, culling them until only eleven remained to copy and paste into an email. No need to overwhelm her on the first round.

After hitting send, I fantasized about visiting San Diego to meet her in person. Maybe by then, my belly would be rounded with pregnancy, and Michele would marvel at my bravery. A cross-country flight in the third trimester? I'd make a joke about what women do for the sake of horses, and we'd laugh together. Then, she'd show me around the Torrey pine–lined pastures and introduce me to her famous pinto Saddlebreds, the ones who grace the Rose Parade every year. We'd sit in the tack room, among the perfume of mink-oiled leather, and chat like old friends.

I stuck the Post-it with Michele's number to the wall above my desk, right next to a horse calendar. April. We had three months until the scheduled vasectomy reversal. V-day. One week after that, I would have my first show with My Queen Bee under the Mike McIntosh Stables banner. After a winter in training with Mike McIntosh, a local trainer with a half century's worth of experience with Saddlebreds and a reputation for patience with young horses, Bee was starting to look show ready. Mike seems like a man transplanted from another era. He rises before sunrise every day, drinking nothing but black coffee until he goes to bed. He collects nineteenth-century literature and spends most of his day engaged in labor that's from the nineteenth century too. Working horses. Putting up hay. Splicing leather to repair his own tack. Like Mitch Clark and Don Harris, and so many successful trainers, Mike is long-legged. He's eternally wearing khakis and a baseball cap. I sometimes wonder if he sleeps in them.

Mike agreed that Bee was about as much horse as anyone could get with a budget my size, so we weren't expecting a blue ribbon, just a decent trip around the ring. I trusted Mike's opinion. He's got a great reputation in the industry. Decades before I called Michele Macfarlane to ask about Sky Watch, Mike had turned down her offer to work for him. Not because he didn't want to work for her, but because he wasn't ready to uproot his young family and move across the country for a job, no matter how promising. My point is that Mike is good. Very good. Good enough that, early in his career, Michele Macfarlane sought him out.

Weeks passed without a word from Michele. I texted. She responded, asking for more time. Her tone was friendly. Approachable. She even sent me a smiley-face emoji. Meanwhile, Mike prepped Bee for me to show. Every Friday, I spent the afternoon at the barn, most of it in her stall, brushing her or just watching her nibble hay after her workout. Every Saturday, I rode her.

"Now," Mike said as I dismounted one Saturday, "with a horse like this, you can't make a lot of mistakes and be competitive." He meant a horse who lacked performance-level talent. "We won't put her in any shows where she'll be outclassed, but still, your rides need to be clean for her to compete, and they won't be clean at first. She's green! Some mistakes are bound to happen. Try not to let them get to you."

Some days, Bee marched beneath me, cranking her head up. Others, she moved like a lesson horse, hardmouthed and stubborn, channeling all her energy into speed instead of action.

"Will she be ready to show?" I asked Mike. "I don't need a blue ribbon, but I don't want to look like we don't belong in the show ring."

"When we hit the gate," he promised me, "she'll be ready. I won't let you go anywhere you'd look out of place. This mare doesn't need to go to Kentucky, but there are other shows."

Finally, six weeks after emailing Michele, her response arrived. Michele thanked me for my patience and included her answers to my questions as an attachment. I opened her email right away, leaving dinner to burn on the stove while I read her replies. When it came to the name, she didn't have a preference. Sky Watch or Skywatch—either worked for her. She used the latter in ads, she said, because it was catchier. Saddlebred registry nerds, the ones who could recite lineages like basketball fans recite starting lineups, preferred Sky Watch. I would have loved to ask Michele how she felt about going against that tradition, but emails don't allow for quick repartee. With email, there's not the back-and-forth of conversation, especially with a six-week delay.

Michele has owned hundreds of Saddlebreds throughout her lifetime. She still owns dozens and is still involved in the day-to-day running of her farm. It wouldn't surprise me to see her clearing horsehair out of the dryer vent before muscling in another load of rub rags. Or wielding a hammer, pounding a stray nail back into a horse's stall. Or on a tractor, spreading manure. Farm work is never done, and answering email is considered a low priority compared to putting up hay and cleaning stalls.

Michele requested that I send any other questions by email too. "No problem," I replied, hiding my disappointment. My fantasy of bonding with Michele in the Scripps Miramar tack room fizzled. "Next set of questions attached." I steeled myself for another six weeks of silence. At least I had my own Saddlebred to focus on. Soon, My Queen Bee would take me into the ring. Her trot would never look like Sky Watch's, but we'd find out what kind of show horse she could be. On the entry form, in the column for "owner," my name would appear next to hers. Bee might not be much of a show horse, but she belonged to me.

After buying Sky Watch in the fall of 1979, Michele had him vanned straight to West Coast trainer Rob Tanner King's Row Acres in Encinitas, just a thirty-minute drive up I-5 from Scripps Ranch. Scripps Ranch is the San Diego suburb where Michele's farm still stands. It's named after Michele's damline: the Scripps family.

In the first recorded horse shipment, in 1500 BCE, an invading Persian army sent horses to Greece by sea for battle. Many of the horses didn't make it. Either restrained in slings above deck or tied tightly in cramped quarters below, the panicked horses threw their heavy bodies against the ropes and walls again and again, beating themselves to death in fury and terror. Many of the ones who survived the fray fell ill on the journey and died. When they arrived in Greece, no unloading ramp awaited the steeds left standing. Soldiers slung them straight from the deck into the sea to fight the tide and find the shore before battling Greek soldiers.

Luckily for Sky Watch, and all horses everywhere, horse transport improved in the roughly 3,500 years between the Persian invasion and Sky Watch's trip west. In Sky Watch's day, horses typically traveled in a truck-pulled trailer, trailer windows open wide to the breeze and noise of the highway. Today, horses can travel in style in climate-controlled, smooth-riding semis that cushion their legs against the bumps and rough surfaces. They can even travel by air, in specially designed stalls in cargo holds.

Rob Tanner was known as Ken Lawson back then, before a numerologist suggested he change his name. Superstitions run rampant in the horse world. *Never leave your hat on the bed. Don't forget your lucky socks. If you say a horse is sound after a period of lameness, knock on wood.* It's no surprise that a major trainer would subscribe to numerology. Some horse people have been known to use animal psychics. Rob didn't need an animal psychic to know how special Sky Watch was. He must have had big plans for him. The whole Saddlebred world wanted to know if the colt could follow up on his stunning two-year-old performance at Louisville. Some two-year-olds, especially ones who are pushed as hard as Sky Watch had to be, fall apart under the pressure and are unsound by the time they charge the gate for the first show of their three-year-old season. Was Sky Watch really a freak, the next great since My-My, or would his body break under its own forces?

The Saddlebred industry is criticized for working its horses too hard, too young. Lipizzans, the breed of choice at the prestigious Spanish Riding School in Vienna, aren't started under saddle until they're four, the age when horses reach sexual maturity. By four, a horse's growth plates, cartilaginous structures that lengthen the bones above and below the knees, are completely closed, so they're less prone to injury. Most of them have reached their adult height, and they're mentally capable of handling the strain of training, performing, and competing.

Most equestrian disciplines don't wait until a horse's fourth year to throw a saddle on him. Hunter-jumpers might start going over jumps as early as three or four, although some say to wait until they're at least five. Jumping can be hard on developing legs. Thoroughbred racehorses start their racing careers at age two, and many are done by age five. The Kentucky Derby, for example, is only open to three-year-old colts and fillies. Some horses, especially ones that run hot, like Saddlebreds and Thoroughbreds, need early training. Depending on the personality, a green four-year-old Saddlebred stud who's been out in the field his whole life could be dangerous.

Sky Watch was one of those horses.

After our lunch at Cheddar's, Mitch and I arrived back at the barn to find Anthio standing with a young horse, already saddled and bridled, in the grooming stall. "I started riding Sky Watch out of self-defense," Mitch had explained. When Mitch appeared, Anthio led the colt out. "This one'll be much easier. Which is good. I'm not as young as I used to be."

"How old is he?" I asked. "Can I say hi to him?"

"He's three," Anthio said softly. "And for sure."

I patted the colt's arched neck, the muscles firm under the soft hide. "Hi, buddy." He cocked his head and flared his nostrils. "You're handsome. Here, give me a sniff."

The colt snuffled my open palm, and my heart dropped and opened as it always did. I turned to Anthio. "He reminds me of the walk-trot horse I had as a junior exhibitor." The colt could have been my old horse Keeper's much-younger brother. Maybe he was.

"Yep, I think this one will be three-gaited."

"He's got the neck for it."

With one hand still on the bridle, Anthio swooped down and scooted a red plastic step stool next to the horse. On cue, Mitch strode up to mount the horse, stepping onto the stool before sticking a toe in the stirrup. "My granddaddy would be rolling in his grave if he saw me using this," he said as he swung up from the stool and into the saddle. "But ever since my hip surgery, the docs say I have to."

"How long ago was that?" I didn't think Mitch moved like an orthopedic surgery patient.

"What was it, Anthio?" Mitch twisted in the saddle, holding the reins in one hand as he walked the colt to the outer ring of the arena. "Nine months ago?"

"Something like that," the young assistant trainer agreed, but Mitch had stopped paying attention. All his focus had shifted to the horse, who bounce-walked confidently on a loose rein, his ears up.

"He's so good with the young ones."

Anthio smiled brightly again. "He's the best. I'm really lucky to learn under him."

For a guy who worked eleven-hour days and had just been left waiting while his boss took a two-plus-hour lunch break, Anthio maintained the same enthusiasm for his work that a Labrador has for tennis balls.

I tucked myself behind a stall to watch Mitch work the necky chestnut colt who reminded me so much of my own Keeper. If I closed my eyes, I could have been back in Virginia in the late 1990s. The scent of hay and shavings. Hoofbeats pounding out a trot.

Under a lemony sun, I climbed on Keeper's back and walked, trotted, and cantered him along the fence line. My then trainer Karin had ridden him first, made sure he was safe enough for my twelve-year-old self. She had approved. "He's game," she'd said, "but you'll be able to ride him. You're just as game." Karin looked just like Alanis Morissette. With a smoker's voice that cracked over its syllables, she sounded like her too.

We bought Keeper of the Stars, then three years old, after that single ride in an open field somewhere within driving distance of Lynchburg, Virginia. After my mom and dad divorced, Mom and I had landed there when she accepted her first full-time job since dancing in Amsterdam in the 1970s. My dad still lived in Indiana, and my brothers had both started college, so suddenly, my family had shrunk to two. Mother and daughter. I'd always been a mommy's girl, though. We shared horses, the only thing that mattered to me. When my dad remarried, my main concern was that the wedding conflicted with a horse show. Lynchburg was five hundred miles away from the only home I'd known, but Virginia was horse country, so the move didn't seem so bad after all.

Keeper had a bright chestnut coat and kind eyes that turned mischievous when the wind changed. He loved bananas, peppermints, and tobacco pulled out of my mom's Winston 100's. He hated puddles and would toss his head and sidestep them as if they were bottomless pits. He half reared at the start of every canter and spooked at dust clouds, but he did it with swagger, not fear. Because of behavior like this, buying a three-year-old is always risky. The horse is still unformed, adolescent. Keeper had promise, but we didn't know if he could live up to it yet.

On Saturdays and Sundays, my mom drove me to Windy Hill Farm to ride Keeper and any other horses Karin let me sit on. The two women talked while I groomed and tacked horse after horse, breathing in their warm animal smell, their hay-scented breath. Once I'd mounted, the leather reins between my gloved fingers turned into telegraph wires, connecting me to my horse's mind. We communicated through shifts of weight, flicks of ears, tension of muscles. After good rides, the ones when I made the horses march with knees level to the chest or cantered Keeper "in a bucket," the one-two-three beat like a slow waltz, my mom clapped her hands together and said, "Good ride, Em." On our way home, we often stopped at a cottage deli for vegetable subs and, for me, a piece of sweet potato pie. If I had a daughter, would we have a post-barn ritual? What type of pie would be her favorite?

As Mitch rode by, still in the bouncy animated walk, he broke my reverie. "Step out here and watch, honey. You'll be able to see better."

I did as I was told. "I was just trying not to spook him. I know he's young."

Mitch urged the horse into a trot. "He's got to learn sometime." As the pair trotted past, the colt eyed me but didn't jump. Mitch's quiet hands held him steady. All afternoon, Mitch worked horse after horse with the same steadiness. His voice never rose. His body never stiffened. His attention never wavered from the animal in front of him. As I drove home that night, I realized the magic that had unfurled in front of me that day. Mitch really was a master horseman.

Rob Tanner was a master horseman too. He had everything it takes to work with a young star like Sky Watch. In 2013, not long after Rob's death, *National Horseman* published four short videos featuring Rob Tanner's horsemanship. In them, Rob exudes the classic combination of gentle firmness. Two of the videos show Rob working directly with a horse, discussing equine locomotion and body mechanics as he works. He knew his stuff. Even when the two-year-old filly he's long lining in the video snorts, switches her tail, and breaks her trot, he remains patient and lets her work out the babyishness before asking her to return to work.

Another video, *Body Language Controls a Horse*, reveals some of the inner workings of the Saddlebred industry. In it, a young Latino groom brushes a filly while holding her lead rope loosely in one hand as he works. She's barely started her training, so the whole process of being handled is new to her. Rather than dominating her and forcing her to stand still, the groom works with her as she moves, allowing both groom and the young horse to be at ease.

Rob, standing off-camera, praises his work. "Now Lupé is really good. He will move as he's brushing her. If she moves, he doesn't try to stop her; he just keeps brushing her to a stop. That way, you never get her hurt, and she learns that brushing feels good."

Like most sectors of the horse world, the American Saddlebred industry uses a lot of Latine labor, with plenty of undocumented workers. Barn owners are always looking for people who will work hard in exchange for living quarters and low pay, and some are willing to turn a blind eye to technicalities like citizenship or green card status. The organizational chart of the typical barn has grooms—who take care of menial labor like cleaning stalls and grooming, feeding, and watering horses—at the bottom. At larger barns, there might be an assistant trainer or two, maybe a lesson instructor, and then the trainer at the top.

Grooms work the longest hours for the lowest pay. They're up before dawn to water, feed, and clean stalls. Then they labor in the barn all day, brushing horses before their workouts and rubbing them dry afterward, pausing midafternoon to hay and water again. Once all the horses are worked, a groom might have to stay behind to help prepare horses for lesson kids or to clean tack and sweep the day's dust and hay from the aisleway. If he's lucky, he gets to go rest for a couple of hours before it's time for the evening feeding and watering. Right before bed, a groom does one last round of the barn, checking water buckets and making sure all the horses are resting quietly. Then, the next day, it's up again in the dark to start all over. They work six or seven days a week, year-round. Horses must be fed and watered, even on Christmas and New Year's Day.

In the barn where I rode as a teenager, the groom in charge of Keeper was also named Lupé. Keeper loved Lupé, probably more than he loved me. Lupé spent the most time with him. Except on Saturdays, when I was there, Lupé brushed him before his workouts and toweled him after. He fed him hay and grain every day and made sure the shavings in his stall stayed fresh and fluffy. Lupé couldn't have been older than nineteen, only a few years older than I was at the time. He seemed to take great pride in his work, creasing his face into a huge smile whenever I thanked him for what he did with Keeper. Keeper never looked anything but his best, his coat shiny, his hooves spotless, his tail soft and full.

The inequities between Lupé and me didn't bother me then, but now, they make me uncomfortable. At horse shows, while I stayed at the Holiday Inn, he slept on a cot in an empty stall, ready to wake at a moment's notice if a horse got into trouble. Over weekends at the barn, while I lounged on post-ride boat trips, Lupé swept the barn aisle. Over the winter holidays, Lupé and I both traveled to Texas, but he continued south to cross the border to Mexico. While the money he made at the barn wasn't much, he sent what he could to support his mother and brothers back home.

Not all barns rely on undocumented workers, but most are run and funded by white people. At Mike McIntosh Stables, three people handle the twenty-five-horse training operation: one trainer and two assistant trainers. The two assistant trainers, Brock Rutledge and Julie Twining, might receive better pay than some grooms, but they still have to sleep in stalls at horse shows and rarely get a full day off. Mike, Brock, and Julie are white. All the customers are white. While none of us would consider ourselves racist and many of us flew "Black Lives Matter" flags in our yards after the George Floyd murder in 2020, a person with Black or brown skin might not feel comfortable strapping on a pair of boots and stepping into such a white space. Across every discipline in the horse world, the racial makeup is similar.

Michele Macfarlane reads as white as a West Hartford housewife, but she's actually the great-granddaughter of a celebrated Buffalo Soldier. Second Lieutenant Paschal Conley boasted a storied military career that included promoting literacy among his fellow Black soldiers. The Conley family is one of the oldest "organized families" in America, according to the Conley Trust, and they have a long history with horses dating back to the early twentieth century. Michele is part of that history.

Sky Watch wasn't concerned with history, race, and ethnicity, though. In 1979, he had a job to do, a new trainer to try to outsmart, and a new owner to impress. Through the winter of 1979–1980, which, in San Diego County, doesn't feel like winter, Rob and Sky Watch got to know each other.

By the early spring shows, Rob had to show the world what he'd done with Sky Watch, and the pair won some three-year-old classes on the West

Coast. However, the colt lacked the magic he'd had with Mitch. In the one photo I can find of Rob and Sky Watch, Sky Watch looks good but not great. In it, he trots high, breaking level, but he's not as up-headed, not as forward and through the bridle. It looks like Rob is keeping him tucked in. Friends from the horse business who look at that picture pronounce it unrecognizable. "I'll take the 'after' photo, please," they say, referring to Mitch and Sky Watch's widely circulated 1984 victory pass. In that photo, the team looks ready to fly straight out of the frame. Where Mitch looks relaxed and half-amused, Rob looks pensive, like he's working on a puzzle. He was.

Difficult horses are puzzles that would make a *New York Times* crossword whiz throw the paper out the window. Mitch agrees that, had he not been at the exact point in his life that he was when Sky Watch jumped off that trailer, he might not have been able to work with him. But, because he'd been desperate to get out of the stereo shop and prove himself as a horse trainer, he put in the time and effort to bring Sky Watch along. When Sky Watch arrived, Rob had already established himself as a trainer, working horses for Michele and other West Coast clients. He didn't have the hunger that gnawed at Mitch.

In her emailed response, Michele explained, "Rob also had a very nice three-year-old gaited mare for another customer, and I think she was more Rob's kind of horse than Sky Watch was. . . . Not all trainers get along with all horses."

To Michele's delight, Rob had even let her show her own colt during that three-year-old season, something most trainers would never do. Typically, trainers show their clients' horses through their junior year. This allows the professional to work through all the behavior that comes with showing babies. The shying. The spooking and sidestepping. The sudden refusal to wear the bridle, even though the damn filly has been wearing the curb at home with no problem for weeks. By the time most horses are five, they're professionals, having shown for two or even three seasons. They can navigate traffic in the ring, trot past an umbrella without being terrified, and stand calmly in the lineup. Some trainers show their clients' horses through the end of their career, especially with a stake horse. The type of fire needed to win at the top levels is thought to be too much for amateur hands to manage—and often, it is.

Michele Macfarlane was no average amateur. She had started riding on the family ranch as a little girl. It was a way of life for her family, so she joined in. Immediately, her competitive nature kicked in, and soon enough, she trotted victory passes with the best of them. By 1979, Michele and her mother, Ellen "Brownie" Scripps Davis, were featured all over the West Coast horse show scene. They sat on show boards and committees, kept horses at home for breeding, and sent out horses for training. Michele lived and breathed horses just as much as her trainers did, but she had the luxury of not having to do it for a living.

I can picture her smiling when she realized she'd get to show Sky Watch at Santa Barbara. "Rob was obligated to show the mare for the other client," she said, and rather than scratch Sky Watch from the show, Rob had asked Michele if she'd like to show him.

Founded in 1919, the Santa Barbara National is one of the West Coast's oldest shows. Held every July, it features multiple breeds competing in three different arenas at the Earl Warren Showgrounds, with the Santa Ynez mountains as a backdrop. Sky Watch must have loved the openness of the outdoor arena, the way the sky went on above his head forever. A horse like that will work up a full head of steam in an outdoor arena, and it takes a strong rider to keep that steam from boiling over.

Luckily for Michele, and for Sky Watch, she was a strong rider. "[Rob] had Sky Watch in very good order for me." In her email to me, Michele was too modest to say how she had placed, but a dive into the archives shows that she won the class. "After the class, Dewey Henderson, the judge, looked me up and said I could win with him at Louisville. Dewey was very excited. I was too!" That victory pass planted the seed of a dream. The California rancher's daughter loved nothing more than winning. In the Saddlebred world, there is no bigger win than the Five-Gaited World's Grand Championship. It had been more than a half century since an amateur took a victory pass in that class. That honor belonged to Revel English, a fellow West Coaster. But a woman—a woman had never won it.

After the excitement at the Santa Barbara National, though, Sky Watch's performances didn't improve through the season. Sure, he won some classes, but he lacked something. Truth was, the red stud didn't spark across the tanbark the way he had at Louisville with Mitch. In fact, he didn't look like the same horse. Could be, he'd burned himself out.

Michele hated to see Sky Watch fading. She had major goals for him. She had major goals for all her horses. Since the mid-1970s, she and Brownie had been on a mission to improve the quality of pinto Saddlebreds until they could compete with their more sedately colored brothers and sisters. In the horse world, *pinto* has nothing to do with beans. Pinto horses have large patches of white on their coat, making them brown and white or black and white. In the mid-twentieth century, "spotted Saddlebreds" were considered ugly and coarse, and even the ones who had talent wouldn't win against a chestnut, black, or bay. However, Brownie loved the flash of pintos, and she'd started using them as parade mounts in 1960. By the time Sky Watch hit the California coast, the mother-daughter team had been, as Michele said, "working like crazy" to breed nicer and nicer pintos.

Over the years, they succeeded. Chubasco, Michele's top-producing pinto site, fathered over two hundred sixty foals that made it into the Saddlebred registry. Fifty-eight of those foals won ribbons at Louisville, proving they were just as good as any other horse in the ring. In 1998, they represented Saddlebreds on a world stage. Eight pinto Saddlebreds flew to Japan to perform in the Nagano Winter Olympics closing ceremony. They'd been trained to rear and walk on their hind legs, and four of them pulled an Old West–style stagecoach with a glowing Michele in the copilot's seat.

For the annual Rose Parade in Pasadena, Scripps Miramar pulls out all the stops. Michele turns out a host of spotted Saddlebreds, with riders in elaborate themed costumes that change every year. Circus clowns and high-wire artist tutus. Dollywood-style Western get-ups. The robes and crowns of medieval royalty. The horses march through the streets along with the floats and brass bands. Michele's mother would be proud. Brownie loved parades more than anyone.

Michele Macfarlane is one of the chief ambassadors for the American Saddlebred, making sure that Saddlebreds are in the public eye whenever she gets the chance. Tens, maybe even hundreds, of millions of viewers all over the world saw Michele and her Saddlebreds in Japan in 1998. Every year, thirty-seven million people watch the Rose Parade in San Diego on New Year's Day. Michele puts Saddlebreds in the spotlight, using her wealth and influence to promote the horses she's built her life around. That exposure means something to a breed whose growth is slowing. The industry needs people like her who can apply their resources and competitive spirit to the problem of breed promotion. The Saddlebred isn't going to die out on Michele's watch.

Sky Watch became part of the Scripps Miramar breeding mission. At the tender age of three, he took his first trips to the breeding shed. Most horses in training aren't simultaneously covering mares, whether through live cover or artificial insemination. The common thought is that it wears them out or dulls them. Show horses show. Breeding horses breed. They're two completely different types of performance.

In a potentially regrettable Google search, I filled out the blank box with "semen collection stallion." Some of the YouTube clips seemed more appropriate for an OnlyFans account, so I skipped over those and chose one with the promise of British humor: *I W*** Horses For a Living*, a short documentary for England's Channel 4 public broadcasting. Artificial insemination is much more popular now than it was in the 1970s, but it was still a common method of breeding. It's safer for the mares, as they don't get mounted by a horny, thousand-pound being, and it's safer for the handlers. Building plans for breeding sheds include escape doors for the humans should things go awry—and when things go awry with large animals in full breeding musk, they go very awry. People can easily be killed with a stray hoof strike or a body check from a sexually frustrated stallion. Any work environment that requires escape doors should include hazard pay for its employees.

Thanks to British public broadcasting, I learned that, for the stallion, artificial insemination uses just about as much energy as live cover. While they don't risk getting kicked by a nonconsenting mare, the stallions still rear on their hind legs and mount a padded, vaguely horse-shaped figure. There, a human technician guides the stallion's penis into an artificial vagina, where semen is collected. A teaser mare, who's in heat but won't actually be bred, stays behind a metal mesh wall. The stud can smell her, which gets him excited, but he's just as happy to mount the equine version of a blow-up doll that he's offered. For both live cover and semen collection, the process doesn't take long—some things don't change between humans and horses—but it still takes a lot of energy out of a male horse. More than that, it can change his mindset. Instead of focusing on training, he's thinking about the next time he'll get to mount something, whether that's a real, live mare or a padded apparatus.

Over the winter of 1980, Michele took mares to Sky Watch to be bred. Only two of Sky Watch's foals from that breeding season, Skylab and The Skyhawk, are registered with the American Saddlebred Horse and Breeders Association. Both boys sired their own offspring, but neither collected Louisville-level accolades. It's possible Sky Watch serviced more mares than just the two who produced foals in 1981, but the record only shows live foals, not breeding attempts. Just as with humans, equine fertility is a matter of timing and luck, and not all pregnancies carry to term. While researching all these equine breeding practices, I started to get nervous about my own prospects in the breeding shed. Would Ben and I be lucky enough to get pregnant the old-fashioned way, or would we need to resort to artificial insemination? What's the human version of a teaser mare? *Playboy*?

According to Michele, Sky Watch might have bred too many mares in his three-year-old year. Still, she sent Sky Watch and Rob to Louisville to try to conquer the three-year-old five-gaited division. All the pieces should have been in place. According to all who knew him and worked with him, Rob was a talented horseman. Sky Watch was a freakishly good horse with an owner who could afford the best for him. He'd had success at Louisville the previous year, so everyone knew he could perform in the energy and noise of Freedom Hall. He'd even had some success on the West Coast circuit in the spring. The colt should have been ready.

When Rob and Sky Watch trotted through the gate, cheers met them and then died down. The wonder colt had grown some since his two-year-old year. His shoulders had broadened. His haunches had filled out, and he stood a hair taller at the withers. Rob worked Sky Watch through his gaits. Trot, slow gait, rack, and canter. Counterclockwise, then clockwise. The horse did his job, but he lacked the smolder that ignited so much fuss after his two-year-old class. Three-year-old Sky Watch looked fine, not out of place among his competitors. But Sky Watch was not a horse to whom adjectives like *fine* apply. Some spectators were so disappointed, they called his performance "a disaster."

The announcer called the class into the lineup, and one by one, each rider high-stepped his horse in until they all stood facing the Freedom Hall sign, a row of slick brown jewels. The organist slowed the tempo while the judges deliberated, and the crowd held their collective breath. The announcer crackled back on. "Looks like we're going to have a workout, folks. The following horses are asked to return to the rail at a trot." He called three horses to the rail, but not Sky Watch. Sky Watch, the colt who'd performed so stunningly the year before that no one could remember who else had competed against him, hadn't even made it to the final round. In the end, he took fourth place.

My own trainer had seen Sky Watch perform that year. At the time, Mike was working as an assistant trainer for one of the greats, Marty Mueller.

Marty had a colt in that class, so Mike stood railside, with a stirrup's-eye view of the whole class. "He was okay," Mike explained. "But just okay. And Sky Watch was not an 'okay' horse." Sky Watch is Mike's favorite gaited horse of all time. He's been known to pull clients into the office to watch Sky Watch's duels with Imperator.

Mike and I stood in the aisle at a horse show, chatting about Sky Watch while we waited for the session to begin.

"I'll tell you," Mike said, "if Sky Watch had been Sky Watch that night, there wouldn't have been a workout. No way." He paused and shook his head for emphasis. "But he was just another horse in the ring. He wasn't Sky Watch, and I can't explain it. Rob was an excellent horseman."

While Sky Watch was disappointing fans at the Kentucky State Fairgrounds, another horse's star was rising. Imperator, the horse who had taken reserve in the World's Grand Championship the year before, had continued to slow-gait his way into crowds' hearts. In the 1980 Five-Gaited World's Grand Championship, Don Harris glided Imperator around the ring, his gaits crisp and perfect. Imperator looked like the picture of what an American Saddlebred should be. Muscular but not overmuscled. Powerful yet elegant. So ideal that Breyer, a company famous for making the realistic, hand-painted model horses generations of girls collected, used Imperator for model #904—a model that still sits on the shelf in my office today.

In 1980, Imperator began a campaign that would go down in Saddlebred history forever. It would be two years before he and Sky Watch met face to face, but the Fates had spoken, angling the trajectory of each horse toward the other. A collision was inevitable.

Part II

1980–1982

5

The People's Horse

On March 11, 1974, at a generational farm in Union, Illinois—population 579—the mare Empress Wing birthed a liver chestnut colt. It was a cold day to bring a youngster into the world. The high wouldn't even hit forty degrees, but Empress Wing's stall walls blocked the wind, and a generous bed of straw kept her maternity ward insulated.

Empress Wing's show career, complete with the silver tray and blue ribbon earned by the winner of the five-gaited stake in Madison, Wisconsin, had given way to the life of a broodmare. Union is surrounded by farmland, just an hour's drive northwest on I-90 from Chicago if the highway isn't too mired with drivers. The city soon softens into green midwestern pastures dotted with trees and soft hills. The stress of mothering is eased with lots of time in those fenced pastures, but I always wonder if retired broodmares miss the show ring, the lights and applause, the popcorn-and-pig stink of county fairgrounds. If Empress Wing did, she didn't tell anyone. Just like any mama, she nuzzled her newborn and urged him to eat, her purpose now to nurture, not perform. All babies are precious to their moms, but maybe she had an inkling of how special this colt would become.

Empress Wing sprang from the loins of the all-time great stallion Wing Commander, making Imperator the grandson of a legend—just like Sky Watch. Another all-time great producer, Supreme Sultan, sired Imperator. His lines trace back to Genius Bourbon King, Della Large's favorite stud and Sky Watch's maternal granddaddy. All of this made Sky Watch and Imperator cousins of sorts, but that's nothing out of the ordinary for top-level show mounts. Trace any lines back far enough, especially on good horses, and most Saddlebreds are related. The same is true for most equine breeds. It's called "linebreeding," which is a nice way of saying inbreeding. Linebreeding can solidify desired traits, but it can be a tricky business, as it can amplify weaknesses as well as strengths. Successful linebreeding requires knowledge of different bloodlines and their associated traits, familiarity with those lines' offspring, and some trial and error. Both Della Large and Wanda Wilkinson Menton, Empress Wing's owner, knew Saddlebred bloodlines as well as they knew their own floor plans.

Della and Wanda must have known each other, both being Illinois horse world royalty. While Wanda didn't have the socialite reputation and heiress-level fortune that Della could claim, she had something dear to the American heart: land, passed down from her family.

Peacock Farm had been in the Saddlebred business since the end of World War II, when Lieutenant Junior Grade Layman John "Wilkie" Cuthbert Wilkinson came home from the Pacific Theater and the USS *Karnes*. Josephine Earlywine, his wife and high school sweetheart, met him back home in Illinois, happy to see him return unharmed. While her husband fought in the navy, Josephine had earned her medical license, becoming a doctor in an era when few women donned a white coat and stethoscope. They'd been married just two weeks after the attack on Pearl Harbor, so finally, Josephine and Wilkie could get down to the business of family—and horses. The couple bred and raised two children, Wanda and her brother. They also bred and raised dozens of American Saddlebreds. Wanda took an interest in the show ring and breeding shed and went on to inherit Peacock Farm. Many Peacock Farm babies grew up to take victory passes in the show ring, but none compared to Imperator, the colt Empress Wing had birthed into the midwestern March chill.

By the time a two-year-old Imperator walked into Don Harris's barn, the Indiana-born trainer had already coached multiple horses to victory passes at Louisville. Don had trotted a horse onto the green shavings for the first time in 1963 and won his first World's Championship in 1967, on a three-year-old mare named Wild and Lovely. From there, Don's reputation solidified. He seemed on the path to Saddlebred trainer fame, joining greats like Garland Bradshaw and Tom Moore, names Saddlebred fans like me know the way Catholics know their saints.

Tall, lean Don Harris also had a knack for that other sport favoring the long-limbed: basketball. He'd turned down a full-ride basketball scholarship to Purdue so he could pursue Saddlebreds instead. He loved the way Saddlebreds performed and rose to their level. After Imperator had proved himself as a champion, Don rode him in demonstration rides, one caught on video. The audience wasn't cheering enough to satisfy him, so he egged them on.

"You can make all the noise you want!" When Don transitioned Imperator to the slow gait, the crowd whooped their approval. Imperator proved his rider's point and pricked his ears as he squatted down and began the one-two-three-four rhythm, the song of the American Saddlebred. The louder the cheers, the higher Imperator stepped, every footfall precise, as if the gelding knew exactly where each hoof needed to land to make the next step as perfect as the last.

Imperator hadn't always been so performance-ready. Dr. Geraldine Meanor, a New Jersey horsewoman who got hooked on Saddlebreds in the late 1960s, picked him out of a muddy field on Peacock Farm. Then, she called him "gangly, long-legged, dirty, and scrawny," according to a *Saddle Horse Report* article. "They thought he was the worst one on the premises, that we were the biggest fools in the world. It was a long trip home, so we asked Lou Teater to put Imperator up for the night. He told us the colt was the funniest looking one he'd seen in a long time. He asked: 'are you sure you bought the right one?'" For the first year, the Meanors kept Imperator at their home farm, Finisterre Farm, in Glen Ridge, New Jersey. Their trainer, Lillard Cox, handled his early education. Lillard had been to blame for the scrawny colt's arrival in New Jersey in the first place. He'd trained Empress Wing, Imperator's mama, and instructed his clients to buy one of her foals if they ever had the chance.

Lillard Cox took Imperator through the usual steps of early training. Groundwork first. Then long lining. Then, once things were going well, a climb onto the colt's back. Lillard could see Imperator had a nice trot and could use his ears, and slowly, he started showing the quality his bloodlines had promised. Eventually, Imperator had advanced enough that he found himself standing in front of the farrier, surrounded by the earthy stink of horse hooves. He eyed the gray crescent trimmings piled around him and huffed through his nostrils. His face, decorated with a thick white snip around the nostril and another swatch of white between the eyes, had always been expressive. Whereas Sky Watch had no markings on his face or body, Imperator's white accentuated his wide eyes and tapered snout. In the horse world, we call bold white markings "chrome." They're a desirable trait.

"Go ahead and set him up to gait him," Lillard instructed the farrier.

A groom held young Imperator steady with a lead rope and halter, the lead rope's chain threaded through the noseband to offer extra control as needed. With a young gelding still learning his manners, that chain could be the difference between the expected sore back for the farrier and the tragedy of a broken bone that would put him out of work for months. Bending over horses' hooves all day left a man—and it was usually a man, especially in the 1970s—achy, that was a given, but also vulnerable. He depended on a steady hand at the horse's head to keep his charge calm while he wielded the hammer, file, and four-inch nails around a thousand-pound animal that wasn't always inclined to stand still while a stranger gave him an industrial-strength pedicure.

The farrier set Imperator up to be barefoot in front and to wear light shoes behind. No horse would show with this kind of setup, but it helped the ones learning to slow-gait to swing their hind feet forward. Classic training for a gaited horse told trainers to take the colt out on a hill, turn his head "upside down," meaning nose in the air instead of the usual tucked chin, and walk him downhill, fast. The terrain and headset helped a horse inclined to shuffle to step that shuffle up to an amble and then into a true slow gait, with each foot moving separately in four-four time. When the slow gait feels rhythmic enough, the trainer asks the colt for some speed and moves him on to the rack.

Once the colt's racking along to the tune of a fast-spoken "chew tobacco, chew tobacco, chew tobacco," he's shod again on all fours. Once he's got the basics down, he stays more balanced that way. From this point, the colt's needs will dictate the type of shoes that get attached to his feet. Imperfections like paddling, where the lower half of the leg wings out from the horse's midline, or interfering, where the leg wings in and risks hitting the other leg, can be improved with shoeing. Hoof angle and leg movement can be adjusted to keep the horse more comfortable and bring him closer to an ideal gait, not unlike the way a competitive distance runner gets fitted for orthotics and customized shoes.

Saddlebred shoeing practices take their share of abuse, some of it only fair, some of it uninformed. It's the shoes that keep Saddlebreds in stalls all show season long. No pasture play for a show-bound Saddlebred, at least not during show season. Over the winters, though, Saddlebreds go on vacation. Trainers take them out of their tail sets and remove their shoes. They get turnout time and a lighter workload each week. Melissa Moore, the daughter of the legendary Tom Moore, posts videos to Instagram of her top show horses on winter vacation. They snort and kick their heels. They canter with their pasture-mates. They graze. They rest.

Saddlebred trainers have their horses shod with heavier shoes than, say, a hunter-jumper would wear. Saddlebred hooves are kept longer too. The extra foot and extra weight emphasize their natural high step and solidify their motion. A longer foot and a heavier shoe mean that turnout in a pasture could result in that shoe coming off and taking a chunk of hoof with it. Horse hooves grow, but not quickly, only requiring trimmings every six to eight weeks. Losing too much hoof during show season could mean the difference between making it to Louisville or not.

Contrary to what the internet would have everyone believe, American Saddlebreds are not subjected to "soring" to emphasize their motion. Soring is exactly as bad as it sounds. In the Big Lick style of showing Tennessee Walking Horses, trainers seek extreme action at the Walker's unique gait, the running walk. The running walk is a cousin to the slow gait and rack, but it's not the same gait. A Big Lick Walker looks like he's walking on a StairMaster, his front legs flailing, his head nodding hard with each step.

I chatted with a Walking Horse trainer, who wished to remain anonymous, at Louisville one year. "Yeah boy, I want action," he said, stirring a whiskey and Coke. We stood at a Kentucky barn's setup, complete with a full bar in front of the stalls. "Their knees need to be hitting their chins, and they need the hocks to match too. If they're not slapping their bellies with those back feet, something's missing."

"Right, I like balanced action too, but—can you get that without hurting the horse?" I asked.

"Listen, honey. Those watchdogs—USEF, the ASPCA, all of them—don't know anything about horses." These "watchdogs" are responsible for making sure trainers aren't abusing horses. They're not popular in certain training circles.

The Walking Horse trainer went on. "They want to take all the show out of the horse. They're coming for y'all too." He meant the Saddlebred community. "Just wait. Pretty soon, no one's going to be showing horses at all. Those pads and wedges y'all use, which we call baby shoes, starter shoes, will be illegal too." Here, he paused to give me a conspiratorial smirk. "I like 'em in big stacks, platforms, two or three times what you put on your Saddlebreds."

He didn't answer my question—Can you get action without hurting the horse?—so, over that winter, I asked my trainer about Tennessee Walking Horses, afraid of what I might hear.

Mike slipped a bridle off the hook hanging next to a young bay mare's stall. "Oh, it's awful. A guy brought one into my barn once and asked me to break him to ride. I did, but when he came in with that mustard oil . . ." He grimaced.

"Mustard oil?"

Mike's mouth turned down as he nodded. "Mustard oil. He told me, 'You got to make sure they can take the oil. Not all of them can. If they're going to be any good, they've got to take the oil.'" Unscrupulous Walking Horse trainers apply this oil to the horse's lower legs. It leaves painful blisters, which throb every time the horse's feet hit the ground, making him pick his legs up higher to avoid the pain. Worse still, these trainers work these already-sore horses with chains clipped around their ankles, so the chains hit the painful spots and exaggerate the action even further.

"That's terrible. What did you do?"

Mike bridled the mare and patted her neck. "I told him I couldn't help him. It was the truth. I don't know anything about training horses like that. I used to see those horses at shows, and it wasn't good. It took four people with whips to get one of them on their feet and out of the stall."

I don't understand how anyone could work with animals every day and cause them so much pain. Tennessee Walking Horses are big, kind creatures. Their blood runs a little cooler than Saddlebreds', so they're steadier, quieter, but just as people-oriented and friendly. Less prone to spooking and shying at, say, a leaf blowing in the wind, Walkers make excellent trail horses. Their special gait makes them a smooth ride, and a rider can stay in the saddle all day. The cross-country rider Annie Wilkins, known as the last of the saddle tramps, rode a Walking Horse all the way from Tennessee to California in the 1950s. They're that comfortable.

Trail-riding Walkers don't look much like the Big Lick contenders at the Walking Horse National Celebration, held annually in Shelbyville, Tennessee, since 1939. To the untrained eye, what Saddlebreds and Walking Horses do in the show ring might look similar. Both step high, and their tack and attire are in the saddle seat style. However, the two breeds have one vital difference.

Tennessee Walking Horses don't trot. It's not in their repertoire. All Saddlebreds, even gaited ones like Sky Watch and Imperator, trot (and yeah boy, could they trot!). They're five-gaited horses, which means they walk, trot, canter, slow-gait, and rack, but Saddlebreds are considered a trotting breed first and foremost. The trot requires two diagonally opposed hooves to hit the ground at the same time. If any of a horse's feet hurt, he cannot trot square. A sored horse can't trot. Period. Every winning Saddlebred trots sound, so soring isn't part of Saddlebred training. Never has been. Never will be.

Every training discipline, from racing to reining, has its own questionable practices, and yes, parts of Saddlebred training are controversial. The shoes that keep them stalled during show season. Even if their shoes weigh as much to them as hiking boots do to us, no one wants to wear hiking boots all day long. The tail sets, which look as comfortable as an underwire push-up bra—again, not torture, but not something I want to wear to bed. The early start for colts. Sky Watch took his first world title at age two and didn't take a break. Couldn't take a break. In an interview with Hackney pony trainer Bill Keith, broadcast on Facebook Live to thousands of viewers, Mitch said he couldn't give Sky Watch winters off like many Saddlebreds get. "He'd get so raunchy I'd have to climb up on his back. He was all stud. I tried to let him down, but he didn't give me any choice." From age two on, Sky Watch had to work. Some horses are like that. Some people call that cruelty. Others consider it part of being in the horse business. If Mitch hadn't given Sky Watch a job as soon as he jumped off that trailer, the stud could have become destructive. Destructive studs tend to get destroyed themselves. If they're too dangerous to handle, they're euthanized. Instead, Sky Watch worked from the age of two on. It's the equivalent of a human starting her career at thirteen.

Imperator, on the other hand, wasn't ready to show at age two. I can picture a two-year-old Imperator: his tail only reaching his hocks, his chest narrow, his long neck thin. In his eyes, though, must have been the spark of the greatness to come, because Don stayed patient enough to work him slow, bringing the colt along at his own pace. Six weeks after Imperator joined Don's string, Don felt good enough about him to call Dr. Geraldine Meanor, his owner. In New Jersey, the name Meanor meant something. The brunette internist was married to a respected judge, but she was also a physician in an era when few women appended their name with *doctor*. Today, at least one New Jersey centenarian credits Dr. Meanor with helping her reach one hundred years old. Both Judge and Dr. Meanor loved Saddlebreds and kept a farm in the Northeast but sent their best to Kentucky. When Dr. Meanor asked if the scrawny colt was working out, Don smiled into the phone.

"You bet," he told her.

In time, Don even began calling him a pet name: "Perry." Many trainers don't use horses' names. They'll call them by the owner's name or use physical characteristics. "The Canaster filly." "The black colt." At my barn, my horse is known as "Emma's mare," not "Bee." This doesn't signify a lack of affection. It's just the way it is. Every time Mike enters Bee's stall, he spends a moment patting her neck while murmuring to her or humming a tune, but he doesn't use her name. It takes something special for a trainer to give a horse a nickname. Perry was that type of special.

Imperator didn't start showing as early as Sky Watch, but the wait paid off. As a three-year-old, he came in second at Rock Creek and Lexington, two top horse shows for Saddlebreds. Don kept working him through the next winter, and, as a four-year-old, Perry hit his stride. At Louisville, he took reserve in the junior stallion and gelding stake and the tricolor in the Junior Five-Gaited World's Championship—the ribbon Sky Watch would soon be vying for. The pretty gelding slow-gaited his way into fourteen thousand hearts that night, and he learned to love the crowd just as much as they loved him. Even at four years old, Imperator knew what it meant when the audience whooped for him. He stepped higher and pricked his ears to parade down the rail for his new fans. Everyone left Freedom Hall that night saying, "Don Harris might just have himself a stake horse."

Today, the Freedom Hall stands aren't so packed. They're not empty, but the big arena isn't standing room only. There are always seats open, even on stake night. I asked Bill Marple, who's been showing Saddlebreds since the mid-twentieth century, what had changed.

"People simply have too much to do," he said, sipping a milkshake. "There are too many options. You can put your kid in soccer or dance instead—which, by the way, might cost just as much as showing Saddlebreds." Debatable, especially when a kid-ready Saddlebred that can win blue ribbons comes with a $50,000-plus price tag, but he's right. Kids' activities aren't cheap. Competitive gymnastics, for example, can set a family back $10,000–$15,000 a year. "And if you don't get the parents involved, then you lose out."

Why go to a horse show on the weekend with your friends when you could do an escape room or play at Topgolf instead? It's true that people are choosing different options for recreation, but that isn't the only explanation. For those who ride, horses are an obsession. Natalie Keller Reinert and Heather Wallace, hosts of the popular *Adulting with Horses* podcast—with fifteen thousand downloads and counting—say that horsewomen are compelled to engage with horses. Something about the animals draws those of us who identify as horse girls, and we don't spend much time questioning it. We're too busy sewing up holes in our horses' blankets and wiping our saddles down with Murphy's Oil. The mysterious pull of horses changes the question from "Should I go to the barn this week?" to "When will I go to the barn this week?" It's like an addiction, with memes to support that comparison. "Horses: more expensive than cocaine and twice as addictive." "Teach your child to love a horse and they will never have money to buy drugs." For a true horse girl, horses are barely a choice.

Of course, horses are only a choice if the horse girl can afford it. I recognize the financial barriers to being involved in the horse world. The average income of a United States Equestrian Federation member is $185,000, with a net worth of $1 million. Mine is nowhere near that, and plenty of horse owners and competitors have a bank account that looks more like mine than like a millionaire's. Many of us make questionable financial decisions around horse ownership. Like taking out a loan to buy a horse (me). Or ignoring the entire idea of a 401(k) to pay board and training (also me). Still, I'm aware of the extreme privilege of having enough disposable income to let me ride in the same arena as people who have nothing but disposable income.

Horses may be a recreational opportunity, but in general, our options for recreation are moving further away from agriculture. Other than the summer tomatoes I grow behind my house, everything on my plate comes from somewhere else. For most of us, farming is something other people do. Fewer and fewer of us live in areas that can be farmed. In 1960, nearly one in every three Americans called the countryside home. Today, the rural population in the United States only makes up 17 percent of the total population. Over the past sixty years, the urban population has doubled while the number of folks in rural areas has dwindled.

Horses, even show ring peacocks like Imperator, connect humans to the land and its history. Americans live further from the land than ever. Not only do I not grow my own food, I've barely even been in a grocery store since the advent of curbside pickup. However, take me to the barn, and I'm suddenly a country girl, interested in the price of hay and happy to wash out a water bucket. Caring for horses—watching their lips wiggle in pleasure while I curry their necks, loosening a knot from their manes and combing them smooth—connects me to another era, when horse care could be the difference between plowing and planting a successful crop or not. America hasn't been an agricultural nation since the Industrial Revolution. The slow dissolve of the connection between people and farming feels inevitable. If only Saddlebreds could stay out of that dissolve.

By 1980, Don Harris was ready to take his first victory pass in the big dance itself, the Five-Gaited World's Grand Championship, and he knew that Imperator was the horse who could take him there.

Don loved the crowd even more than Imperator did. To make sure he stood out, he wore a unique hat: a beige, turned-down fedora. In the conservative fashion world of saddle seat, it was a bold move, and only someone with Don's charm could pull it off. Don Harris is the type of man whose slacks stay crisp, whether he's spent the day training horses or cheering for Indiana University basketball. Even in his early nineties, he still matches his socks to his shirts and wears designer sunglasses under his hat brim. The man knows how to make an impression.

That year, Don campaigned the gelding with intention, giving Perry more show experience without taxing his engine. There are enough horse shows within driving distance of Simpsonville, Kentucky, the home of Don Harris Stables, that a horse could compete every weekend from early spring through midfall. Such a grueling schedule can wreck a horse, so trainers choose carefully, visiting a few smaller shows early in the season to test their horses and see what a winter's worth of work has done for them and then ramping up to larger shows in preparation for the World's Championship in Louisville in August. Building a horse's recognition with both audiences and judges is important but not worth the cost of dulling his shine.

Perry is a horse who needed to shine. At six years old, he collected blue ribbons at shows like Rock Creek, the season's first big-time show, and Lexington, the first jewel of the Saddlebred Triple Crown. Then, when Louisville rolled around, he took a first in the gelding stake, the qualifying class for the big one, the Five-Gaited World's Grand Championship. In the 1980 Five-Gaited World's Grand Championship class, Imperator entered the gate as the crowd favorite. The volume in Freedom Hall hit a new high as soon as he hit the ring on Saturday night. Imperator loved the noise, lifting his head high and making a pass.

As he trotted, slow-gaited, racked, and cantered, no one could look anywhere but at the liver chestnut gelding. The other horses contending for the title were no less impressive. The beefy bay Titleist, representing the stallions. The elegant mare Candle Dance, a large white star on her forehead highlighting her wide eyes. The French brothers French Wine and French Commander, both with white stockings behind, each of whom could rack up a storm. All eight of the horses in the ring that night were the best of the best, the top-performing show mounts in the country—no, the world. But none compared to Imperator. He had that impossible-to-describe quality the American Saddlebred Horse and Breeders Association rule book says every performance-level Saddlebred should have: brilliance.

Don Harris's coattails flew back from his body as he glided Imperator around the ring. He rode with long reins, keeping his hands close to his body. When Don asked for the slow gait, he stuck his elbows out and sat upright in the saddle, keeping his face composed. Don knew his horse would beat any other at this gait. He barely had to try. Even when other horses passed him, Imperator came out looking better, stronger, more elegant. Not that Perry lacked fire. At the second-direction rack, Perry came off his feet and broke into a canter for a few steps. His own brilliance became too much for him. The whole stadium groaned.

On the TV recap of stake night at Freedom Hall, Louisville television anchor Ryan Halloran asked horse show announcer Bill Carrington if the mistake would hurt Perry. "It all depends on how much the judges saw," Bill explained. "They don't have eyes in the back of their head." What Bill didn't say: sometimes, a judge can turn away at the right moment, making sure they don't see their favorite horse bobble.

Ryan asked if a mistake would separate the winner from the rest. Bill clarified: "To win the world's championship, to be the best, you've not only got to be able to do everything right; you can't do anything wrong. It's like the Super Bowl. If a team makes mistakes, they're going to lose, even though they're a very good football team."

The eight contenders lined up, and the gates reopened to allow each horse an entourage of grooms, who ran in at speeds that would make a track coach reach for his stopwatch. After the trainers dismounted, the grooms removed their horses' saddles and upended them nose down on the green shavings, a towel protecting the precious leather from the dust. Then they set to work, wiping sweat from necks and foam from mouths. The trainers slipped the reins over their mounts' heads and stood in front, asking their horses to "park out," meaning to stand with hind feet extended, front feet planted beneath the shoulder, and neck arched up and over. It's the equine equivalent of a runway pose. Some horses posed as if they were made for the model life. Others broke form to jig in place. The three judges walked the line of nostril-flaring horses, each still blowing from the effort they had just expended. When the judges reached Perry, the crowd burst into applause and cheers.

The announcer called three horses back for a workout: French Wine, French Commander, and Imperator. In any class, if the judges are struggling to determine a winner, they can call horses back to the rail and put them through their paces again. It's tradition for the Five-Gaited World's Grand Championship to have a workout, so no one was surprised. The three horses, already tired from a long class, amped back up for an encore. Saddlebreds are known for their stamina, and a workout on Saturday night at Louisville is the ideal place to showcase that trait. The geldings trotted to the rail, slick with sweat but still stepping high.

In 1980, no one had iPhones or GoPros. All we have of the landmark class is an old video filmed for the Louisville news and preserved online by Richfield Video, a company that films Saddlebred shows today. As Imperator moved into the slow gait, his long neck swanning up from his shoulders, his eyes brightening, Bill Carrington narrated. "There he goes at that slow gait, that famous high-climbing gear. I guess forty years from now, if Imperator wins it, they'll say, 'He sure could slow-gait.'"

While French Wine and French Commander moved like the high-class horses they were, Imperator strode on a level all his own. Don Harris sure had been busy in the year between Imperator's reserve World's Grand Championship and this class. The gelding looked like royalty, and the crowd cheered for him as if it were his coronation day. The three horses lined up in the middle for the judges' final deliberation, but it didn't take long. Imperator won the crown.

Bill Carrington was right. It's been forty years, and anyone who knows Saddlebreds still praises Imperator for his slow gait.

Don turned Perry to make his victory pass, but between the spotlight, the screaming audience, the streaming tricolor ribbons, and the blanket of roses shedding blossoms with his every step, the new king of Saddlebreds broke his gait and jumped off his feet, the whites of his eyes wheeling. Don smiled. Luckily, he'd already won the class. Ever the showman, Don turned him around and took another shot at it, this time circumnavigating the ring without a misstep. He'd earned his turn presenting a Champion of Champions to the world.

Researching Imperator is like researching an American ambassador. Imperator is respectable, gentlemanly. He's the picture of what a twentieth-century Saddlebred was supposed to be. An icon. One photo in his archive at the American Saddlebred Museum is of him lowering his nose to sniff Elizabeth the bulldog, the barn mascot. Another shows Dr. Geraldine Meanor leaning over to kiss the white spot on his nose. He looks like the type of horse I could introduce to a baby girl, if I'm lucky enough to have one, to let her reach out a chubby hand to stroke the white snip on his nose. Magazine clippings call him "The People's Horse." Renowned sculptor Linda Rankin cast his image in bronze. E. R. Wasemiller carved him in wood at a full-on rack, only one foot on the ground, hindquarters bulging, tail floating behind him like a flag. *Imperator* means "commander in chief" or "emperor." Someone official. Royal. Irreproachable. Appropriate for Perry, a horse who, in the eyes of his fans, could do no wrong.

At a restaurant near the Kentucky State Fairgrounds, one Texas couple recognized the Meanors, Imperator's owners. They'd chosen the Kentucky State Fair as their family vacation destination. "It was worth the trip from Texas," they told the Meanors. "We have three children, and we'll probably get a Saddle Horse because of Imperator." The gelding even started receiving fan mail. One little boy addressed his letter directly to Perry, asking him for one of his horseshoes.

After the green shavings of the 1980 World's Championship Horse Show had been raked away, the banners and bunting boxed up, Sky Watch found himself on a trailer again, but not to California. After his disappointing three-year-old class at Louisville, Michele approached Mitch. At the end of Sky Watch's trailer ride, he wouldn't see eucalyptus trees and palms. Instead, Sky Watch returned to the rolling hills of Danville, Kentucky, and a stall in a familiar barn off Hustonville Road. Mitch and Sky Watch were reunited.

By then, Mitch's training string had grown enough that he didn't need to sell stereos in the afternoon. The commission check from Sky Watch's sale had planted the seed, and the word of mouth from Sky Watch's incredible two-year-old class at Louisville had watered the soil. Mitch's career was sprouting. Money was tight, but he could work full-time at the barn and get the bills paid.

Mitch worked Sky Watch for three weeks and then did what any self-respecting horse trainer would do. He took him to a horse show. Quietly. In Atlanta, Sky Watch looked more like himself than he had all year. The colt, it seemed, just needed the right set of hands on his bridle. He won, thrilling the small crowd lucky enough to see his comeback. Mitch got to call Michele back home in San Diego and share the good news: Sky Watch was back. Unfortunately, show season was almost over.

Mitch won't say how much he had to work to get his colt back in order after his year with Rob Tanner, and he had nothing bad to say about the West Coast trainer. Everyone seemed to agree that Rob "just didn't get along with the colt." Even Don Harris, Mitch's soon-to-be rival, said so. Horse training is a gentleman's sport, and the boys protect one another, at least in the public eye. I'd love to hear the conversations that happened in tack rooms, no one there to hear but the horses.

Next season, the 1981 season, would be Sky Watch's junior year, an important year in a horse's development. Sometimes, the ones who burn hot as two- and three-year-olds fizzle out by the time they turn four and achieve sexual and physical maturity. Others only get better. This next year would be a chance for the stud to reclaim the greatness his two-year-old season had promised—or, like most horses, to simply get by. These horses pass from owner to owner, showing at smaller and smaller shows, sometimes making it in the ribbons and sometimes not. Every season, a new barn. A new trainer. A new owner who may or may not ride them, who may or may not ride them well. These horses' names don't stay on trainers' lips. They may make a victory pass or two, but in the end, they slip into oblivion.

6

The Red Mile

Something about the fair seems vitally American. Where else can you, in a single day, eat a deep-fried Twinkie, marvel at the world's largest hog, enter a hot dog eating contest, admire a butter sculpture of Tiger Woods, scramble your brains on the Gravitron, and watch a free concert by the Beach Boys? Fairs are all about excess. Since their birth in the United States in the nineteenth century, state fairs have been a place for American farmers to show off their best and biggest. Pumpkins as tall as a man. Pies with crusts so evenly browned, they look painted. Sheep wearing head-to-toe spandex, only their eyes and mouth visible, like woolly superheroes.

When the fair is in town, the fairgrounds become a miniature city. Temporary livestock stalls divide pavilions into hundreds of squares and rectangles. In the horse barn, stable staff dolly in heavy wood and fiberglass trunks, filled with blankets, clippers, groom boxes, shampoo, ribbons, leather cleaner, and tack. The staff demographics vary depending on the barn. The biggest barns hire out the labor or send grooms to the shows in advance. Barns with big lesson programs use student workers, usually teenage girls helping to earn their horses' keep. At smaller barns, like mine, the trainer and assistant trainers do all the work themselves.

No matter the laborers, the work stays the same. They staple-gun heavy polyester curtains around an empty stall. Inside, they hang saddles, bridles, surcingles, harnesses, girths, and saddle pads. They erect a shelf and stack it with bins of bobbles for the horses' tails, bottles of show sheen for their coats, sanding blocks and shoe polish for their hooves, towels for everything from drying the horses to soaking up spills. Back in the aisle, they snap open folding chairs with logo-bearing canvas backs and hang decorations: silver Saddlebred silhouettes, a banner monogrammed with the barn's name, flower baskets trailing lobelias. All the barns do this, turning the rows of stalls into festival tents, done up in the barns' respective colors. There's purpose beyond the rah-rah team spirit: hiding the thousands of dollars' worth of equipment in the tack stalls. At horse shows, stealing is rare, but it happens. Better to prevent it than to do damage control.

Meanwhile, at the midway, semitrucks rumble in, Tetrised full of everything it takes to make a Ferris wheel or spinning cups. Tattooed men and women, the ink faded over their tanned skin, unload steel poles, joists, and joints. Out of these scrap piles, metal miracles rise, slowly becoming rides, the types of things parents hope are safe enough to strap their kids into. Next to the rides, a similar process unfolds with the food booths, gyro stands, and lemon shake-up stations popping up like boxy flowers.

In broad halls, women set up folding tables and cover them with the tablecloths they ironed the night before. On them, they lay out their garden and kitchen bounty: zucchini with radial symmetry, jars of browned onion chutney, and tarts a Victorian architect would admire. These halls become havens for the livestock workers and midway staff, who risk side-eye from the farmers' wives for lingering in the chill of an air-conditioned bathroom.

In a week or two, those halls will be empty. The midway will turn back into pavement. The pavilions will be stall-less. Everything at a fair, from the funnel cake booth to the stall housing the world's largest hog, is meant to be temporary. Celebrated for the duration of a fair—days, sometimes weeks—then packed away until the next one. It's a performance, not that different from a play, complete with sets, costumes, and actors. The transience of a fair gives it a sense of magic. The show might be repeated next week, but it will never look exactly the same.

The American Saddlebred first found his show home at the fair. Since the mid-nineteenth century, these highly trained animals have competed at fairgrounds all over the country, judged not on speed or ability to complete a task but on their exhibition. Show horse—not track star, and certainly not beast of burden or warhorse. Even though their ancestors worked in the fields and carried soldiers into battle, a show-quality Saddlebred today wouldn't know what to do with a plow and would buck at the sound of buckshot. The breed's journey from functional farm animal to pampered performance pet is complete.

I'd promised myself to wait six weeks after emailing Michele my second set of questions. That's how long it had taken the first time. Once those six weeks ended, no matter how many times my mouse clicked the refresh button, the Scripps Miramar email address never popped into my inbox. How to nudge her without seeming pushy? A call? Text? Email? Finally, I spent twenty minutes composing a single text, hesitating one last time before hitting Send.

When I reread the text the next day, it sounded groveling. Anxious. Something about Michele brought out all my fears about where I belonged in the Saddlebred world. She, the woman rider I've admired my whole life. I, the nobody with a low-budget horse. Michele has everything it takes to succeed with Saddlebreds. Land, money, time—but most importantly, talent. That's the deepest fear, a black egg in my belly. What if I had no talent? What if my horsewomanship didn't chalk up?

Then, within twenty-four hours—relief. Michele texted me back. She didn't hate me. I spent most of a morning thinking about my own response, trying to make it sound warm, composed, and anything but desperate. Is a comma between "Hi" and "Michele" too formal? Does a text message even need a greeting? Does punctuating "Thank you" with two exclamation points sound polite or overenthusiastic? What about "You're my role model"? What kind of punctuation does that deserve? Finally, I hit the blue arrow and watched my words appear in the blue bubble of an iMessage.

In the second set of questions I'd sent Michele, the first two asked about her background rather than her horse's. How had her mother inspired her? How did she feel about inspiring others? Michele is a fascinating figure. No one else in the country is a newspaper heiress with a Buffalo Soldier heritage who can outride most professional trainers in the morning and breed champion show horses in the afternoon. No one could blame me for wanting to know more, for wanting to learn more about everything she and her family have accomplished. Except Michele.

Ten days after our text exchange, Michele emailed me back. Gone were the smiley faces. The tone, too, seemed unsmiling. "I'm sorry," she wrote. "But I'm afraid that I am unable to answer any more questions or give you additional help."

My heart sank. I'd overstepped. Everyone I'd talked to had warned me about how shy Michele could be, how little she liked talking about herself. Mitch had even mentioned stepping in and speaking for her at restaurants to save her from her admiring fans. The woman liked her privacy, and my fandom had invaded that privacy. Her final email didn't reprimand me for my faux pas. She didn't tell me to go to hell, as she could have. Instead, nicely, she told me to mind my own business and focus on the horse, not her.

That much I could do.

As he entered the 1981 show season as a four-year-old, Sky Watch looked less coltish. His shoulders had broadened. His neck had thickened, looking even more studdish than it had before. His tail had grown. Even when braced, it hung down to his ankles. In Phoenix, the first show of Sky Watch's junior season, Mitch must have been taking deep breaths before he trotted through the in-gate. Had that win in Atlanta been a fluke, or would Sky Watch keep redeeming himself?

He did, racking up a victory with Mitch while Michele watched. Given that Michele calls herself "competitive by nature," she must have been pleased to see the star colt she'd bought rise to the level of her expectations for him. I'm sure that from a spot on the rail, her eyes lasered onto Sky Watch, only flashing away to check out the competition. No other horse in the class could touch her now four-year-old. I picture her after the class, ducking back to the Scripps Miramar barn aisle, the stalls full of pinto Saddlebreds who were beginning to make their way into the ribbons. Michele and Brownie had a mission, and they didn't waver from it. Pintos might not have been winning at Louisville yet, but Scripps Miramar women weren't going to stop until a spotted Saddlebred stood in the winner's circle at Freedom Hall.

Next, at Rock Creek, Sky Watch trotted his way to another win. A winter of work with Mitch had done the trick. Michele couldn't always make it out to her horse's Kentucky shows, so she heard about the win via a phone call with Mitch, the news coming to her across time zones and state lines. If Mitch called her after the evening class, it would have been dusk in San Diego, the sun descending over the western pastures of the ranch. Michele might have answered on the barn phone, listening to the horses chewing their dinner in the background as she took in the good news.

Now, Mitch let himself think bigger. He entered Sky Watch in the first jewel of the Saddlebred Triple Crown: Lexington. The Lexington Junior League Charity Horse Show began in 1937, founded by the local ladies of the Junior League, a women's charitable and civic organization that's really a hobby for wealthy wives seeking social status. Next to Louisville, it's the biggest party of the year for Saddlebred folks. A ringside table for six, complete with catered cocktails, hors d'oeuvres, and a buffet dinner will set today's spectator back $2,500—if she reserves early. For decades, the Red Mile hosted the Lexington Junior League Horse Show. The Red Mile is the second-oldest harness track in the world, with red clay footing that lends the one-mile oval its name. For the horse show, a six-hundred-foot section of the track was fenced off to create a long, narrow outdoor arena with plenty of room for showgoers to gather in the grandstand. In 2018, Lexington moved from the Red Mile to the Kentucky Horse Park's Rolex arena. While the new arena is safer for the horses, with generous turns and better footing, many old-school Saddlebred fans miss the Red Mile days.

Just as it is at the Kentucky Derby, Lexington's grandstand could be a show of its own, especially in the late twentieth century. Women donned cocktail dresses, heels, and hats. Men wore light-colored suits. All gussied up, they picked their way along gravel paths dotted with the occasional pile of horseshit, both literal and conversational. At their table, they'd drink a few too many bourbons, whoop for the winners, and snark about who spent how much on which horse. While a few outlandish outfits were always in the stands—as a teenager, I packed a sequined tube top for stake night at Lexington, but Karin marched me to the mall to buy a black dress instead—the real stars have always been the horses.

In 1981, both Imperator and Sky Watch stood in stalls at the Red Mile. Lexington is always an oven, and 1981 was no different, with temperatures hitting ninety degrees by Monday afternoon. In just a few hours, Sky Watch would enter the ring with fifteen other four-year-old stallions and geldings. Those bright track lights would hit him full in the face, and he'd see a crowd, the biggest he'd seen yet, packing the ringside boxes and filling the stands.

Sixteen horses were a lot for the Red Mile Lexington ring. I should know. In 1999, at age thirteen, my teeth still strapped with braces, my eyebrows and nose too large for my face, I showed my horse Keeper of the Stars in a sixteen-horse class at the Red Mile. In the warm-up ring, I tried not to look at the other horses and riders but couldn't help it. Keeper picked up on my nerves and pricked his ears, which was good. That gelding's ears usually swiveled on his head like satellite dishes looking for a signal. In all my photos with him, he's got one ear back and one ear forward. Sky Watch's sire, Flight Time, also fathered Keeper's mama, which made Sky Watch Keeper's uncle, although the two looked nothing alike. The red stud stood muscled and powerful, while Keeper, a much lighter shade of chestnut, giraffed up from the ground, his slender neck and low back making him look taller than his 15.3 hands.

When the judge called the canter, I panicked. A knot of horses, seven deep, minced in front of me. None of them were cantering yet. Good ringmanship dictates waiting until the horse in front of you has taken their lead before starting your own, but a rider can't wait forever. Another horse came cantering alongside me, too close and too fast, and Keeper sidestepped, his body tense and springy between my legs. Now a full horse's length away from the rail, I let nerves get the best of me, and instead of waiting, I angled Keeper's hips toward the center, nudged him with my right leg, and said, "Canter." Railside, Karin shook her head. Wrong decision.

Keeper popped up in a half rear. Then he took off down the middle of the ring at a too-wild three-beat gait that made the judge step back to stay out of our way. My back, usually supple as a dancer's, turned stiff and tilted forward, seeking control over the creature beneath me. To horses, however, leaning forward means "Go faster." Keeper picked up speed, and I could barely steer him around the others. As we careened around the ring, sweat pooled in my sports bra. The light poles flashed by, dizzying, and the campy organ music turned sinister. An eternity later, the announcer asked for the walk. Every cell of my body sat heavy, willing Keeper to slow down. Finally, he did.

At the reverse, two horses almost collided. The whole class had gone wild. At least it wasn't just me. I aimed my own horse down the rail and tried to keep the smile pasted on my face. By the time Keeper and I lined up, he was soaked with sweat, his chestnut darkened to amber. He stepped from side to side as the judge walked the lineup. On the other side of the rail, Karin stood in front of me. Out loud, she soothed me. "It's okay, Emma. You did good." Internally, she must have been seething. Her rider had blown it, and we both knew it. The announcer called first place. Applause and cheers. Another tuxedoed young girl leaned down and hugged her horse before trotting to the winner's circle. Second, third, fourth, fifth, sixth, seventh, and eighth. My number, hung on my back with tiny gold-plated Saddlebred pins, remained uncalled, eliminating my chances at the championship. My shot at Lexington had ended.

Back in Keeper's stall, I gave him peppermints and threw my arms around him. Not placing was disappointing, but the smell of him, the earthy-dirt whiff of his hooves, the sweet grassiness of his breath, rewarded me more than any ribbon could have. In the barn aisle, Karin dissected the class with me. The Red Mile's tight turns and long straightaways have defeated many blue-ribbon contenders. Keeper wasn't the first.

"First of all, that was a crazy class," Karin said. "They should've split it."

She wasn't wrong. The show officials could have cut the class in half, making it two classes of eight instead of one of sixteen. Safer for a group of thirteen-and-under riders. That didn't change the fact that I'd screwed up.

"There's one thing you have to remember with this horse, Emma," Karin said, smiling the whole time. She could chew me out and make it feel like a compliment. "Keeper needs to follow the leader. But you have to pick the right leader. In there"—Karin pointed to the ring—"you didn't. You took off cantering after that horse came galloping past you. Monkey see, monkey do—so Keeper galloped away too. I was yelling at you to take your time."

"I'm sorry. I didn't hear you." I inhaled. Exhaled. "Okay. Follow the leader. The right leader." I broke eye contact. "I can't believe we almost ran over the judge."

Karin laughed. Her voice, always throaty, cracked. "You're lucky you didn't get kicked out! There was so much going on, no one even noticed. Did you see those two horses almost run into each other? Out of control." She stood, hands on hips, pretty in her boatneck top and jodhpurs. "They should've called a time-out right then and made them take the gate."

Karin lit a cigarette, tucked a stray strand of hair back into her scrunch-ied ponytail, and started walking back to the ring to watch the next class. "Don't beat yourself up. This is a tough arena, and that was a tough class. Now you get to relax and enjoy the horse show instead of worrying about the championship."

As hard as the Red Mile could be for a horse like Keeper, who only had to perform three gaits, it was harder on a gaited horse like Sky Watch. Those tight turns force horses to check their speed to stay upright. They make the four-beat gaits a challenge to maintain. The clay footing isn't as forgiving as tanbark, and a horseshoe can get sucked right off a horse's foot, sometimes taking a chunk of hoof with it. It isn't abnormal for a Lexington gaited class to have multiple time-outs for lost shoes, keeping the farrier busy as he works against the clock to get the shoe hammered back on. Meanwhile, the show goes on along the rail, even though officially, no judging can happen during a time-out. Everyone knows, though, that a horse can win a class during a time-out. If he makes strong passes and gets the crowd whooping, the judges can't help but notice.

As he trotted along the rail, Mitch had noticed Sky Watch paying attention to the crowd, the other horses, and the judges' stand in the center. He would have preferred the stud focus on him. These shifts in attention could turn the class's tide if Mitch didn't reel his stallion back in, but so far, only Mitch could tell how precarious the situation could become. Had it been me on Sky Watch's back that night, it would have been a disaster. I would have ended the night in a Kentucky jail cell for involuntary manslaughter, having left stallion-size hoofprints all over the tuxedos of two of the three judges. Mitch, of course, was a professional, and he made it through the class as a professional would. Even though Sky Watch "didn't show with as much expression," as Mitch told the *Lexington Herald*, he still ran away with the qualifying class and won with a unanimous vote.

Later that week, Sky Watch would have to face off with a feisty mare, Mirror Mirror, who had already been pegged as a junior horse to watch in 1981. She sailed through the junior five-gaited mare class and, by Friday, had been training hard all week to meet Sky Watch head-on.

The bugle rang out, and the announcer called for the junior five-gaited championship. Mirror Mirror and Sky Watch cranked through the in-gate. There were other horses in the class, but they faded into the background. The mare, her face stamped with a white star and snip, whipped her legs up and raised her head high. She owned her passes, earning big cheers from the crowd packing the grandstand and approving nods from the railbirds with their elbows hooked over the ring's white fence. Sky Watch zipped around the other horses, throwing mud in their faces. By the reverse, the audience had crested to its feet, some cheering for Sky Watch, some for Mirror Mirror, some for both. Why not? They were seeing one of the best contests between two young horses that anyone had seen in years. The track became "slick and gummy," according to *Saddle and Bridle*, but Sky Watch kept on, working up the crowd each time he sailed down the long straightaways.

Most young ladies don't like mud being flung in their faces, and Mirror Mirror let the crowd at Lexington know that she remembered her blue-ribbon ride earlier in the week and she considered the ring hers. Young horses, or at least the ones destined to become show ring greats, gain confidence once they've been to a few shows. They put together the puzzle, understand what the training has been all about. They still snort, but out of fun, not fear, their expression playful, not worried. Their eyes still widen, but they're focused, looking ahead, not wheeling around or staring at the stands, starstruck. Even non-horse people can see the change. It's the same difference you'd see between the new girl at high school walking into the cafeteria and the head cheerleader doing the same. They're both walking, both moving their legs and swinging their arms, but the movements are nothing alike. When we see this transformation in horses, trainers will remark, "I think she's starting to like herself." After her win in the junior mare division at Lexington, Mirror Mirror liked herself plenty.

When the judges called everyone into the lineup, the announcer called two horses back to the rail. The class might have felt like a two-horse class all along, but now, Mirror Mirror and Sky Watch had to face off. Still blowing hard, the two horses left the lineup at a trot, their energy testifying to the Saddlebred's stamina. Sky Watch's trot elevated Mitch out of the saddle, his feet barely skimming the stirrups. Veins popped out of the stallion's neck and chest, and lather foamed under the saddle. Later, Mitch would sponge away that lather with warm water, maybe even liniment. These baths cool a horse's temperature and keep his skin from rashing, but they're also aromatherapy for anyone standing within range. There are few odors better than hot horse and liniment, a combination that hits the nostrils like warm straw and eucalyptus.

Sky Watch wasn't ready for his cooldown bath yet. He'd just begun.

The stallion's nostrils flared with each step, sucking air, but he showed no sign of turning his assault on the ring down. Mirror Mirror strutted with the same determination, but where Sky Watch revved, Mirror Mirror crackled. The filly electric versus the stallion powerful. They hit the rail, and the crowd flew to their feet, ready to whoop at the first passes of the workout, and—Mirror Mirror pulled up. The track, which sucked as many as six shoes off in one night earlier in the week, had lived up to its reputation. Mirror Mirror had cast a shoe. In the most intense moment of the most closely watched class of the night, the announcer called a time-out so the farrier could enter the ring and nail the mare's shoe back on. By the time David Becker, her rider and trainer, stepped back into the stirrups, Mirror Mirror's sparkle had faded.

After the time-out, each trip around the ring made it clear that Sky Watch's undefeated record with Mitch would stay that way. Mirror Mirror never resettled, never clicked back into rhythm. The judges voted for Sky

Watch. Against any other horse, Mirror Mirror might have come out on top, but Sky Watch was becoming more than a horse.

In his victory-pass photo, Sky Watch's ears are pricked forward. His right front leg is popping so high out of his shoulder it looks unhinged, but Sky Watch is focused, all his power under control. Mitch, dapper in his dark suit, is connected to his mount, his body rising at the top of his horse's trot. Mitch's mouth is ajar, his eyes boring into the back of Sky Watch's neck. The ribbon flaps from the bridle, standing out against Sky Watch's red coat, wet and sweat-slick. The box-seat holders behind him stand, staring with smiles on their faces, their hands frozen forever in applause.

Friday night at Lexington in 1981 might have belonged to Sky Watch, but Saturday belonged to Imperator. The only two horses who stood a chance of beating him had been scratched from the championship class. While some might have whispered that Mitch could beat the reigning champ with his four-year-old colt, Mitch knew better than to throw his youngster into the deep end. Not yet. There'd be plenty of time for that next year. According to the *Lexington Herald*, Imperator "made a shambles of the field" and won the class "easily." Don Harris enjoyed the victory, but it would have been sweeter if the other contenders had suited up and trotted through the in-gate. As it was, the class turned into a demonstration of Perry's superiority. Had a horse ever slow-gaited with such precision? Had a Saddlebred ever maintained such a headset? Was such a perfect set of ears even possible? At seven, the gelding was hitting his prime.

Don Harris, too, was hitting his prime. Over the past decade, he'd won with horses like Well Chosen, who'd won the fine harness stake at Lexington that year; Finisterre's Gift of Love, who'd won Three-Gaited Horse of the Year four years in a row in the late 1970s; and Giddy-Up-Go, who'd campaigned hard in the early 1970s and become known as the best five-gaited horse to never win the big one at Louisville. The showman had been honing his gifts, and his name appeared in every issue of the industry magazines of the day.

In full-page glossy images, the handsome Don Harris appeared on horseback, a Saddlebred trotting or racking along underneath his long, slender frame. The horses' names and accolades blazed across the bottom of the page, along with the owners' and trainers' names in the bottom corners. The owners paid for these photo spreads, which in turn paid for the magazine. They served as advertisements. Judges read *Saddle and Bridle* and *National Horseman*, and if they had seen a horse's name in a magazine, they might remember it when that same name appeared on their judge's cards. The photos also served as "For Sale" ads, and no one sold horses better than Don Harris. Among the photo spreads, articles on all matters Saddlebred, and pages of horse show coverage, you'd find the Transactions section. Trainers and owners reported their sales and acquisitions, and magazine subscribers could keep up with who was adding to their string. From the 1970s on, Don's name riddled that section, usually as the selling agent. He sold so many horses that the archives of the American Saddlebred Museum credit him with single-handedly turning Simpsonville, Kentucky, the home of Don Harris Stables, into the Saddlebred hotbed it still is today.

Along with the rest of the crowd at Lexington, Mitch watched Don Harris and Imperator dominate the five-gaited championship. Mitch knew he'd be pinning Sky Watch against the unbeatable gelding the following year, God willing. He watched Imperator the way a boxer watches his rival. Mitch needed to learn his ticks and tells, his habits and tendencies. He might not have said it out loud, but he must have been thinking it: *Sky Watch could beat this horse. Might be the only horse who could.* Mitch scanned the crowd, wondering who else was thinking the same. For now, all eyes fixed on Imperator as he paraded through his victory pass.

Only one audience member didn't stand at his usual spot along the rail.

That March, before show season launched into its frenzy, Danville Emergency Medical Services received a panicked 7:30 a.m. phone call from the white-columned home at the farm on Hustonville Road. In the early spring chill, the sun barely up, the ground still damp from rains the day before, an ambulance transported the man known as the ultimate Kentucky gentleman to the Ephraim McDowell Memorial Hospital. Garland Bradshaw had suffered a stroke. A bad one. A man who relied on a fully functioning body had suddenly found himself incapacitated, one side of his body nonresponsive.

Three weeks later, Garland had to take another ambulance ride from the small local hospital to Cardinal Hill Hospital in Lexington, which specialized in stroke rehabilitation. His condition had stabilized enough that he was ready for their programs, for occupational, recreational, and physical therapy. At seventy-six, Garland was still lean, still in good shape for a man in his seventies. Maybe there was hope.

Garland returned home, and briefly, that hope rose. For the first time in his life, Mitch didn't have his mentor at the barn with him. The day before Garland had the stroke, he'd worked nine horses. Now Mitch added those nine to his own string. He'd trot the horses out of the arena and up to the house. There, he'd ride them back and forth in front of the door where Garland could look out and see them from his chair. The pupil still needed his teacher's help—and he hoped that seeing horses might infuse his grandfather with new life. But the king of Saddlebreds could only nod, his mouth slumping down. Still, Mitch held out hope and kept bringing horses to the back lawn. Lena, Garland's wife, kept him shaved and dressed for the day, his shirts still crisp, the pleat in his pants still sharp.

Then, another stroke. And another. With each onslaught, Garland deteriorated a little more. Eventually, he had to return to nursing care at Friendship House nursing home. The facility was on Mitch's route from the farm to his house, but many nights, to Mitch's shame, he couldn't bring himself to stop and visit. How could he connect with a man known as the ultimate Kentucky gentleman when that man, all of a sudden, couldn't shave his own face?

Still, every day, Lena drove across town to spend the day with her husband, making sure the aides kept him bathed and fed. Garland couldn't communicate the way he was used to, so he needed an advocate. Stroke victims struggle with movement and speech, but even basic functions like eating and going to the bathroom can become difficult. Garland was not a man who discussed bathroom functions, and here he was, needing help on and off the toilet. Maybe he would have welcomed the visits from Mitch, but it's also possible that he was grateful to have been spared the embarrassment.

Garland should have been standing next to Mitch at the Red Mile, watching the judges give Imperator their approval, but he wasn't. Mitch made his way through that show without the guiding hand that'd been there since he was old enough to toddle through the stable. For the first time, Mitch was navigating a show season all on his own.

After my lackluster class with Keeper at Lexington in 1999, at one of the endless exhibitor parties held under a tent near the Red Mile arena, I eyed the beer bottles behind the bar but was too chicken to swipe one. An older boy approached me, all boy-band bowl cut and whatever the Y2K version of Axe body spray was. He might have been sixteen or seventeen, which, in my fourteen-year-old eyes, made him infinitely cool. He drove a road horse, making him even cooler. We talked horses, and he complimented mine, which won me over. "Want to go for a walk?" he asked, following my gaze to the Budweiser beers. "I know where we can snag a couple of those."

"Sure," I said, and let him lead me away from the tent to stand behind a cluster of trees in the center of a roundabout.

"So," I asked, trying to sound tough, "how about that beer?"

"We'll get some later," he said. Then he leaned in to kiss me, flicking his tongue like a lizard. *Gross*, I thought, but instead of pushing him away, I let his lips meet mine. It seemed easier. His hands roved over my body, and his fingers tickled the hem of my dress, pushing it up. My muscles stiffened, but my voice seemed to have disappeared. The *no* beating in my chest stayed silent, so the boy kept going, probably thinking he'd hit the jackpot. Then, the announcer's voice boomed.

"Emma Faesi, you need to report to the horse show office."

"Oh my God," I said, pulling away, "that's me." I ran back to the crowded part of the fairgrounds, my hair tousled, my face puffy from necking with the Backstreet Boy. My mom stood in the show office, the lines in her face drawn tight. Someone had seen me leave the party with a boy and then disappear. A mother's worst nightmare. Later, a lecture about right and wrong, safety and fear, disappointment and expectations. But for now, she led me back to the barn, to our stalls, to my horse, wordlessly. The silence was worse than any other reprimand.

"Give your horse a peppermint," she commanded. "He deserves it. Then, we're going back to the hotel." Keeper's gaze hit mine, and the shame that had been coursing through me dissipated. Here, in front of me, stood the only male in my life who mattered. I held out my hand and let him lip the peppermint from my palm; then I turned to my mom. She must have been terrified. What fate had she saved me from? What plans had that older kid made for me behind those trees? We'll never know. I never saw him again.

Keeper had talent, but, just like me, his adolescent antics could be dangerous. His rough canter departs turned into jumps that could take us halfway down the rail. Once, at a show, he reared as we approached the arena chute, dumping me into the dirt behind him. Karin legged me back onto the horse, but the ringmaster closed the gate before we could enter. We missed the class, which disqualified us from the championship on Saturday night.

Bit by bit, my adolescent behavior turned riskier than my horse's. The little girl Dearie had spoiled grew into a devious teen. Drinking. Hooking up. Sneaking cigarettes. Thanks to straight-A grades and blue-ribbon rides, I got away with it. To pay our mortgage and Keeper's training bills, my mom worked six days a week, often well into the evening. I wasn't aware enough to be grateful for her sacrifice, but I made the most out of the unsupervised time it provided. After school, I hosted parties at our house, with liquor stolen from parents and cigarettes filched from the drugstore. By the time my mom returned to cook up a late dinner of whole-wheat penne made sticky with feta and tomatoes, the crowd had dispersed, cucumber-melon spray had been applied, and enough Bagel Bites had been consumed to soak up the booze.

Outwardly, I looked like a model daughter: good grades, clean room, active extracurricular life. My dinner plates included spinach, and I always rinsed them before sticking them in the dishwasher. On my nightstand stood stacks of books, everything from nineteenth-century literature to the latest fantasy novel. My desk held color-coded folders filled with completed homework. No one knew that my school-day afternoons looked like the first half of an after-school special.

In spite of my troublemaking, I never missed an opportunity to go to the barn. The barn was one place where I always behaved. Had to. On horseback, rules mattered. The wrong signal meant my butt landed in the dirt. With horses, danger is ever-present, so there was no need to put myself in its path. At the barn, the relationships are defined. Keeper was my horse. Karin was my trainer. Together, they kept me in line.

Keeper and I walked, trotted, and cantered through a few seasons of decent showings—top three, mostly. One blue ribbon stands out in my mind. We were at a county fair show in the rain, the night floodlit and roaring with the tractor pull on the other side of the fairgrounds. Usually, Keeper hated the wet, sidestepping the puddles as if they held hot tar, but that night, Keeper strode into the muck like a prizefighter shucking his robe. When we took our victory pass, blue ribbon whipping in the drizzle, mud splashed his belly with every step. He ignored it and stepped high. But after we left the arena, Keeper jiggered around the first puddle he saw, nearly unseating me.

As Keeper's misbehavior escalated, so did mine. After my mom fell asleep, I'd open my window, climb onto the roof, and shinny down to the ground to meet friends at the trailhead at the end of our street. There, we'd roll a joint or pass a bottle around. Usually, my mom didn't know a thing.

She slept on, unaware of what her daughter was doing in the night. But once, when I tried to slide back in the window, it didn't budge. Locked. Busted. Caught.

Eventually, Karin and my mom decided to pull me from the horse. It was hard to tell if the decision came as punishment for my behavior or as concern for my safety on a horse I couldn't control. Probably both. My trainer and my mother agreed. Keeper wasn't ready for a young rider—which, I understand now, was true. My mom sat me down in our terra-cotta tiled kitchen and tried to explain, her eyes meeting mine. "He needs more training, Em. He's not the right horse for you right now."

Tears stung my eyes. Not the right horse? I only wanted Keeper. I feared what this might say about me: *You're not good enough to ride him.* But instead of asking why, I internalized the fear. The adolescent rebellion that had been stirring spilled over. Horses were my container, my structure. But without Keeper, why bother?

My barn weekends turned into an hour on Saturday mornings. Karin let me groom Keeper and watch her ride him, but she put me up on barn-owned mounts, lesson horses and homebred show horses in training. None of them as exciting as the young chestnut I'd first ridden in a sunny field. In my mind, depression turned *you're not good enough to ride him* into *you're not good enough to ride.* So, instead of sticking around for an afternoon trail ride, I drove back to town to smoke weed with my new boyfriend, who drove a white Chevy S-10, blared Lynyrd Skynyrd from its speakers, and piled friends into the truck bed for trips up the Blue Ridge Parkway.

With his dark curls and five o'clock shadow—my sixteen-year-old self thought stubble swoon-worthy—my new boyfriend looked nothing like the Backstreet Boy from the horse show. In fact, he knew nothing about horses. Didn't know the difference between a canter and a gallop. With him came excuses to skip Saturdays at the barn. Homecoming. A pool party. A camping trip with friends, which really meant drinking beer in the woods. Outwardly, it looked like I was having fun. Inwardly, I shriveled.

You're not good enough to ride warped into *you're not good enough.* The friends who had replaced horses didn't see me sitting alone in my room at night, listening to Simon and Garfunkel's "The Sound of Silence" on repeat and writing poems about gray weather and lost daughters. They didn't know I sometimes drew bloody lines on my wrist with a Gillette Venus, the razor of choice for early-2000s girls doing the cry-for-help thing. When my scared mother drove me to the emergency room after I overdosed on aspirin, those friends didn't visit me in the hospital.

Finally, I stopped taking the road to the barn at all. I turned my back on Saddlebreds.

At the end of my senior year of high school, Keeper was sold. At a profit. He'd made good on his talent. Numbed by depression and hurting with a hangover, I felt nothing.

"Great," I responded when my mom shared the news. "Maybe we can use the money to buy me a car. I'll need one for college."

Imperator may have been undefeated all season, but Don Harris didn't take his success for granted. With each victory pass, the pressure rose to make sure he could take another one at the next horse show. Because he'd become the horse to beat, anyone who thought they had a shot at him rode right at him, trying to cover him along the rail or cut him off in the corners. But so far, no one had come close to taking the gelding's place in the winner's circle. That didn't stop eight entries from storming the gate at Freedom Hall on Saturday, August 22, 1981. Following tradition, the announcer called in the entries one by one.

Valley Venture boomed in first with Nelson Green up. Valley Venture was the first horse ever to have a company formed just to buy him. Nelson Green's clients joined forces and created the Valley Venture Partnership so their trainer would have a contender in the Five-Gaited World's Grand Championship. The big chestnut trotted in, then slowed to a bounce walk in the far turn. Next, in came Redd Crabtree with French Wine, the previous year's reserve champion, ready to try to outshow Imperator for the second year in a row. Following French Wine, Candle Dance zoomed through the in-gate with Bob Ruxer posting along with her. She'd won mare classes all over the country and represented the best of her sex, but she'd be the only gal to challenge the guys that year.

The announcer called French Commander, French Wine's full brother, in fourth. Then Rare Treasure with Mike Brannon up, then Stonewall's Diamond Gem, a West Virginian entry. Finally, the moment the crowd had been waiting for: Imperator's entry. No one could hear the announcer over the audience's roar, but Imperator didn't need to be announced. Instead of slowing in the far turn and notching his energy down to wait for the final contestant to enter, Don Harris called for more, making another pass down the homestretch straightaway. The audience ignored the last horse's entry. Unlucky guy, having to follow Imperator into Freedom Hall.

Imperator and Don Harris moved as one, flying around the ring as the announcer called the gaits. Suddenly, the noise from the audience crested. Had REO Speedwagon entered center ring through a trap door? No, just Imperator, rocking back into his slow gait. Don Harris carved up the ring at Imperator's signature gait, cutting corners to get in front of the other horses. By the time the class reversed, Imperator must have circled the judges' stand twice as often as the seven other horses in the ring with him.

On the reverse trot, Rare Treasure, a long-strided stud with extreme action, challenged the reigning king. He outstrode Imperator on the rail, but Don cut the corner short to catch Rare Treasure on the next straightaway. When he passed him, the crowd screamed their approval. This was Imperator's class to lose, and by God, Don wasn't going to let that happen. Especially not in the four-horse workout that ensued.

Once again, Imperator faced off with brothers French Wine and French Commander, but this time, the jointly owned Valley Venture joined the fray. In the workout, Don grew more determined, making extra passes every chance he got. After all the other horses had lined up, he called on Imperator for one extra slow gait, zipping behind the rest of the horses. Pure showmanship. Would it pay off?

The pause between the announcer calling the lineup and announcing the winner was longer than Don Harris would have liked, but at the end of it, the announcer called Imperator's name. The audience's cheers filled the arena as Don held his hat to his chest and took Imperator to the winner's circle. In the post-class interview, Don admitted to having been a little worried in the workout. "There were some nice horses out there," he said. Don needn't have worried. With two World's Grand Championships now under his girth, Imperator was on his way to meeting the six-win records set by My-My and Wing Commander.

After his second win in the big one at the Kentucky State Fair, Imperator's fan club grew. So did his accolades. Doug Shiflet, one of the industry's best horse show photographers, advertised a limited run of Imperator prints laminated on canvas. In the photo, Imperator is trotting, his gait collected, his ears punched forward. Don holds the reins at shoulder height, drawing Imperator's energy up, up, up. Don's face is cool, as if he doesn't have a half ton of high-energy horse beneath him. Sculptor Linda Rankin cast

Imperator's image in bronze in a limited run of five, with one for the Meanors and one for Don Harris. At year's end, the United Professional Horsemen's Association once again voted Imperator the Five-Gaited Horse of the Year. He'd earned it. How many horses received visiting requests from Muhammad Ali? And then nipped at the Champ himself when he brought his fists up for a photo op?

Mitch saw Imperator's win in 1981 and walked away knowing the horse he needed to beat next year. With eight horses at Louisville in 1981, Mitch must have missed his grandfather more than ever. At the same time, Garland's absence let Mitch step out of his granddaddy's shadow and make a name for himself—which, of course, had been Garland's plan all along. Garland's barn was known as "Garland Bradshaw University" in the Saddlebred community because, along with a generation of great horses, the man brought along a generation of the best trainers in saddle seat. Names like Jack Nevitt, Lee Shipman, Jim Koller, Larry Hodge, Bill Becker, and Carter Cox rang out during the championships in Freedom Hall every summer. Each of those trainers traces his education back to Garland. Garland's brother Frank was also a legend for lovers of long-necked horses. Among others, he trained My-My, the only Saddlebred mare to win six Five-Gaited World's Grand Championships. Training the Bradshaw way brought out the best in horses, and no one had spent more time learning the Bradshaw way than Mitch.

Mitch had hung out his own shingle as a trainer in 1978, when he was twenty-five, but until Sky Watch came along, the name Mitchell Clark Stables hadn't appeared in the newspaper. Sky Watch changed everything. Before him, Mitch had maintained horses in his string like Maplewood's Night Gambler, a promising three-year-old, and Seventh Avenue, a big-going three-gaited horse, but Sky Watch made Mitch. The red stallion became the comprehensive exam at the end of Mitch's tenure at Garland Bradshaw University. So far, he was passing, but the final test would come in another year, when Sky Watch would face Imperator on a Saturday night at Louisville.

7

No Other Horses Will Do

The week after Michele emailed me to politely yet firmly decline to answer any further questions, I drove to the Shelby County Fair and Horse Show. In just a month, Ben's vasectomy would be reversed. By the time Louisville rolled around at the end of August, the hope of pregnancy could become a reality. On the way to Shelby County, I wondered how a seat belt would feel buckled around a pregnant belly. Would my favorite cowboy boots still slide onto swollen feet? What would it feel like to look in the rearview mirror and see a car seat—to see a baby's wide eyes gazing back at me? My baby, I decided with the parenting certainty that only nonparents have, would travel well. She'd handle car trips with ease.

The show I drove to is called Shelby County—not to be confused with the Shelbyville Horse Show held at the same venue in August. It might sound trivial, but to Saddlebred diehards, that distinction is crucial. Shelby County is an early part of the Kentucky County Fair circuit. It's a little rougher, a little wilder. Shelbyville is a county fair show too, but it's one of the last pre-Louisville showdowns, the place you take a contender to work out the kinks before hitting the green shavings. To an outsider, though, the two shows would look identical.

It was 2020, in the first summer of the COVID-19 pandemic, so posters of hand-drawn Saddlebreds with medical masks stapled over their muzzles sprouted up all over the showgrounds. The show manager rode around in a golf cart, reminding people that masks needed to be worn in group settings. My own mask hung on my wrist as I strode, solo, over to Mitch's stalls, reminding myself with every step that I belonged, that I had the right to be curious about this horse and this sport even if Michele had declined to answer any further questions. Michele was right. The person I really needed to talk to was Mitch. He'd spent the most time with Sky Watch. With over an hour to go before the show would start that evening, I'd probably get Mitch all to myself.

Anthio greeted me from a chestnut walk-trot horse's stall. While the horse stretched his neck and groaned with pleasure, making the same noise my Labrador does when I scratch her ears, Anthio moved a white loop of tubing along his neck, hovering over it without touching skin. The tubes emitted clicks and connected to what looked like a stereo cabinet on wheels but was actually a MagnaWave, a machine that produces electromagnetic pulses and, supposedly, aids in muscle recovery. A MagnaWave can set you back $20,000.

"Hi, Anthio. Looks like someone likes his MagnaWave," I said.

"Hi! Good to see you. For sure. They all love it. We do this for them every time they have to trailer anywhere. It works out all the kinks."

Mitch appeared from behind the curtains of his tack room. His horse show attire of khakis and a polo shirt was a step up from the jeans and chaps he wore at home. The horseman's equivalent of business casual. He still wore a broad smile—and his signature ponytail. "Nice to see you again, ma'am." It had been four months since my initial visit to Mitchell Clark Stables on Hustonville Road.

We sat in the navy-blue director's chairs on either side of the tack trunk and watched Anthio move from stall to stall with the MagnaWave, giving each horse a treatment. None shied from the clicking machine and its tubing.

I started in with my questions. "You've said Sky Watch had lots of personality. How would you describe that personality?"

"Hmm." He paused as if searching for the right words. "Strong. He had a strong personality. He was all stallion."

"How so?"

Mitch leaned back, making himself comfortable. "You should've seen what he'd do in his stall."

Most mornings, Mitch had had to spend time untangling Sky Watch from his equipment. I would love to have been a mouse in Sky Watch's feed bin, taking in the scene.

"All right, you tricky son of a buck," Mitch would have said, standing in front of Sky Watch's stall. "You won this round."

Sky Watch snorted and jerked his head. His tail set dangled from him by the surcingle, the metal crupper inches from the ground instead of secured to his backside. Sky Watch reached back to snap at it with his jaws, his teeth clicking. He snorted again, throwing his head toward the rafters. Most horses would be foaming with sweat and running in circles to escape the foreign object hanging from them, but the stud wasn't scared of the equipment. He was pissed at it. More than that, he was proud of himself for outsmarting it.

"Guess you're first up to work again this morning. You've earned yourself that dubious honor." Mitch would be working the horse twice that day, as usual, so Sky Watch was almost always the first one the trainer led out of the stall.

If it was a Friday, most trainers would have been working Sky Watch up to that day's workout all week. Saddlebreds work six days a week, with Saturdays for owner exhibition and Sundays off for stall rest. Fridays can be the hardest workout of the week. On a Monday, trainers do a lot of long lining, driving the horse from the ground where they can see him. Long lining is the least strenuous form of work for a horse. There's no rider to carry, no cart to pull. The movement is pure, unhindered. It allows the trainer to watch the horse, see how he travels, notice any imbalance that needs to be corrected.

Sky Watch wasn't most horses, and Mitch wasn't most trainers. Mitch spends more time in the saddle than his colleagues. He also works his horses longer. If the training session is going well, most trainers will have a horse warmed up, worked, and cooled down within fifteen minutes. When I spent the day with him in February 2020, Mitch spent double that with each horse. That much time with a rider in the saddle can be hard on a horse, but none of Mitch's horses hitched their hind legs or humped their backs. How? Because Mitch gave them a long warm-up and cooldown at each ride, they stayed sound. The only horse I saw Mitch long line was a liver chestnut filly with more go than whoa, but, as Mitch explained, "This is just to take the edge off of her, make sure she don't kill me when I climb up there."

So Sky Watch was in for at least one ride every day. Mitch mounted up and bounce-walked the colt over freshly dragged footing, Sky Watch's footfalls pockmarking the dirt furrows. Until the first frost, Kentucky can be sticky, but the mornings are fresh, the dew sparkling on the bluegrass. The chill in the air kept Sky Watch's ears sharp, flicking back and forth, but never lazily. Sky Watch always seemed to be paying attention to something, even if that something wasn't, to Mitch's dismay, his trainer.

Two workouts a day wasn't enough to keep Sky Watch from expending extra energy in his stall overnight. Eventually, Mitch had had the horse fitted with steel bars that ran from his halter to his tail set.

"Thick as my finger, they were," Mitch explained, holding up his index finger. "They were supposed to keep him from turning 'round and tearing things up."

In between snoozes—horses only sleep in short bursts, most of those happening on their feet—the stud colt started bending his neck, first to one side and then to the other. With the determination of a toddler fighting a nap, he kept flexing and turning. He stretched his jaws and snapped his teeth toward the equipment hemming him in. After minutes of effort, he huffed air through his nostrils, let his head drop, and lowered his eyelids. When he woke up, he'd be back at it. Those metal bars kept Sky Watch from reaching his blankets and tail set and doing damage to them and to himself, but they hadn't stopped him from trying.

"Every night, he'd bend the steel. Every morning, we'd spend a good amount of time at a hammer and anvil straightening them back out." Mitch laughed, but I'm sure he hadn't been laughing on those mornings. With stalls to clean, feed bins to fill, hay flakes to hand out, and horses to work, losing a half hour to basic equipment maintenance must have been devastating. But Mitch believed that Sky Watch was worth it, so he spent the extra time the stud colt demanded. These antics had earned Sky Watch the nickname "Tricky."

Luckily, Sky Watch applied the same level of effort to his work as he did to his attempts at destruction.

"You can't get mad at him," Mitch explained, leaning forward and opening his arms, palms up. "You have to live with this part so he's happy enough to give you what he gives you out here." He angled his head toward the show ring.

"The same drive that made him bend metal bars was why he could go in and do what he could do, though, right?" I asked. "He had that much energy and that much go."

"Yes, ma'am. He had more than any other horse I've ever seen. I knew just how lucky I was. My grandfather spent thirty years looking for another Lady Carrigan." Garland Bradshaw had ridden Lady Carrigan, a "little brown mare" with a big personality, to World's Grand Championship titles in 1954, 1955, 1957, and 1958. "That lesson was not lost on me, so I appreciated every minute I had with that horse." Mitch meant Sky Watch. "I knew it was a privilege just to crawl on his back. To drink in that kind of work ethic. I was mindful enough to appreciate how lucky I was to even be able to touch that horse."

I glanced at the three horses Mitch had brought to Shelby County. They looked like nice horses, much nicer than anything I'd ever be able to afford, but none had the magnetic pull of Sky Watch—even after their MagnaWave treatments.

Anthio hung up the machine's white coils and wheeled the whole contraption back into the tack room. He emerged with a bridle, a rag, and leather cleaner, then sat down and got to work. The task list of an assistant trainer is endless. Anthio's diligence made me want to ask for a saddle to polish, my own lack of effort embarrassing me. But I was too shy.

"Sky Watch was the type of horse who inspired people to go out and buy horses. Why was that?"

Mitch's eyes grew serious. "There's two horses." He meant Sky Watch and Imperator. "And they're better than anything you're to going to see— ever—and they're about to be in the ring at the same time."

In November 1981, after winning the gelding stake with Imperator at the American Royal, the third jewel of the Saddlebred Triple Crown, Don Harris made a point of being ringside for the junior five-gaited class on Wednesday night. He'd been keeping an eye on Sky Watch all season long, of course. He lived in Kentucky, not in a cave, and he knew the young stallion might be the only thing who could beat his seemingly unbeatable gelding.

The American Royal is held every November in Kansas City, Missouri, and is the official end of the Saddlebred show season. After Kentucky, Missouri is the next Saddlebred hot spot in the country, mostly thanks to Tom Bass, a man born into slavery in 1859 who became the nation's best horse trainer. Tom Bass loved his Saddle Horses and showed them all over the country, becoming the first Black man to compete in horse shows.

The American Saddlebred has a complicated history with race. Famous horses of the Civil War—Grant's Cincinnati, Lee's Traveller—were early Saddlebreds, then called Kentucky Saddlers. Because Saddlebreds grew out of horses that settled in the South, if Johnny Reb was lucky enough to be cavalry instead of a foot soldier, he was probably on a Kentucky Saddler. Gaines' Denmark, one of the foundation sires of the breed, belonged to General John Hunt Morgan, who led the infamous, bloody, and ultimately doomed Morgan's

Raid into Indiana and Ohio. Gaines' Denmark is so influential, his blood runs through most Saddlebreds who are alive today.

While the American Saddlebred Museum touts the presence of Kentucky Saddlers in the Confederate Army, one part of Saddlebred history practically goes unmentioned. The Saddler must have been a plantation horse, ridden by slave-owning Southerners. Saddlebred historians avoid the topic, but the geography and time period would make the ancestors of the American Saddlebred part of the fabric of the brutal system that built America. The development of the American Saddle Horse happened alongside slavery. The horses can't be blamed. They were property too. But what does it mean to own a horse whose grandpa twelve generations back might have pulled a cart full of slaves to the auction block? Whose breed is immortalized in Confederate statues? Trace just about anything in America back far enough, and slavery is caught up in its roots. Perhaps the horse world feels especially tangled because it's already so class-stratified and whitewashed.

Dave Hysaw, a Black trainer in Minnesota, has been working with American Saddlebreds since the late 1980s. He started as a groom, and when he realized he didn't see many other Black men at horse shows, he decided he would "set a mark." Today, he is the owner and trainer at Willow Falls Farm, and trainers and owners from all over the country send him horses to work. In a phone interview, he told me that he hasn't dealt with too much blatant racism because he's "always affiliated himself with the right people." For him, the hardest thing about the show horse industry has been the judging.

"Two people can have equal horses, but one person is going to be a little more successful because of who they are than the other person," Dave said. As of 2022, no Black trainer has won the big one, the Five-Gaited World's Grand Championship. "In my heart of hearts, I feel that it's coming. There have been so many great African American trainers before me."

One of those greats is Mike Spencer, who owned Gold Leaf Farm in Simpsonville, Kentucky. In 2004, he took a mare named Spider Red on a victory pass in the five-gaited mare stake in Freedom Hall, earning her a World's Champion title after an intense four-horse workout. However, when Mike came back the next year, gunning for the Five-Gaited World's Grand Championship, Spider Red came in sixth.

Dave Hysaw said, "I think he got robbed. That mare was a sight." Still, he's optimistic about the future of Black horsemen and horsewomen in the industry, even considering the history behind it. "These are the most beautiful horses in the world. Bad things have to turn around to become good things. In the nineteenth century, a lot of the people working with these horses were Black grooms. The African Americans built this industry, but the grooms never got the recognition. It's not the horses' fault."

For Dave, it's not about ribbons and recognition. "We do it for the horses," he said.

Today, the American Saddlebred Horse and Breeders Association runs a prominent social media campaign every year during Black History Month, showcasing the Black horsemen who made their mark on the breed. In 2018, the association made the short film *Out of the Shadows*, which identifies the racism that kept Black people out of the show ring until the mid-twentieth century. The film is well-made and does some important work in uncovering history that might otherwise have stayed hidden. It's a start, and a good one, but my own complicity still deserves some examination. I don't condemn the horses for carrying Confederate soldiers to war, but I hate that something I love has connections to this country's deepest shame.

While visiting with a friend last year, a poet who prefers books to barns, I described the conflict I feel about the Saddlebred's connections to slavery. He and his wife are old enough to be my parents and are better read than I'll ever be, but they've always treated me like an intellectual equal. That evening, we sat in the living room, its walls lined with books from floor to ceiling.

I started rambling. "They're this beautiful breed of horse, all showy, like models on a catwalk—but athletic. No other horse is anything like them. They're super-American too. The first horse breed developed in the US. Paul Revere supposedly rode one on his famous midnight ride. Civil War cavalry rode them—more Southerners than Northerners—"

"Why is that?" my friend asked, glancing over his glasses and looking every bit like the academic he is.

"They were probably plantation horses. The breed grew out of nineteenth-century Kentucky. In fact, you know those Confederate statues that are finally being taken down?"

He nodded. "It's about time."

"Yes. I agree." I looked down, suddenly squeamish. "Well, if the general or lieutenant or whatever is on horseback in the statue, the horse is probably a Saddlebred."

"How awful." He grimaced. "Can't you ride a different type of horse?"

My chin tucked back into my neck the way it does when I don't like what I'm hearing. I blinked.

"No. I mean, it's not the horses' fault." Right? I asked myself. "There's something special about Saddlebreds. Other horses aren't the same."

My friend nodded and smiled as if he understood, but I knew my explanation didn't really explain anything. My connection to horses, to Saddlebreds especially, only made sense to those who had been bitten by the horse bug. There's no academic analysis that can wrestle my compulsion into logic. Other horses didn't compare. Not to me.

A year before the New Rider Special that led me back to Saddlebreds, I'd tried other styles of riding, other breeds. My friend Angela, an English professor who loves Jane Austen, Great Danes, and Baroque horses, lives in a Victorian cottage on the edge of Yellowwood Forest, where she keeps two gray horses—a Lipizzan and an Andalusian mix. Angela can quote Michel Foucault and Dave Chappelle in the same breath and, even though her student loan payments take up most of her income, can manifest a gourmet meal for six out of whatever happens to be in her fridge. Angela is twenty years my senior, and she became the horsey, intellectual aunt I'd never had. For a full year, she made me lunch and let me ride in her field every Friday, asking for nothing in return. Friday afternoons meant driving to the country, laughing with the blue-eyed, blond-haired Angela over couscous, then tying her horses to a tree to groom, saddle, and ride under a blue Indiana sky.

While Angela graded papers, I trotted and cantered in circles and figure eights, avoiding the tall grass and the molehills it might hide. When the ride ended, a slow walk back to the pasture gate, where Angela met me with dessert, a Perrier, and compliments about my riding style. She would have brought a glass of wine—Angela is the type of person who knows which bottle of red to pair with dark chocolate—but she knew I'd given up drinking, so sparkling water it was. That's the type of love she showed me: fully aware, fully compassionate. Angela gave me space and support to find my place in the saddle again.

Horses didn't reenter my life like Sky Watch hitting the gate in Kansas City. They returned gently, through the kindness and compassion of another horsewoman, more than fifteen years after I'd chosen boys and booze over weekends at the barn. Sober, married, and starting to make my way in the world as a writer, I was ready for them. Horses require coherence, Angela told me. In my early thirties, my brain and body were finally starting to realign.

Horses have always connected humans to something larger—some animal energy that fosters joy and releases pain. They're mirrors for our very selves, and no wonder. Horses can hear our heartbeats from up to four feet away and can synchronize their own ten-pound hearts to ours. While I'd like to tell a story about Keeper and me reuniting and rehabbing each other, it didn't happen that way. Instead, Keeper found his path, and it led him straight to a victory pass in Freedom Hall. Mine took a little longer to find, and it took the generosity of another horsewoman to nudge me back into the saddle. Without Angela, I might not be riding today.

Trained in dressage, not saddle seat, Angela's horses taught me to ride differently, with more contact on the bit than I was used to. The ideal Saddlebred rides with a feather touch. A Saddlebred's way of going is different too, with intense vertical motion as well as horizontal.

Angela introduced me to Ali, a local dressage trainer, who gave me lessons in exchange for cleaning stalls. When Angela and I traveled to a local dressage show to watch Ali compete, a Saddlebred in full saddle seat glory swaggered by, her energy barely contained. My lips parted. "Look! A Saddlebred!" My eyes followed her from barn aisle to warm-up ring. Angela and Ali looked at each other and raised their eyebrows. "We've lost her," Angela said. Ali nodded. Weeks later, I signed up for that fateful New Rider Special, abandoning the smooth-moving grays in Angela's fields for long-necked chestnuts.

My answer to my poet friend's question was true, down to the core of my being. "Why not ride a different type of horse?" Because, to a Saddlebred fanatic, no other horses will do. Even so, my conversation with him left me shaken, wondering at my complicity. What if, every time a Saddlebred took off at a trot under me, his hoofbeats echoed the Confederacy? Like the millennial I am, I took to Google.

The American Saddlebred Horse and Breeders Association, known then as the National Saddle Horse Breeders Association, became official in 1891, founded by—and here, I gulped—a Confederate general. John Castleman presided over the association for twenty-five years. Today, I pay annual dues to the ASHBA. It makes me a little queasy to think that I'm supporting an organization a Confederate general founded and ran, even if, according to a 1918 article in the *Wisconsin State Journal* (my Google game runs deep), Castleman recanted his support of "state's rights." Castleman expressed gratitude to Abraham Lincoln and credited him with changing his mind. "[Lincoln] gave me the light to see the wrong cause I had championed, the right cause that he battled for." At least the man had the wherewithal to repent. It would be up to me to determine how to reckon with my own misgivings about the breed, the organization I support.

The ASHBA is handling its own reckoning. In 2021, the association launched a Diversity, Equity, and Inclusion Committee that has stayed busy. So far, the committee has highlighted the importance of diverse racial representation in association media, scheduled a Diversity, Equity, and Inclusion workshop for horse show judges, and committed itself to building principles of diversity, equity, and inclusion into ASHBA itself.

It's true that we have a whiteness problem in the American Saddlebred community. The entire horse world does, and the Saddlebred barns are no more or less white than those of any other equestrian discipline. On the surface, just about everyone in the horse world claims to be antiracist, and for most, that's the truth. But Black equestrians report receiving lower-ranked ribbons at shows, and a majority of the horse show workforce is made up of underpaid Latine laborers. The association's leader today isn't a Confederate general—he's a businessman, a successful one—and he attends every meeting of the Diversity, Equity, and Inclusion Committee. The association's Facebook page regularly features equestrians of color, holding true to the commitment to diverse racial representation. Tom Bass's legacy lives on, both through the doors he opened for nonwhite equestrians and through the gentler, safer curb bit he developed that's still used today. The community has much, much more work to do, but it's at least made a start on that labor. I wish there was more transparency and discussion about the Saddlebred's Southern roots. Recognizing the complexity and dark history behind the horses I love doesn't mean I need to renounce them. Understanding where they come from can only deepen my relationship with them today.

Standing at the rail in Kansas City in 1981, Don Harris wasn't thinking about slavery, or racism, or Tom Bass—although he surely used Tom Bass bits. He had one horse on his mind, a red stallion, just four years old. Over the high white walls of the Royal's arena, Don watched Sky Watch take yet another victory pass and solidify an undefeated season. Once Sky Watch hit the gate, no other horse in his class really had a shot at winning. Everyone else was competing for second place, for the rights to say they took reserve to Sky Watch and Mitchell Clark.

When Don returned home, he called Dr. Meanor. The slender physician, her dark hair worn short and set with bangs that curled over her forehead, was always happy to talk to her favorite horse's trainer. Perry had just won at the Royal, too, sailing away with the five-gaited championship the way he had all season long.

"Listen," Don said in his twangy tenor. "That Sky Watch will be hard to beat."

From her New Jersey home, Dr. Meanor laughed. "Oh, Don," she said, "nobody can beat Perry." She knew who Sky Watch was, of course. She was part of the Saddlebred world too. After the season her World's Champion gelding had just finished, though, it was impossible to imagine any horse racking into the winner's circle while Perry slow-gaited out of the arena with a reserve ribbon instead.

Sky Watch's five-year-old season started with victory passes in Phoenix, his sharp-eyed owner watching every step. Mitch's daily two-workout program seemed to be working, but with a horse as athletic as Sky Watch, the potential for injury loomed. High athleticism combined with big energy and a strong work ethic could produce aches and pains that would only show up subtly, if at all. A missed step in an arena turn. Heaviness on one side of the bit. A hind foot cocked to rest just a hair longer than the other.

Some horses are so driven to perform, they ignore the pain of injury. Ruffian, a thoroughbred racehorse, could have challenged the legacy of horses like Man O' War and Secretariat, but she died as a three-year-old. Jane Schwartz documented her too-short life in the book *Ruffian: Burning from the Start*, a book I devoured as a teenager and return to regularly as an adult.

In the greatest race of her career, a one-on-one match race against another talented thoroughbred, Foolish Pleasure, Ruffian broke two major bones in her front right leg. The great mare continued to run on the injured leg, pushing even harder as her rival pulled ahead of her. Ruffian's jockey stood in the stirrups, trying to pull her up, but she continued, her hoof flapping at the end of the broken leg. She demolished her bones so badly that four veterinarians and a twelve-hour surgery still left the leg in questionable condition. As the mare woke up from anesthesia, the race continued in her mind. From her spot on the floor of a padded stall, Ruffian's legs thrashed, still trying to finish the race she'd started. She destroyed the plaster cast on her leg and brutalized her shoulder in the process, injuring herself so badly that she'd never recover. The vets had to humanely euthanize Ruffian.

Horses with that much heart will let their own drive to win destroy them. Nothing—not fatigue, not pain, not the breakdown of their own bodies—can stop them. Horses are also very good at masking pain. It's a survival tactic. In the wild, predators will look for prey animals that are injured or seem to be in pain because they're easier to catch. I'd hide my pain too if it increased my likelihood of living through a wolf attack.

Sky Watch was like Ruffian, with an engine too big for his body. At Shelby County in 2020, with the MagnaWave clicking behind him, Mitch described the type of care he had required to stay sound.

"That horse took more time than any other horse in the barn. Because he was so athletic, he was always hurting himself one way or another. The boy who had him"—Mitch meant his groom—"had fewer in his string but more work than anyone. He was always wrapping or icing his legs, you know, doing something to him."

I leaned forward, eager to hear more about Sky Watch's caretaker. "What was his name?"

"Emiliano Ocharia. I ran into him three years ago. He's rocking and rolling, running a lawn and garden business in Versailles."

I looked up every landscaping company and garden shop in and around Versailles, Kentucky, but couldn't find an Emiliano Ocharia. According to the phone book, he didn't exist. Same for Facebook. Ocharia seems to be a very uncommon surname, most prevalent in Uganda according to the Forebears.io website, so perhaps there'd been a misspelling. Mitch confirmed that I had the correct name, but more digging only led to dead ends. The only one of Sky Watch's caretakers whose name appears in the archives is Solomon Gallegos, known as one of the greats, and honored with being inducted into the UPHA Caretaker's Hall of Fame in 2015. His tenure with Sky Watch didn't begin until later in the horse's career.

In the horse industry, these laborers can fall through the cracks, and it appeared Emiliano would fall through the cracks of my research too. Sometimes, grooms are acknowledged in those big photo spreads in the magazines, but just as often, they're not. They spend more hours with the horses than anyone and receive the least amount of credit.

"In the early days with Sky Watch, though, he didn't have a groom, right? When it was just you and your grandfather?"

"That's right." Mitch chuckled. "I was the groom."

At the start of 1982, that had changed. Garland Bradshaw never made it back to the barn. On March 14, almost a year after the initial stroke, Garland Bradshaw died at Friendship House nursing home, leaving Lena a widow. Mitch and Lena didn't mourn alone. The entire Saddlebred community grieved the loss of a man who, according to one of his protégés, George Gwinn, never had a fault.

"During the last 50 years I've known all the top horsemen but you would have to put Garland right at the top of the list," Gwinn told the Danville *Advocate-Messenger*, who printed an article announcing Garland's death on the front page. The article calls the master horseman a member of the American Saddle Horse Breeders Association and First Baptist Church—in that order. Garland might have appreciated that. For him, Saddlebreds certainly were a religion.

Tom Moore, a show ring great in his own right, added, "He was one of the men who made the business what it is today. . . . He could also appreciate a good horse no matter who had it or what color it was. He was just a great showman and a great person."

Bill Wise, another Danville horseman who's ridden horses to victory passes in Freedom Hall, seemed to agree. "He was a great trainer . . . he was the best teacher ever to come along in our business. He was a hard taskmaster, sort of like a drill sergeant in the army. But no matter whether you loved or hated him at the time, you learned your lessons."

Garland's most devoted student couldn't take bereavement leave. Mitch might have lost his mentor, but he'd pay tribute the best way he knew how: working. No matter who had died, the horses needed to be fed and exercised. Stalls needed to be cleaned. Working was the best way to honor the man who liked to greet Mitch with a "Mitchell, good afternoon. How was your morning?" if Mitch was as little as five minutes late for the 7:30 morning feeding.

Mitch dreamed of another way to honor his grandfather too, but he didn't dare say it out loud. With Sky Watch, he could win the big one—the Five-Gaited World's Grand Championship. With twelve World's Grand Championship titles in his family, Mitch knew better than to let that thought out of his head and into the air. Master horsemen kept their plans to themselves. Winning the big one took a great horse but also some chess-level planning, and Mitch knew Don Harris played a good game of chess. So, as Mitch mapped out his show season, he skipped some of the major early shows.

Instead of entering at Rock Creek, Mitch entered Sky Watch at Devon, in Pennsylvania, far from Don Harris Stables. The two shows run almost back-to-back, so if a horse goes to one, he isn't hitting the other.

In the 1980s, Devon didn't draw the Kentucky crowd as it does today. Classes were smaller there than they'd be at Rock Creek, filled with horses from the Northeast, who usually didn't meet their Kentucky rivals until Louisville. The Devon Horse Show and Country Fair is, according to their website, "the oldest and largest outdoor multi-breed horse show in the country." Other than a pause for World War II, the show has run continually since 1896. Like many horse shows, Devon is also a charity. During World War I, in 1918, the horse show raised $9,000 to donate to the war effort. The next year, a group of women took over show management and added a country fair, but East Coast style, complete with tea sandwiches. Bryn Mawr Hospital became the new charitable recipient, and with these women at the helm, the 1919 edition of Devon raised nearly three times as much as it had the year before. In the century since then, Devon has been responsible for more than $15 million in donations to the hospital.

With white picket fences around the outdoor ring, hat contests on Ladies' Day, and events like four-in-hand driving, Devon is one of the classiest shows in the country. In four-in-hand driving, one person drives four horses from a seat in a nineteenth-century-style carriage. It requires excellent driving skills, excellent horses, and an excellent amount of money. The period costumes alone will set an exhibitor back thousands. The carriage could be upward of $30,000. Add harnesses and bridles—another $15,000. Michele Macfarlane excelled at four-in-hand.

Michele watched Sky Watch burst into Devon's newly rebuilt Dixon Oval, one of the country's nicest outdoor rings. The late-spring Pennsylvania air cooled his nostrils and added an extra pop to his step. Sky Watch showed well in any conditions, but he appreciated the break from the Kentucky humidity. He held his head so high, his crest sat almost in Mitch's lap, Mitch's tie inches from the stallion's mane. In his matching red polka-dotted patent leather browband and cavesson, Sky Watch smoked his four competitors, including The Talk of the Town, a bright chestnut stallion who some had said could challenge Imperator. Only the true Saddlebred fans stayed late enough to see the victory pass, but Sky Watch rewarded them for their patience. Spectators who were there that night remember the chess-piece headset, the motion that "no photograph could do justice to."

Meanwhile, a few days later, Imperator racked by the Rock Creek Riding Club House in a victory pass of his own. That show already belonged to Don Harris. In the early 1970s, he rode the dark chestnut gelding named Giddy-Up-Go to seven straight championships there. Imperator, too, took more than his fair share of victory passes at Rock Creek. According to some, Imperator "bore an eerie resemblance" to Giddy-Up-Go, who, although he never won the five-gaited championship at Louisville, is still remembered wistfully by old-timer horsemen. Don had the home court advantage at Rock Creek, no doubt. It's no wonder Mitch skipped that show.

A month after the organ's last note had faded over Rock Creek Riding Club, sending Imperator back to his stall for a rubdown and a visit from barn mascot Elizabeth the bulldog, Don Harris loaded the gelding on a trailer again. Lexington. Both Sky Watch and Imperator had shone at Lexington the previous year. Don was counting on taking Imperator all the way to the championship, but rumors about Sky Watch were circulating. Mitch had said he'd take his wonder stud to the stallion stake at Lex but had waffled about the championship, saying he might choose to gear for Louisville instead.

With a horse who works as hard as Sky Watch, injury is always just around the corner. Mitch knew he needed to choose his pre-Louisville classes carefully. Every time he hooked Sky Watch to a jog cart—because yes, he could finally jog the stud—he studied him. Left hind, left front, right hind, right front. Did he place weight equally on all four? That pull on the bit— was that soreness in the right hind, or did Sky Watch want to move faster? When on top of him, Mitch felt for the horse's movements through his hips. Did Sky Watch reach equally through both hocks? Did he land squarely under each shoulder?

Imperator knew the grounds at Lexington, the old wooden stalls for the harness-racing horses, the tented temporary stalls, the Red Mile itself. He knew, too, the level of excitement that the horse show brought. By then, Imperator was a horse show veteran. I'll bet, like many show horses, he'd get excited at the sight of barn staff packing equipment, at the sound of the trailer pulling around. He probably flattened his ears in disappointment when Don trailered off to the shows in between Rock Creek and Lexington—like the Shelby County Fair and Horse Show—and left him behind.

At Shelby County 2020, Mitch asked me the question I'd been dreading. "Have you been in touch with Michele?"

"I have." I could feel myself hunching forward. "She's answered some questions for me already." Not untrue, but the full truth hurt too much to say. How could I tell Mitch she'd shot me down after ten questions? What did that say about me?

My last name wasn't Teater, Moore, or Wheeler. My family was no Saddlebred dynasty. The box of ribbons labeled "Emma" in my mom's attic didn't hold any blues from Lexington or Louisville. My only Louisville ribbon wasn't a blue first but a fifth, pink as my lipstick in the ten-and-under equitation qualifying class. The only horse I'd owned worth remembering had earned his World's Championship title with another little girl, not me. My current horse would never show at Louisville, and, with a baby looming in my future, who could say how long Bee and I would show together at all?

Yet here I was, obsessed with Sky Watch, a horse who had retired a month before my mom fired up her mixer to make my third birthday cake. That moment in the American Saddlebred Museum, when the footage of Imperator and Sky Watch flashed across the screen, returned. *This is why Saddlebreds matter.* Sky Watch was worthy of my obsession, no matter my pedigree. That's what made him great. He inspired everyone, from Hall of Fame trainers to people who'd never even touched a horse. Saddlebreds—and horses everywhere—were fading. He was their starring act, deserving of every YouTube view and Facebook comment he earned.

8

A Dance of Sensation

So far, Mitch and Sky Watch were undefeated together. The summer stretched out before them, blue-skied and sticky over the bluegrass, week after week of twice-a-day training relieved only by horse shows and their various ovals. Burlington's almost circle. Shelbyville, with its wooden tunnel of a chute. Mercer County, with its perfectly banked turns, newly built after a fire in 1981. Fire is every horseman's nightmare. Losing that ring to it would have been tragic, so horsemen and horsewomen from Kentucky and beyond celebrated the rebuild. Sky Watch wouldn't go to any of these smaller shows. Instead, Mitch hauled others from his string to the county fair circuit and took victory passes with them. He needed to save Sky Watch's spark. Lexington first. Then Louisville.

One morning, right before the Lexington Junior League Horse Show, where Don Harris hoped to overtake Sky Watch on the Red Mile, Emiliano found the stud standing on three legs. His right hind barely held weight, only the toe touching the ground. Something was very, very wrong. When Mitch led him out of the stall, he could barely walk. Mitch had already turned in his entries for Lexington. He'd listed Sky Watch's name under the stallion stake.

While no one saw the injury happen, Mitch was convinced that the horse had gotten down in his stall and hurt himself getting back up. Even in a twelve-by-twelve box intended to protect them, horses can do a lot of damage. At Shelby County in 2020, I saw it in person. Before setting out for Mitch's stalls, I stopped by Mike's. Bee isn't Kentucky caliber, not even for the county fairs, so she wasn't there, but my trainer's stalls still served as my home base, their tan curtains my banner. There, I belonged, a privilege bought with each month's training bill.

No sculpted head appeared above the first door on the left, so I peeked in. The horse was stretched out on the ground, his sides heaving. Uh-oh.

Julie, one of Mike's assistant trainers, walked in. Thank goodness. "Julie," I said, "something's not right."

Julie, tortoise calm, stepped over and looked in. "Yep. Excuse me." She opened the stall door. As soon as she did, the gelding's eyes wheeled and his legs paddled—three of them. One was caught in his tail set. The horse was trapped. Sweat darkened his coat. He'd panicked himself into a trance, but Julie's entry had broken through it. Because they're prey animals, horses carry an innate need to run from danger. With his equipment hemming him in, the poor guy couldn't run. Some horses will let the panic take over and break their own bodies to get free. Others find solace in stillness, seeming to know that a human will be there to help and if they just stay still, they'll be okay. This one oscillated between the two.

Julie stepped back and slid her iPhone out. "Mike," she said, "we've got a horse down in his stall." This, Julie had decided, was above her pay grade.

Horses are large enough animals that, in the confines of a stall, they can lie down next to a wall and end up stuck, unable to heave their feet underneath them enough to stand up. In the horse world, that's known as getting *cast* in the stall. It's a dangerous situation for both horse and human. The horse needs help, but getting too close to those thrashing legs could be deadly. I had no business trying to save a downed horse, which was why I had called for Julie, who'd decided to escalate the issue up to Mike. The gelding needed to be freed from his tail set first. With any luck, he'd rise on his own after that. But how to maneuver close enough to the horse without taking a hoof to the temple?

When Julie hung up, I offered to help. "I could probably slip through the stall next door and sit on his head for you." Sitting on a horse's head, or, more accurately, planting a knee in his neck, prevents him from trying to rise.

Julie knew better than to let an amateur into the stall with a hurt horse. "No, we'll just wait for Mike." Julie's got shoulders like an oak, so if she didn't feel comfortable in there, there's no way my five-foot-five, 130-pound frame could or should provide equine restraint. Besides, I didn't have the technique or knowledge.

Moving slowly and deliberately, Julie propped a fan in the stall door. The horse remained still. The least she could do was make him comfortable while we waited for Mike. Minutes later, he pulled his white truck in front of the stalls and jumped out. Best practice would have been to leave the scene and let the professionals handle things, but my curiosity got the better of me. From the aisle, I watched Mike slip into the stall, keeping his body close to the wall to stay away from those hammer-hard hooves. The horse, miraculously, didn't move, as if he knew the help he needed had arrived. Mike crouched and pulled a knife from his pocket, murmuring all the while. Then, he knelt down, within striking range if the horse had felt like it, and, with one quick motion, cut the tail set's strap and jumped back.

The big gelding groaned and rolled to his chest. I let out a breath. He'd made it. A horse on his side is in strife. Even when sleeping, horses only stay in that position for a few minutes at a time. But a horse on his chest—that horse is going to be fine. In seconds, he slung his back legs under him and rose to his feet, cocking his left hind foot. He was hurt, but not gravely. Julie clipped a lead rope to his halter and walked him off. To a horse, forward movement, even at a limp, is soothing.

What's most miraculous about the whole scene at Shelbyville was how calm the horse became when Mike entered. With me, and even with Julie, whose knowledge and experience dwarfs mine, his panic had only increased. With Mike, the big horse calmed. No teeth were gnashed. No ears were pinned. Matching the right personality to the right horse is half the battle. Julie has horses in her training string that match her perfectly, ones who are always at their very best when she's handling them. That's why it helps to have multiple trainers in one barn. When a trainer meshes well with a horse, we say he or she's "got the key" to the animal.

Mitch had the key to Sky Watch.

Injured, Sky Watch wouldn't perform at Lexington in 1982, which disappointed Don Harris. He'd hoped for a confrontation between Sky Watch and Imperator, but when Mitch's trailer pulled into the Red Mile, his star horse wasn't on it. Naturally, the papers got curious. Mitch told the *Advocate-Messenger* he wouldn't be able to ride the stud for thirty days. A horse like Sky Watch taking a month off in the heat of show season, in the last six weeks before Louisville, was like a quarterback tearing a hamstring during playoffs. Those Super Bowl dreams would have to wait until next year.

At Lexington, Imperator continued his winning streak. All three judges voted for him in both the gelding stake and the championship, giving the liver chestnut twenty consecutive blue ribbons with unanimous votes. The crowd, too, voted for him with their cheers and applause, their devotion bordering on religious. *Here*, their hollering said, *is a true Saddlebred, the best of the breed*. The reigning king would be hard to dethrone. Fans might have been curious to see what Sky Watch could do, but truth be told, a show horse had to stay sound. If he couldn't cut it, he might as well stay on stall rest or retire early to stud like his own sire.

Sky Watch's daddy, Flight Time, the son of the immortal Wing Commander, had gotten hurt at age four. As a three-year-old, he took first place in the five-gaited three-year-old stake at Louisville, winning the class Sky Watch would lose with Rob Tanner fifteen years later. Like Sky Watch, he'd been labeled a young horse to keep tabs on. After his injury, he couldn't enter the gate to win, place, or show at the four-year-old stake at Louisville in 1966. By 1967, the Teater family had decided to make use of his other gifts, the genes coded into his DNA, and they started Flight Time in the breeding shed.

When a stallion is injured, his owner must make a decision. A stud's primary value comes from breeding, not from showing. A winning show record might drive up the stud fee, but the real proof is in the quality of his get. Some stallions tear it up in the show ring but don't pass their talent to their colts and fillies. Others barely have a show record, or none at all. Undulata's Nutcracker, who became the youngest stallion to come in at the top of the World Champion Sire Rating, never entered the show ring, but there isn't a class at a horse show in America that doesn't include at least one horse whose name puns on "Nut," indicating the relationship with the great Undulata's Nutcracker. Just Maybe a Nutter. This Is Nuts. Nutorious. Stallions don't need to prove themselves with ribbons. No one would fault Michele for retiring Sky Watch after a short but brilliant career. Rumor had it, she'd turned down offers upward of $500,000 for him, making him the most expensive Saddlebred in history. What else did he have to prove?

Michele might be shy, but she liked to win. While she and Mitch agreed that it would never be worth the cost of Sky Watch's health or career to push for a Louisville show in 1982, they decided not to pull him from competition, at least not officially. After thirty days of rest, they'd still have two weeks before Louisville. Showing wasn't impossible. Just improbable. No one had high hopes that after so much time off he'd be ready for the show ring, but maybe—just maybe—Sky Watch would surprise everyone.

Stall rest did not agree with Sky Watch. Life at Mitchell Clark Stables became miserable for everyone. Emiliano's horsemanship skills were considerable, but he couldn't keep his charge calm. I can only imagine the ruckus a frustrated Sky Watch would have made when penned up in his stall for days on end. Horseshoes on stall walls can be loud as gunshots. Sky Watch's jaws, working at every crack and crevice he could find, weren't exactly silent either. None of the horses around him could have been getting any rest. Their workouts were probably suffering. With all his energy, Sky Watch could do considerable damage to a stall. It was only a matter of time until he did damage to himself. Mitch had to step in.

I picture Mitch standing in front of the stud's stall, muttering, "We can't keep you on stall rest." Hands on hips, staring Sky Watch down as the horse pawed and pinned his ears. "We can't hand walk you for shit. What am I supposed to do with you?"

As a colt, Sky Watch had destroyed multiple sets of harnesses before Granddaddy Bradshaw stepped in, but as a five-year-old, he'd accepted the training tool. Most days, Mitch jogged Sky Watch in the morning and rode him in the afternoon. In the jog cart, though, Sky Watch didn't look like Sky Watch. He settled in, settled down, and let Mitch put some quiet miles on him. With a cart behind him, Sky Watch reverted to shuffling along the way he had before Mitch put a mouth on him. His knees didn't pop; they plopped. Mitch could have been jogging any old plug, not the stallion ready to steal a world title.

Now Sky Watch stood, restless, his hurt rear leg cocked as his trainer strapped down the shaft loops and hooked the traces. Mitch grabbed the lines and, fluid as an egret, swung one leg and then the other into the cart as the horse walked off. It's a movement ubiquitous among horse trainers, one I might never master. When I learned to drive, the horse had to be at a full stop for me to climb in. Then I hopped on backward, thumping my butt into the cart's seat before heaving both legs around at once. Heavy-bottomed mammal, not graceful bird. The jog carts most trainers use have metal stirrups and a seat no wider than some women's hips. They look like the result of a bicycle's affair with a gynecologist's table. Soon enough, I'd be spending a lot of time on one of those tables.

With all of Sky Watch's pent-up energy, it would have been no surprise if he had taken off with the cart, reverting back to his two-year-old antics. To Mitch's delight, he didn't. Sky Watch didn't buck or jump. He kept to a bounce walk, although there was a definite hitch in the rhythm. He rolled his trainer around the arena counterclockwise, then bounce-walked through the middle to head the other way. After they'd circumnavigated the oval a few times in both directions, Mitch said, "Whoa," pulling his horse up. "That'll do for today. Maybe that'll take the edge off, you raunchy son of a buck."

It didn't. Mitch had to hook him two more times before Sky Watch stopped clanging around his stall like a pissed-off gorilla.

Strict stall rest had been the prescription, but, as usual, Sky Watch defied expectations. He needed some activity. Bounce-walking in front of a cart might be as close to total rest as a brush fire like him could get. So, every day, three times a day, Emiliano slung the harness on the stallion's back. Then off the horse would go with Mitch in the driver's seat, bounce-walking along, often with Mitch's German shepherd, Nick, trotting alongside. Sky Watch still two-stepped in the crossties, but he'd quieted some since his two-year-old year. Emiliano learned, as Mitch had, to step along with the horse while brushing him or tightening his girth.

All through July, Mitch walked Sky Watch in the cart. August came, and they kept walking. While Emiliano packed tack trunks for Louisville, Sky Watch walked. On the day he hauled into the Kentucky State Fairgrounds, Mitch strapped the jog cart to the top of the trailer. He didn't know if the stallion would be sound enough to compete, but he'd reserved a stall for him and entered his name in the stallion stake. He'd be in Louisville all week. Whether or not Sky Watch hit the ring, Mitch needed to keep walking him in the cart.

What would it take for Mitch to hop on his back and ride down the chute into Freedom Hall? He told the *Advocate-Messenger*, "He'll have to give me two straight workouts where he feels like his old self. The horse is trying. He wants to go. But he's rusty."

Mitch never got his two straight workouts. Over the weekend, he'd kept up with the slow jogging, and the hitch in Sky Watch's step had improved, but not so much that Mitch felt like climbing on his back. The night of the stallion stake arrived, the clouds an upturned bowl in the sky that kept the humidity clamped over the fairgrounds. Horses and riders alike steamed like noodles. All day, Mitch debated. The class came at the end of the session, so he could change his mind at the last minute. In Freedom Hall, the classes rolled along. Junior five-gaited mare. Amateur ladies' fine harness. Amateur three-gaited under 15.2. Mitch pressed his hand against Sky Watch's stifle, palm flat, feeling for heat. The flesh felt warm but not hot. With a nod, he signaled Emiliano. Tack him up.

As the sun set over the Louisville skyline, Emiliano saddled Sky Watch, and Mitch stepped in to brace and bridle him. Mitch hadn't been on the horse's back in six weeks. He might have to jump off as quickly as he'd jumped on. Or the stud might dishonorably discharge him from the saddle. Or he might hit the warm-up ring for the first trot and stop. No matter what, if the stallion wasn't sound, he'd scratch.

In the warm-up, Sky Watch moved with more confidence than Mitch had expected. *Well*, he thought, *we'll see how it goes.* Mitch knew he could win the stallion stake without calling on the horse's full power. It would be a test. If Sky Watch could make it through the class that night, maybe he'd be strong enough to go up against Imperator on Saturday.

Seven other studs hit the gate for the stallion stake, including The Talk of the Town, who'd just won the stallion class at Lexington and had challenged Sky Watch at Devon the previous spring. Sam Stafford, aboard the bright chestnut, knew that his horse stood the best chance of beating the unbeatable. He knew Sky Watch was recovering from an injury. He knew this could be his chance.

Sky Watch and The Talk of the Town stood out as the two top horses in the qualifying class, but no one in Freedom Hall questioned who would end up in the winner's circle. Mitch might have called Sky Watch "rusty," but the stud shone like new steel. He burst through the chute and down the straightaway, Mitch working his lines through the arena. What looked like a simple straight line was more like a negotiation.

MITCH: See that red banner at the end? We're aiming for that.
SKY WATCH: No, we're not. We're going to cut that turn.
MITCH: Sure, but let's not take it too sharp. How about we hit that blue banner instead?
SKY WATCH: Didn't you hear? We're cutting the turn.
MITCH: Okay, we'll cut the turn. But we're taking the rail down the other straightaway.
SKY WATCH: Only if I choose the angle.

This back-and-forth happened every step of every trip around the ring. Mitch has said that when he watches his classes with Sky Watch, he sees two trajectories: where he meant to go and where he wound up. To an observer, the difference is invisible, but to the rider, the two lines are miles apart.

The Talk of the Town stepped high with a wild look in his eye. He had talent, passed down to him by Yorktown, his daddy, another Saddlebred great, but he couldn't quite match Sky Watch. Looking at photos of the two side by side, I can see that The Talk of the Town carried a longer foot and more shoe. According to *Saddle and Bridle*, Sky Watch's front feet stayed trimmed to a modest three and three-quarters inches. On them, he wore a single pad and a twelve-ounce flat shoe. Behind, his toes stayed a little longer—four and a half inches—and held a little more weight—eighteen ounces. The Talk of the Town would have trounced any other stallion, but Sky Watch, even in his first postinjury ride, had him beat. As he walked Sky Watch back to the barn, blue ribbon in hand, Mitch breathed in relief. He'd made it through the class.

On Saturday night, Mitch still wasn't taking chances. He'd hate to do it, but he'd scratch in the warm-up ring if he needed to. He feathered the reins, testing the new curb bit he'd buckled onto the bridle, hoping to make the negotiations with Sky Watch a little less one-sided. As he warmed the stallion up, weaving around the seven other horses he hoped to beat, including Imperator, he called to the trainers watching railside.

"Is he sound? Does he look as square as he feels?"

Mitch knew he might only have one shot at a horse like this, and he wasn't going to screw it up for the sake of a win that night. That would have been greed. *I am not going to hurt him at any cost, including for this class*, he said to himself. If he needed to pull the horse and come back to challenge Imperator the following year, he would. He'd hate it, but he would. His horse's health meant more than a victory pass, even a victory pass on Saturday night in Freedom Hall.

Mitch moved Sky Watch into a slow gait. Sky Watch rocked back and shimmied into it. His neck sucked back, just inches from his rider's body. One, two, three, four. Yes. Mitch trusted the rhythm beneath him. Sky Watch could show.

By the time the crowd clapped the Five-Gaited World's Grand Championship contenders into Freedom Hall, they'd already had quite a night. Twice, they'd seen a father-daughter showdown. Tom and Melinda Moore showed against each other in the Three-Gaited Grand Championship and the Fine Harness Grand Championship. In the former, the father triumphed, but in the latter, youth trumped age, and Melinda Moore took Shadow's Creation for a victory lap around the ring. Mitch's wife, Cyndy, sat among the fifteen thousand people packed into the stands, along with Mitch's great-uncle Frank, the Bradshaw brother who piloted the fabulous My-My to six World's Grand Championships. Cyndy normally didn't mind standing on the rail, but at nine months pregnant, she'd taken a seat to rest her feet. The Teater family joined the spectators, excited to see what their "unremarkable" baby, now turned wonder horse, would do in the class that determined the World's Grand Champion of Champions.

The fifteen thousand people packed into Freedom Hall only grew louder as each Five-Gaited World's Grand Champion hopeful entered the ring. Both French Wine and French Commander had returned for another shot at the big one. So had Valley Venture and Rare Treasure. One of two mare entries, The Rose, bucked on her way in, almost unseating her trainer. Rhythm 'n Jazz, the other mare, trotted in slick. No hump in her back. Fine horses, all, but the two everyone really wanted to see had yet to enter.

The sound in Freedom Hall hit a new high as the announcer called Sky Watch in. Mitch couldn't hear anything. It was so loud, he might as well have been working in silence. Sky Watch flew down the rail; then, as he hit the turn, the announcer called Imperator, the two-time defending grand champion. If the sound had been deafening before, it became flattening, a palpable thing. Mitch realized he would be communicating with his horse by feel alone. If he needed to cluck or say whoa—too bad. Sky Watch wouldn't be able to hear him. This would be a dance of sensation.

The noise didn't faze Don Harris and Imperator. Don always said, "He likes it," and he was right. The gelding, fresh off the best performance of his career in the gelding stake earlier that week, moved proudly as a ship's figurehead, cutting through the arena as if it were his own private bay. His first slow gait carried the crowd, every micromovement perfect, his ears up and tethered forward.

Sky Watch, too, was unafraid. As he moved him into the rack, Mitch felt Sky Watch magnify. Even at his modest height, he looked like a giant as he racked around horses like Valley Venture—a good horse, one worth forming a whole damn company to buy, but next to Sky Watch, he might as well have been ambling down a trail. With every step, Sky Watch's strength grew. Mitch breathed deep and shifted his seat. Go time. His horse was sound. He knew it, now, in a place beyond doubt. He needed to plead his case to the court.

With a teardrop reverse that razored between Rhythm 'n Jazz and the rail, Mitch angled Sky Watch out of the corner and cut across center ring. Sky Watch's legs looked unhinged, their length and fineness accentuated as he reached and pushed, reached and pushed. His ears swiveled forward and stuck there, lasering on the space in front of him. The crowd stomped in the stands. If the judges hadn't been paying attention before, they were now.

Mitch locked eyes with Jim Koller, who stood outside the center ring with his judge's clipboard, and pointed Sky Watch right at him. Jim stood, goggle-eyed, as Sky Watch moved with so much motion he thought the horse might throw his shoulders out of their sockets. Even with a thousand pounds of energy coming at him, the judge didn't yield. The ground shook. Between each step, Sky Watch caught four inches of air, making him look a full hand taller than fifteen-two. The stud thundered by, close enough that Mitch could have kicked the card out of the judge's hand.

That night, Jim Koller didn't need a judge's card. No marks could describe the pageant unfolding in front of him. Everyone lucky enough to be in Freedom Hall knew they were seeing history in the making. Each time the announcer called for the walk, Sky Watch and Imperator accelerated, adding an extra pass at the trot or slow gait, each showing off his favorite gait. Underneath Mitch, Sky Watch flew, all power, no pause. If there had been a hitch in that hind stifle, it had evaporated. Imperator's neck lathered with effort, but Don pushed him, leaning back in the saddle and driving him forward. He counted on winning the class, so he asked his favorite gelding for his all. Imperator, generous, gave it, sucking his chin in and squatting low. Had a horse ever loved performance more than Imperator?

At the second-direction rack, the class almost over, Mitch had to hold Sky Watch back. Unbelievable. Imperator adored performing, but Sky Watch moved for the love of movement. Had the arena been empty and silent, it wouldn't have changed a thing. After a month of rest, the stallion carried energy to spare.

The announcer called the lineup, and the class filtered in, some trotting, some racking. The two horses everyone watched ignored his request. Instead of slowing down and turning for center ring, they sped up for another pass, then turned to make another, Imperator headed one direction and Sky Watch another. Finally, they aimed straight for each other, Imperator at the slow gait, Sky Watch at the trot, and nearly clanged stirrups.

Don Harris's gelding had been at his very best all week. As he dismounted to let his grooms remove the saddle for the conformation portion of the class, Don was sure he'd already won. The judges walked the line of horses, each of which posed like a runway model. Minutes later, to Don's dismay, the announcer called two horses back out for additional work. For six horses, the class had ended. For Imperator and Sky Watch, the second round began.

The two horses hit the rail, and Freedom Hall reverberated with sound. Sky Watch's neck, too, was lathered with effort, but it didn't stop him from making extra passes whenever he could. Mitch plotted out a cut on the rack and chased Imperator down the rail, never quite catching him. The announcer called the reverse, and Mitch cut again to move behind Imperator. Don cut Imperator even deeper and avoided the stallion. Back and forth, one outside, one inside, the two horses egged each other on. Eight minutes into the workout and nearly twenty minutes into the class, Sky Watch showed no sign of tiring. He could have kept it up all night.

All summer, Mitch had been watching Don Harris show Imperator, seeking weakness. He didn't find one. Imperator really was the perfect horse. Mitch knew it was an honor just to be in the ring with him, but that didn't stop him from painting a target on Don's back. He saw signs that the gelding might be tiring, so at the rack, Mitch increased Sky Watch's speed. Imperator lost collection as he worked to maintain the furious pace, but his heart loomed larger than his engine, and he kept at it. Pass after pass, the horses traded places, their legs churning, their nostrils blowing as if they were dragons, not horses. At last, Dick Morgan called them in. The judges had seen enough.

Saddlebreds show at 75–95 percent effort for however long the class goes, and the duration is up to the judges. There's no real way to prepare for the length of any specific class. Sometimes, a horse throws a shoe, adding an extra five minutes. Others, the judge calls a time-out to excuse a horse from the ring, breaking the expected cycle of trot, walk, canter, reverse, and repeat. Sometimes, there's a workout. Sometimes not. The shortest classes clock in at under ten minutes. The longest might go for forty. For comparison, Grand Prix dressage horses have no more than nine minutes to complete their tests, which aren't performed at speed. A jumping course might take less than a minute. Racehorses go all-out but finish in two minutes. Bucking broncos—eight seconds. Compared to these styles of competition, the Five-Gaited World's Grand Championship is an endurance event.

An entire entourage, including the Kentucky state governor and his wife, walked into the ring to present the trophies for the World's Grand Championship. The winner would need an extra tack trunk to cart home all that silver and the blanket of red roses. While the judges made their final deliberations, discussing who would take the remaining six ribbons after champion and reserve, the eight contending horses circled in the far turn. Cooling off—they'd earned it—or, for one lucky horse, warming up for a victory pass.

Finally, Dick Morgan spoke into his microphone. "Moving to the upper ranks, it's the challenger—Sky Watch." The rest of his announcement went unheard. A tsunami echoed through the stands as the crowd once again took to their feet. They stayed there and sent Don Harris and Imperator out with a standing ovation. The king had been dethroned.

In his post-class interview with TV announcer Bill Carrington, Mitch looked like he might cry.

"Here we have Mitchell Clark. What about it, partner?"

"Well, I'm very happy." Happy couldn't have described it. Mitch had just achieved something he'd wanted so much he couldn't even breathe it into words. "We weren't sure whether or not we'd make it tonight, but all the work has paid off."

"I would be remiss if I didn't point out that a gentleman passed this year who would be awful proud of you tonight."

"Yes, sir." Mitch's mouth tightened. His gaze dropped. "I tell you, I picked up everything I know about the horse business from my grandfather Garland Bradshaw."

With two spotlights trained on Sky Watch as he took to the rail for one final pass, Mitch felt another presence riding alongside him. Garland Bradshaw's spirit must have taken that victory lap with him, racking Lady Carrigan for all she was worth.

After making his way around the ring, Mitch and Sky Watch exited, but a slew of fans blocked their passage and forced them back into Freedom Hall for an encore. Sky Watch didn't mind. He liked the lights, trotting high and then, impossibly, even higher while the crowd thundered for him. As he made his exit, Mitch removed his hat in a last salute. Together, man and horse left the stadium and entered the night, the same pair as before but forever changed.

By James L. Crow, 1982. (Courtesy of the American Saddlebred Museum.)

Sky Watch at the Devon Horse Show, 1983. (Photo by Doug Shiflet.)

Sky Watch at the World's Championship Horse Show, 1983. (Photo by Doug Shiflet.)

Sky Watch at the World's Championship Horse Show, 1984. (Photo by Doug Shiflet.)

Sky Watch at the World's Championship Horse Show, 1988. (Photo by Doug Shiflet.)

Study of Sky Watch at all five gaits at the Devon Horse Show, 1985. (By James Walls.)

Imperator at the World's Championship Horse Show, 1985. (Photo by Doug Shiflet.)

My Queen Bee and Emma Hudelson at Four Willows Farm. (Photo by Ben Hudelson.)

My Boogie Nights and Emma Hudelson. (Photo by Brooke Jacobs of Jacobs Photography.)

Part III

1982–1985

9

The Horse He'd Wanted to Beat

After losing to Sky Watch, Don dismounted from Imperator and handed the gelding off to Myrtle, Imperator's caretaker. Sky Watch had just succeeded where Imperator had failed. Three years before, when Imperator was five, he had taken reserve in the Five-Gaited World's Grand Championship. After that class, his caretaker at the time, Tom Heron, had told *Horse World* he believed the gelding would only get better. After all, he'd said incredulously, "Can you imagine a five-year-old winning the big one?"

Now no one had to imagine a five-year-old wearing the roses at Louisville's grandest class. Sky Watch had just checked that box—with fifteen thousand witnesses.

Myrtle took Perry back to the stall and unbuckled the throatlatch, curb chain, and cavesson. Cavesson last, as always. Then he slipped his fingers through the headpiece and eased it over Perry's perfect ears, allowing the horse to open his mouth as he cradled the bridle off, careful not to let curb or snaffle stick in the bars, that magical toothless spot in a horse's mouth that makes it look like God made a slot for the bits to sit in. Myrtle's hands had performed these actions so often, he didn't have to think about them. Good thing, because after the class he'd just seen, he could hardly think.

While Myrtle slipped a wool cooler over Perry's back and brought him out of the stall for a walk that would slow the gelding's heart rate, lower his blood pressure, and bring his body temperature back to normal, Don Harris set his chin to do what needed to be done. He had to congratulate Mitch on his victory. After all, he was a gentleman. Before setting out for Mitch's stalls, he swung his coat off his shoulders, hung it on a bridle rack, and tugged at his famous turned-down hat. He'd hoped to toss it to the crowd during his victory pass. Instead, he rested it on a tack trunk.

Mitch stood in the stall with Sky Watch, lending a hand as Emiliano completed the same routine Myrtle had just finished. Bridle off first, then saddle, then tail brace. Only a handful of others had beaten Don there, but they grew silent and parted for the celebrity trainer.

"Congratulations, son." At fifty-one, Don could have been twenty-nine-year-old Mitch's father. "You've got one heck of a horse, there."

Mitch met his eyes. "Thank you, Mr. Harris. You know, I'm your gelding's biggest fan. I was awful worried going out there with you and him. I thought you might teach me a few lessons in front of all those people."

"It wasn't for lack of trying." Don glanced over his shoulder. "I'd better get out of this stall. Looks like you have a lot of folks headed your way." He turned, then paused at the stall door. "Enjoy it. And again, congratulations."

"Thank you, sir. I sure appreciate it."

As Don left, it looked like all of Freedom Hall was heading for Sky Watch. On the asphalt sat a program, thick as a picture book, for the 1982 World's Championship Horse Show. Imperator gazed out of the full-color cover, his ears pricked, his eye sharp, his legs hefted at the trot. The cover spot always goes to the previous year's Five-Gaited World's Grand Champion, so Imperator's image had represented the show for two full years. Now it splayed on the ground, discarded.

Don returned to his stalls. His grooms had already started packing the tack room and tearing down the curtains. He joined in, wrapping bridles in towels before stacking them for travel and folding up the director's chairs, which sat in a semicircle. Normally, Dr. Meanor would be standing there, feeding Perry treats and delivering kisses on his nose, but she'd been thrown from her horse in the warm-up ring earlier that week and broken her leg. The physician, probably against doctor's orders, had been brought to Freedom Hall that night on a stretcher. Doctors always make the worst patients.

Don stood in front of Imperator's stall. Rubbed dry, with his show sheet buckled around him, the gelding dropped his head to nibble hay.

"Perry," Don said, "we've got work to do."

Louisville might have been the high point of the show season, but it wasn't the end of it. Kansas City's American Royal, the third jewel of the Saddlebred Triple Crown, still glittered in November. Don had already started planning the rematch. If he closed his eyes, he could picture the Royal, the fairgrounds sprouting up from that city of brick and smokestacks.

The ring, its white walls festive with yellow-and-blue bunting. Perry liked to march around it as if it belonged solely to him. Yes, the Royal. Don might not be able to reclaim Imperator's World's Grand Champion title there, but he could reclaim his pride.

Back in the barn aisle, the one Garland Bradshaw had held for years at the Kentucky State Fair and the one Mitch still uses today, a crowd hemmed Mitch into Sky Watch's stall.

"They stood three, four, five deep around me," he told me at Shelby County in 2020, spreading his arms. "I couldn't get out. And I didn't let anyone leave without a handshake or an autograph—whatever they wanted. I owed them that. To be a part of something like that, it's special. I didn't take it for granted then, and I don't now."

I thought about how generous Mitch had been with me, a woman he'd never met. The man had a farm to run and horses to work, but he'd spent hours answering my questions so far, never giving me any indication that he needed to be doing something else. Whenever I sat in front of him, he gave me his undivided attention. "I wish I could've been there," I said, my imagination filling in the scene he'd just described to me.

His eyebrows rose and his mouth dropped open as if the spectacle were unfolding in front of him. "The energy was like at a baseball game. Everybody walking out of there wanted to raise a colt, wanted to breed a mare, wanted to buy a horse."

"Sky Watch has that effect," I agreed. "After seeing footage of that duel at the American Saddlebred Museum, I drove home and started horse shopping. Why do you think that is?"

"To have two horses of that caliber in the ring at the same time, showing against each other . . ." Mitch's gaze hit the ground, then rose to meet mine. "It's a once-in-a-lifetime thing."

Uncle Frank, the other Bradshaw Saddlebred wizard, had stood among Mitch's congratulators at Louisville in 1982.

"Well, Mitchell, you broke the tie," Frank said, his hands in his pockets.

"Tie? What tie?"

"Teaters and Bradshaws had been tied at twelve wins each." Frank meant the big one, the Five-Gaited World's Grand Championship. "You just broke that."

Mitch threw his head back. "Well, I'll be damned. I knew y'all had twelve wins, but I didn't know about the Teaters."

"That's right." Frank grinned. "I'll be spending most of tomorrow morning on the phone telling them all about it." He turned away, letting his nephew get back to his fans.

Two boys, one seven and one eight, approached Sky Watch's stall, their parents behind them. They thrust out their programs. Mitch knelt to the ground to look them in the eyes.

"Young man," he said, addressing the older one, "did you have a good time tonight?"

"Yes, sir, I did."

"And you? How about you?"

"Me, too! I really like your horse."

"I can tell. I think he can too." Mitch glanced up at Sky Watch, who stood with his ears pricked toward the small humans at the front of his stall.

"How do you get him to trot like that?" asked the older boy.

"He's a special horse," Mitch replied. "And we practice a lot. I'll bet you have something you practice at. Let me guess. Football? Baseball?"

The boys nodded.

"It takes time to get good at something, right?"

They nodded again.

"But it's worth it." Mitch signaled to the parents for a pen, catching their eyes and pinching his index finger and thumb together, scribbling an imaginary signature. "Here. Can I sign those programs for you?"

Next in line stood Lee Shipman, an Arkansas native who'd fallen in love with Saddlebreds at age sixteen and had worked under Garland Bradshaw in the late 1940s and 1950s. "Well, Mitch, you just dethroned me."

"Mr. Shipman. Nice to see you, sir. I did what, now?" Mitch replied. He'd finally made it out of the stall, and he stood in the aisle with his coat off. His white shirt, translucent with sweat, stuck to his wide shoulders.

"I used to be the youngest trainer to win a World's Grand Championship." In 1959, at twenty-nine, Lee had won on Plainview's Julia. "But you're a month younger than me, so now that honor goes to you."

"I'm tickled. You've given me big shoes to fill."

Cyndy Clark braved the crowds and walked toward Mitch with her hands resting on her belly. A brunette with a wide smile, she had started working as a travel agent just the previous year, but she'd be taking a break from the working life soon. *Not soon enough*, she thought, shifting on her feet. The young couple embraced. After a night like that, maybe she wouldn't need to go back to work at all. Her horse trainer husband might end up with some new clients, ones like Michele, who had money to spare and wanted only the best for their horses.

On and on into the night, a crescent moon rising above him, Mitch accepted congratulations and good wishes. Michele preferred to avoid the crowds, but she must have made her way to the stalls too. I can picture it, that moment, the two regarding each other. The quiet female owner with unimaginable wealth and a stable full of champions. The tall male trainer she'd entrusted with her best horse. She was five years older than him, but her wide brown eyes made her look younger.

"We did it, didn't we?" she said, smiling.

"Yes, ma'am, we did," he replied.

The Scripps fortune helped pay Mitch's bills, but Mitch needed Sky Watch in his string for more than the money. In his soul, he needed Sky Watch. Once you've sat on a horse with that much fire, it's hard to picture giving up that seat. No one could ride Sky Watch like Mitch. Rob Tanner, an expert horseman with a string of champions, couldn't get the job done. Michele, who knew her way around a horse as well as most professionals, won on the West Coast on board her stud but wanted Mitch on board for the cutthroat competition of Kentucky. She might have wanted to be back in Sky Watch's saddle, but more than anything, she wanted to win.

For now, at least, Mitch was her ticket to winning with Sky Watch. After his performance that night, it seemed anything was possible. Only one burr stuck in the evening: it turned out that the win hadn't been unanimous. One of the judges, C. E. Peppiatt, known better as Pep or Peppi, had voted for Imperator. A minor flaw in a perfect night, but still a flaw. Perfectionists like Michele don't like flaws. Next time, that vote had better be unanimous.

At the 2020 Shelby County, Anthio asked me if my mare would be showing.

"Oh, no," I said. "She's not ready. She's not exactly Kentucky quality."

"That's okay," he said. "She looked good in that picture you posted on Facebook."

I smiled and looked down. "Thanks. We had a good ride that day."

In that photo, her mane is flying, and she's stepping high. Not Sky Watch high, but high enough. Her ears are forward, and her head is up. I remember that ride. The air late-spring warm against my skin as Bee shifted into her first trot. The molecules of her body moving in time with mine. My friend Angela says that riding requires coherence, but some rides leave me feeling more coherent than I felt before stepping into the saddle. In the photo from that day—a screenshot from a video—Bee looks like a show-quality Saddlebred. If every one of her steps looked as good as that one, I might have shipped her to Shelby County.

"I'm hoping to show her in Ohio at Dayton," I offered, unasked. "She's just a four-year-old, but she should be ready for me by then."

"Cool!" Anthio turned back to the bridle he was cleaning. "That'll be fun. For sure." His enthusiasm seemed genuine. He respected riding—at any level.

Shelby County might not be the show for Bee and me, but other, smaller shows could be her chance to shine. Nice horses entered these shows, too—sometimes just for practice, sometimes for serious competition—but not in the depth or numbers I'd see that night at Shelby County. Maybe then, my chance would come. Not to win, not even to get in the ribbons, but to ride well, to sync up with my horse, and to make some passes in front of a judge. To, as Mitch would say, "plead my case."

Plenty of riders pleaded their cases at Shelby County. From my spot in the stands, surrounded by the group of women from my barn who make up what we call our barn family, I whooped for my favorites. We all cheered for our trainer as he entered the ring. Mike rode a black filly in the junior park pleasure class, what would have been Bee's division, but those fifteen horses moved in ways Bee could only approximate. He and the black filly walked out with a ribbon, seventh place. Not bad for the young lady's first time off the farm.

Later that night, my friend Linda took to the ring. She rode a leg-waving nut-brown chestnut in the country pleasure division. "When I first tried him, Mike asked me what I thought." Her eyes sparkled. "The only bad thing I could say is that he was brown!" Champ, as she calls him, doesn't have any white markings, and his shade of chestnut isn't chocolate like Imperator's or red like Sky Watch's. He's brown as Indiana dirt, but his talent makes up for any lack of coloring.

Thirteen other horses joined Champ and Linda in the ring. As she weaved through the traffic jams and guided her gelding through the walk, trot, halt, and canter, a smile illuminated her round face. Even when another horse and rider crowded her in the turn, Linda maintained her grin.

"A little space, please, Nancy?" she called over her shoulder, bending her leg to scoot her horse's butt away from the horse walking alongside her. She looked up at us, her barn family, her cheering section, and raised her eyebrows. We nodded back at Linda, elbowing one another. We'd seen it. The two had practically knocked stirrups. Geez. What was Nancy thinking? Eyes up, Nancy. Not that I knew Nancy, but I joined in the ribbing, anyway.

Linda didn't get a ribbon in the class that night, but she didn't care. "That was so fun!" she blurted as she returned to us in the stands, drink in hand, her three-piece suit exchanged for denim shorts and a sleeveless top with a hand-painted Saddlebred in tropical colors. Virgin Islands, but horse show style. "So fun. Champ is just the best."

Michele Macfarlane might have declined my questions, but in those stands, surrounded by other women who love Saddlebreds, passing a paper plate of greasy potato wedges drenched in ketchup, she didn't cross my mind. I was home.

If you want to reach Don Harris, make sure he's eaten lunch first. After my conversation with Mitch in Shelby County, Don was next on my list to interview. When I first called the legendary trainer, now ninety-one, he asked me to give him some time. He was feeling a bit weak that day, so how about sometime the following week, maybe around 1:00 p.m.? He needed to make sure he had a chance to eat before we chatted.

The following week, I tried again. "Hi, Mr. Harris," I said. "This is Emma Hudelson, the gal who's writing about Sky Watch."

"Yes, yes." Don sounded every bit of his nine decades, but he was still sharp. "Thank you for calling me back. However, the day's gotten away from me, and I'm just now sitting down to my bacon, egg, and cheese sandwich. Can you give me a half hour?"

Who was I to keep a man from his eggs? "Of course, sir. I'll call you then."

I pictured the elderly trainer sitting in his Simpsonville breakfast nook in khakis and a white button-up shirt. Did he wear his fedora at the table? Probably not. As a gentleman, he would lay it beside him or hook it over the back of a spare chair. On his walls hung framed photographs, paintings, and drawings of the great Saddlebreds he'd worked and showed. Giddy-Up-Go.

Starina. Protégé. Prize Contender. Finisterre's Gift of Love. The Executor. Enlightening. Shoobop Shoobop. Reedann's Box Seat. And, of course, Imperator. None of those horses could top Imperator.

When I called back, Don was ready to talk. I was ready to listen.

After his loss at Louisville in 1982, Don hoped to meet Sky Watch at the American Royal. All week, Imperator had worked better than ever, but his rival didn't even trot into the warm-up ring. According to Mitch, he needed to show Michele's gaited horse New York, New York instead, so Sky Watch stayed in his stall. Don understands the need for a trainer to take care of his clients, maybe more than anyone, but still, he was disappointed. Rather than turn his own gelding around, though, he knew he would enter the ring. He felt an allegiance to the audience. They too had been hoping to see another showdown between the best two show horses in the country. Without Sky Watch there, the people might be let down, but Don could still give them one hell of a show. He might even win back the crowd who would have been rooting for Sky Watch. Don believed in the purest form of equine exhibition. A horse show was a show, after all. Like all performers, he knew the show must go on.

Go on, it did. Imperator gave the best show of his career thus far. He looked better than he had on Saturday night at Louisville, better, even, than he'd looked in the gelding stake that week. At eight years old, the horse was in his prime. Old enough to know his way around a show ring but not so old that the aches and pains of performance could slow him down. The victory might have been stunning—Imperator cranked up and back, his muscles popping as he paraded, his fourteen-foot tail sailing behind him, the whites of his eyes showing—but it rang hollow. Don hadn't beaten the horse he'd wanted to beat.

After getting stood up at the American Royal, Don wasn't backing off the gas pedal. He knew Sky Watch would come gunning for him the following year, so he made a plan for the offseason. When Myrtle brought Imperator to the arena at Don Harris Stables one winter morning, Don watched the gelding walk in. "I think you could stand to lose a few pounds, Perry. We've got to stay in front of that Sky Watch at the trot. You'd like that, wouldn't you?" He mounted up and turned to Myrtle. "Let's cut his grain back, see how he does." Everyone was talking about Sky Watch's unbelievable trot. Well, Imperator could trot too.

Under saddle, Don worked the gelding's trot, bouncing him back off the bits in the corner and keeping him straight as a laser beam down the straight-away. He sat back and deep in the saddle, inviting the horse to impel himself from his hind end. Perry liked to work. He enjoyed the challenge and worked to please his trainer. If Don thought he could do more, then he'd step up and do it. Imperator didn't have a half ounce of quit in his body.

To finish the workout, Don slow-gaited Perry around the arena. Once, then twice for good measure. The slow gait didn't need work. The heavens had gifted Imperator with the perfect one-two-three-four rhythm and the strength to elevate through every step. He could maintain the gait all day, easily, happily. No stress.

The rest of the week, Don jogged Perry. Five, six, seven miles a day. No break to canter or slow-gait. Just trot, with a pause for a walk here and there as needed to let the gelding blow. Then back to the trot. The weight of the jog cart helps horses with hind-end impulsion too. Without Don on his back, Perry could move freely. Each week, he seemed to trot a little bigger.

The diet, too, seemed to be working. For the first few days, Perry nosed around his bin, looking for the missing grain. Like anyone on a diet, he might have been a little sour. He gave Myrtle some dirty looks in the crossties while he tacked him up, but he never landed a kick or a bite. In his workouts, Don felt him pick up speed. He nodded. Good boy. He'd need that speed in the show ring.

As show season crept up, Don lightened the workload. To beat Sky Watch, Perry needed to be fresh. After four months of conditioning, Imperator bulged with muscle, his chest, shoulders, and hindquarters like something an architect would design. Of course, he ate only the best hay, mown locally, and the finest grain, dark and molasses sweet, so his coat glistened. While both Imperator and Sky Watch are listed as chestnuts, officially, their coloring looked completely different. Sky Watch shone red as an ember. Imperator's coat could have been dipped in Swiss chocolate— a rich, warm brown. By the spring of 1983, he looked as kingly as his name. The judges would decide, but Don had a feeling all his hard work would pay off.

Mitch, too, continued to work his horse hard through the 1983 offsea-son, but only because he had no choice. If he didn't, Sky Watch would tear down his stall and tear himself up in the process. The stallion's energy knew no bounds. After a morning of kicking the stall wall and pulling at the crosstie anchors, Sky Watch could still go out in the arena and yank Mitch around while he motored down the straightaway.

"Because of the pounding he gave his legs when he worked, we were constantly fighting inflammation in his tendon sheaths," Mitch explained to me at Shelby County. "Emiliano spent five times as much time with that horse as any other because of all the work he had to do on his legs."

"I'll bet Sky Watch was hard on himself. The best athletes are."

"Yes, ma'am." Mitch passed a hand over his forehead, which carried the thirty-eight years' worth of wrinkles he'd earned since 1982. "And you couldn't give him time off, or he'd get too raunchy for me to do anything with him. He was worth it, though. All the extra time he took—I wouldn't trade it for anything."

I thought about Anthio and the MagnaWave. MagnaWave didn't exist in the 1980s. Hyaluronic acid, the go-to treatment today for inflammatory musculoskeletal issues in equines, hadn't yet been approved for anything beyond eye surgeries. That meant the treatment of choice would have been old-fashioned coldness. Ice baths or wraps. More often than not, cold water from the hose. Some old-timers even liked to take a horse and stand him in a cold creek for a while, but I couldn't imagine Sky Watch standing quietly in the pasture's retention pond.

After Sky Watch's workouts, then, Emiliano took a hose to his legs. He crooned to the stallion as he yanked the pump handle up, holding the lead rope close to Sky Watch's head, the chain passing over his nose to maintain light but constant contact with that pressure point. As the hose gurgled in his hand, Emiliano aimed the jet of water at Sky Watch's lower legs, in the space that would be the shin on a human. Some horses are afraid of hoses—snakes!—and water—cold!—but not Sky Watch. Instead, he thought himself above such obstacles. That didn't mean he stood quietly.

"Whoa, whoa," Emiliano said. "Easy, fella." He stood to the side of the stallion, moving with him as he dodged left and right, all while maintaining the flow of water on first one front leg, then the other. When holding a horse, especially a horse like Sky Watch, it's better not to stand directly in front of them unless you enjoy being knocked down and run over. Equine restraint is more about attitude than physicality, anyway. In a bodily battle between horse and human, human always loses. It's physics. Like all good caretakers, Emiliano maintained a gentle firmness with his string of horses. He didn't have to demand respect. He and Sky Watch didn't need to work together to win, the way a trainer and horse must, but they still needed to work well around each other.

Sky Watch might have made working around him difficult, but he accepted all the coiffing and doctoring show horses receive. He would let Emiliano fork manure from his stall, stepping around him while he worked. He took the rubdowns, the comb run through his mane, the braiding of his tail, Emiliano's soft speech, sometimes English, sometimes Spanish. Horses don't care what language they hear. They understand tone more than words. Sky Watch still two-stepped in the crossties, but Emiliano moved with him, not trying to stop him or hold him still. Sky Watch's only sticking point? Injections. Sky Watch hated shots. Whether it was a vaccine or a cortisone shot for his joints, if Sky Watch saw a syringe, may God have mercy on the man holding it. Only Mitch could administer injections, and he had to walk in with the syringe hidden under a washcloth to get the job done. Even with the offending piece of equipment hidden, Sky Watch knew what was coming, and he'd strike out with his front hooves and snap his teeth like a dragon, ears pinned. He could look pretty in the show ring, but show him an equine influenza booster, and Sky Watch's face turned ugly with rage.

Mitch hated giving Sky Watch shots. Not because he was afraid of the stud but because he needed to get along with him when he climbed on his back. For this reason, many trainers don't do much of their own dirty work. They let someone else, a groom or assistant trainer, trim the fuzz from a horse's ears or the whiskers from her chin. The only battle a trainer wants to fight happens in the saddle. They don't need baggage from bickering with a horse in the stall over a haircut. Especially if they're working that horse twice a day, six days a week, as Mitch was with Sky Watch.

In February 1983, Sky Watch won in Phoenix, surprising no one. There, though, he'd shown more speed than anyone had seen from him before. It was hard to believe, but Mitch had found Sky Watch's sixth gear. Everything he'd done until then had been in fifth, maybe even fourth. More speed, and without sacrificing collection or action. If anything, the faster Sky Watch zipped around the arena, the farther back his neck snapped and the higher he stepped.

After getting wind of that, Don decided to give Imperator the call in his next workout. He'd had a hunch that the horse was faster, that he trotted a little higher, but he hadn't asked the gelding for his all. Not yet. One morning, when the sun rose to air that was already a little warmer than it should have been in late winter, Don bounce-walked Imperator out of the arena and to the outdoor track, a larger oval than his indoor ring.

"All right, Perry," he said. "Let's see what you've got."

Outside, the chocolate-brown gelding perked up. He widened his nostrils and snorted. *Good*, he seemed to be saying. *I've been waiting for this.* The pair barely made it to the ring before Imperator started trotting. His knees popped high, even higher than before, and he moved with more confidence than he'd had before. Don stuck his elbows out to the side and jiggled the reins left and right to ask for the slow gait. Imperator lifted his head and squatted, getting right to it. Even though his best gait hadn't changed much, Don swore he felt some extra power coming from behind. Then—rack on. Don squeezed his long legs along Perry's barrel and asked for some speed. Imperator zipped out of the corner and down the rail, a flash of dark brown glinting under the Kentucky sun. One by one, the grooms paused at their jobs and peeked out the windows to see what the boss was up to. Down the hill, they saw Imperator tearing up the track, Don barely checking him in the turns before sending him down the straightaway again. Both Don and Imperator were exactly where they wanted to be: surrounded by bluegrass, warmed by the sun, and working hard for an audience.

"Mitch might have been the youngest trainer ever to win the big one, but I was the oldest," Don told me, referring to his 1993 win with Protégé. Don paused, and I gave him time to collect his thoughts. "Thank you for waiting. I'm going off the top of my head here, and all this was a long time ago."

I didn't mind the wait. Talking to the nonagenarian trainer, the one my mom had watched show against her own trainer, Dale Milligan, was an honor. I sat on the daybed in my office and gazed at my own horse photos lining the walls. Two of My Queen Bee at horse shows, then a headshot of her at the farm. Keeper of the Stars, of course. Hello Dolly, a pleasure pony I'd won with as a teenager. Dutch, a big Friesian I'd been lucky enough to show for Roselane Farm, the barn where I took lessons. Then two of Faith, the walk-trot mare who'd stolen my heart when I returned to riding as an adult. None of these horses took victory passes at Louisville—except for Keeper, and that wasn't with me on board—but they were the best horses I'd ridden. Nothing like Don's string.

"Have you talked to Mitch, by the way?" Don asked.

"Oh, yes, sir. He's been great. I just talked to him at Shelby County. Earlier in the year, I drove to Danville, and he worked some horses for me and gave me an interview."

Don chuckled. "I wish you were doing this when I was a little younger. I would have liked to work a few horses for you."

I smiled. Ninety-one years old and still the master showman, ready to upstage his young rival.

As the 1983 show season rolled on, Mitch refined one more trick. He knew his horse could trot like a demon, so he needed to find ways to show off that gait as often as possible. Over the winter, he'd discovered that extra gear, that little bit of speed that would help him pass and cover up whatever horse he needed to in front of the judge—even, hopefully, Imperator. What he needed were a few extra steps of trot in the show ring to get the job done.

In five-gaited classes, the judge asks for the trot, then the slow gait, the rack, and the canter, with a walk between each gait. Then, reverse and repeat. In the open division, most trainers barely walk, if at all. Some stop their horses, giving them a full rest before asking for the next gait. Others keep trotting or walking. Some bounce walk. While this wouldn't fly in a junior exhibitor or amateur class, no one cares if a stake horse walks or not. Their job is to perform. In their first showdown, Don would ask Imperator for an extra slow gait every chance he got, and Mitch asked Sky Watch for a trot. What if, instead of pulling the stud down to a bounce walk from his rack or his canter, he could trot straight off instead? Mitch knew he'd ask Sky Watch for the extra trot at every opportunity. Might as well get an early start.

The problem was, the trainer couldn't force the stallion to do Mitch's will. Sky Watch worked best when he felt like the ideas came from him and not the guy hanging off his back. An old horseman's adage goes, "Tell a gelding, ask a stallion, discuss it with a mare." The testicles hanging between Sky Watch's hind legs demanded that he be treated differently. If Mitch asked and Sky Watch refused, well, Mitch had better think fast and find something else to do.

After a few false starts, in which Mitch thought he might end up plastered to his own arena wall, he found the key. One old trick to help a gaited horse catch his trot is to pinch his withers or even pull at the base of the mane. The attention to the front end breaks a horse out of the four-four rhythm and into the two-four of the trot.

Mitch didn't think Sky Watch would like him grabbing mane, so he tried pressure on the withers. Bingo. When he was ready to drop into the trot, Mitch lowered one hand enough to press the space just behind Sky Watch's neck. Combined with a shift in weight and a pressure release on the legs, it was enough to make Sky Watch stop one gait and move into the other without coming back to a walk for the transition. Mitch tried it out at Devon, in the Dixon Oval, where he found himself again because Michele needed more opportunities to take out her four-in-hand. In those days, she was willing to haul the whole shebang—carriage, harness, costumes, and all—from one coast to another, and why not? Her carriage turnout was flawless. Naturally, Michele had wanted her star gaited horse at Devon too. Mitch, on the other hand, liked Devon because it let him avoid Don Harris at Rock Creek.

Mitch's trick worked. While the three other horses in the ring stumbled down to a walk from their canter before pushing back into a trot and heading the other way, Sky Watch broke into a trot and sailed halfway down the rail while they were still getting turned around. Sky Watch left Devon with two blue ribbons. Michele, of course, was pleased. So was Mitch, but Mitch had something else to be excited about at Devon.

Sky Watch's sire, Flight Time, had been busy since Sky Watch's win in the two-year-old five-gaited stake in 1979. Della bred Aries Golden Gift back to him, and Mitch bought one of her fillies, named Sky Blue, for himself. At Devon, he trotted her into the show ring in the three-year-old five-gaited class, just to see what she could do. She moved like her big brother, all trot, all fire, and seemingly built for speed. While she didn't win the class that year, Mitch knew he had something special underneath him. And this time, he owned her. One hundred percent. He got to call all the shots and make all the decisions—and he'd collect all the money if she ever made it big and got sold. Michele might have turned down $500,000 for Sky Watch, but Mitch wouldn't reject an offer like that. That much money could buy the farm, maybe even buy a few more nice colts to invest in. After all, he was a father now, and he was tired of living in a house in town and driving to the barn every day. He wanted to raise his boy among the pastures at Ridgefields, where he could walk up to the house at lunchtime and kiss his tiny brow.

Show season ambled on. Imperator won at Rock Creek and Lexington, with Sky Watch nowhere in sight. After Rock Creek, Don told the *Louisville Courier-Journal* that Imperator "was like a horse running through a field" at that show. It had been that easy, that relaxed. "People are starting to talk about his trot, too."

In July, after Lexington, Don Harris wondered out loud why Mitch hadn't shown up for a rematch yet. "I really don't know why Mitch has avoided me," he told the Danville *Advocate-Messenger*. "I'm going in with as much confidence as a person can have. Imperator is the best he's ever been. If Imperator got beat at Louisville [in 1982] I still think it was more Mitch Clark beating Don Harris than Sky Watch beating Imperator."

One hundred pounds lighter and trotting better than ever, Imperator's 1983 show season had been almost embarrassingly good. It was understandable that Don Harris blamed himself for Imperator's loss the previous year. He conceded to the *Advocate-Messenger* that he'd worked the gelding too hard between the stake and the championship and asked too much of Imperator in the championship itself because he hadn't expected a workout. "I want to get to it," he said. He meant Louisville. He meant beating the boots off of Sky Watch.

Just a week before Louisville, in another interview with the *Louisville Courier-Journal*, Don threw down the gauntlet. "I have all the respect in the world for Sky Watch and Mitch Clark, but I think I have a plan to change the results. And time will tell."

Mitch read the papers. He knew what the elder horseman had insinuated: *I'm better than you, I'm more of a showman than you, and I've got the better horse to boot.* Mitch cut out those articles and stuck them to his refrigerator at home. Whenever Cyndy reached for the milk jug, she had to get past Don Harris quotes. Her husband used them for motivation. He'd read Don's words, turn around, and head back to the barn. Surely there was some tack to clean or a bridle to put together. Surely he could do more to get ready for his meeting with Don Harris and Imperator at summer's end.

Newspapers had reached out to Mitch too, but he'd kept his mouth zipped. After Sky Watch's win at Devon in June, he'd responded to the Danville *Advocate-Messenger*'s interview request with "Just say that he's in training and that he's 100 percent healthy. There's not much more to say right now."

Unfortunately, by mid-August, Sky Watch wasn't 100 percent healthy. One morning, when Emiliano led him out of the stall, he noticed a softness in the stallion's step. Not lameness, not exactly, but enough that he told his boss. Mitch watched the stud walk. "Damn," he said. "There's something going on. I'll hop up and have a feel. Maybe he'll work out of it."

Soft tissue injuries tend to improve with gentle work. Joint injuries don't. Same for hoof issues. Sky Watch's gait didn't smooth out after a trot and canter. Instead, it seemed worse. At least Mitch had identified which leg—the right front. He dismounted and passed his hand up and down the leg, pressing gently, his palm seeking heat or sensitivity, pausing at the fetlock, where the tendon sheaths tended to get irritated. Swelling, very subtle, and warmth.

"Let's get the vet in here, see what's what," Mitch told Emiliano. "Until then, get some cold on it. I'll just jog him today, keep my weight off him." Mitch set his chin. "I'll be damned if this son of a buck doesn't choose the worst times to get hurt."

Horses are unpredictable. At any second, things can change. A horse can get sick, get hurt, or even die. Accidents, illness, and injury are part of the gamble when working with living, breathing beings. Every trainer knows this, so they take it in stride when one of their string has to take time off. It happens to every athlete. Mitch understood and would give his horse as much time off as he needed. He accepted the setback, even if he didn't like it. Don Harris might have to wait another year for his rematch.

One athlete who never handles time off gracefully is my husband. In July 2020, the day before his vasectomy reversal, he sat on the couch, scowling at the recovery instructions the clinic had emailed him. "We recommend three weeks before lifting over thirty pounds or any exertional, heavy exercise, for example, running or sports," Ben read, grimacing. "Three weeks. That really sucks."

"What about walking? Can you walk?" I asked. Part of the benefit of running is getting outside. Fresh air. Sunshine. The breeze. Seeing trees. We'd chosen our neighborhood because it's bounded on all sides by trails, one that's made from former mule tracks along the Indianapolis canal. The mules used to pull the barges downtown, twitching their long ears to shake off the flies and mosquitos that still congregate on the waterway. Mules haven't plodded down the canal in over a century, but their trail remains, covered in gravel that's tracked with bicycle wheels and Nikes, not hooves. Still, that trail is proof that equines once shaped the city's landscape. Ben runs it, and together, to wind down from our workdays, we walk it, sometimes for miles.

"I don't know," Ben replied. "We'll have to ask. I'm guessing no. There's a whole paragraph here about the importance of scrotal support."

"Nice alliteration." I giggled.

Ben stared up at me from under his eyebrows, reminding me that he was about to undergo surgery so that we could create life. "For the return to other activities, we recommend two weeks to resume sexual relations."

"No baby making in the first two weeks," I replied. "Got it. I'll keep my ovulation chart to myself." Ben didn't laugh—didn't even smile. It's hard to find things funny with genital surgery looming in front of you. I scooted onto the couch next to him. "Seriously, though, I'm grateful you're willing to do this. For eight years, you handled our birth control. I didn't have to take the pill or get an IUD. That's a big deal. You changed your body so that we wouldn't have a baby before we were ready." I slid an arm around Ben and squeezed his shoulder. "Now that we are, you're changing it again." He exhaled hard, relaxing into me. "Not all guys would do that. I appreciate it."

"It's no problem, sweetie," Ben replied. "Just doing my part."

During the surgery, Ben was sedated but awake. The doctor let me stay at his side, where I couldn't tear my eyes away from where his tenderest bits rested, sliced open on a blue surgical drape. "Don't look down," I advised Ben.

He gritted his teeth. "I have no intention to. I can't feel what he's doing down there, but there's a lot of pressure." The doctor tugged at something tubelike and bloody. "Fuck. Shit. This is awful." In his sedative haze, Ben's language became unfiltered. "I'm sorry, Doctor." Our surgeon was clearly a conservative Christian. Before the procedure, he'd asked us if he could say a prayer. Ben and I are in that annoying "spiritual but not religious" category. We both meditate. We trust in a vague power greater than ourselves and believe in spiritual ideals like honesty, service, and compassion, but we haven't found a religious body that fits. Still, we'd agreed to the prayer. It wouldn't hurt to have God's help in all this.

"That's all right, son," the doctor said from behind his mask, sounding more like a preacher than a doctor. "We're getting close to the end, now."

He sent Ben home with a jock strap (for that all-important scrotal support), an ice pack, and instructions for a postoperative test in four months to see if the reversal had been successful. In the weeks that followed, Ben chafed at the inactivity, as restless as Sky Watch on stall rest.

"Why not come to the horse show next weekend?" I asked. "You won't be able to go for your long run, so that would give you something to do." Ben preferred not to watch me show. Horses made him nervous, and seeing me on one amped his anxiety, so we'd come to an agreement. He'd support me in this whole horse thing, but he'd do so from afar. "If we have a girl," I teased, "you know she'll be a horse girl. It'll be good practice."

Ben agreed and drove the two hours to the Clark County Fairgrounds in Ohio. There, he sat next to me and watched an afternoon's worth of classes.

A group of Hackney ponies trotted in, hitched to two-wheeled carts, their drivers in colorful racing silks and caps not unlike what jockeys wear in the Kentucky Derby. Hackney ponies are much smaller than Saddlebreds. "Wait," Ben said, "what are these? Are they young?"

"No." I laughed. "They're full grown. Those are ponies. That's what our Realtor drives." The Saddlebred world brings referrals of all types. Since I'd started riding again, my barn family, and the extended barn family of the entire Indiana Saddlebred scene, had helped Ben and me find, in no particular order, a tailor, a real estate agent, a hardwood-floor guy, and a new flood insurance quote. We watched in silence for a few minutes as the ponies worked, warming themselves up at the jog and then the faster road gait.

"Why are they dressed like they're in Mario Kart instead of in suits like you wear?" Ben asked.

The tinkling organ added to his Mario Kart analogy. The horse world can be foreign to an outsider. "Those are racing silks," I explained.

The announcer called for their grand finale: "Drive on!" He growled over the r in *drive*, letting his voice rise as if in a commercial for a weekend used-car sale.

"Oh," Ben said, nodding. "I get it. So this is a race?"

"No, not really." I fumbled. "I mean, not at all. They're borrowing from the racing tradition. They're fast, and they're judged on speed, yes, but form still comes first. There's no finish line."

Ben watched the ponies zipping around the ring, their drivers' faces set as they glanced over their shoulders and urged their ponies on to avoid getting passed. Ben looked even more confused. "So our Realtor does Mario Kart with very small horses and goes fast, but it's not a race?"

"Ponies," I corrected. "Hackney ponies. And she doesn't drive a road pony. She drives a harness pony." As if that would mean anything to him. The announcer tooted into a whistle, signaling the ponies to slow back to a jog. "She wears regular clothes, but fancier than she'd wear to show houses in. She doesn't have to wear silks like them or a suit like me."

The ponies lined up in center ring, their nostrils flaring, their little rib cages heaving. As I struggled to explain the spectacle in front of us, Ben laughed. He adjusted his hat, cocking it down and to the right. Ironically, and unbeknownst to him, his flat tweed hat is known as a driver's cap, originating in the nineteenth-century United Kingdom, to be worn when driving a team of horses for fun on a Sunday. So much of history is tied to horses. Even men's fashion. "Horse people are weird," he said. "You know that, right?"

"I know. We all do," I said, gesturing to the small crowd in the stands around me. "But we do it anyway. Just wait. Keep watching, and it'll make more sense."

By the time my class rolled around, my first with Bee since we'd been under the Mike McIntosh Stables banner, my heart pumped hard enough that I could see it through my vest. My entire suit, vest included, was another throwback to nineteenth-century men's fashion. Astride Bee, I stood in the center of the warm-up ring with Mike at her head. His assistant trainer, Brock Rutledge, stood behind Bee, combing her long tail.

Brock and I had grown up riding together. He'd taken one of his first riding lessons from my mom, who moonlighted as a riding instructor when our then trainer needed a hand. While I'd chosen mind-altering substances and college, though, Brock had chosen Saddlebreds. He'd started apprenticing under Mike when he was still in high school. Seventeen years later, the two men still worked together, familiar enough with each other that they barely needed to speak to get through a day of working horses. Brock looked the same as he had when he was ten, just rounder around the middle. His sense of humor hadn't changed either; his fashion choices were mostly in the vein of T-shirts with "You Can't Ban These Guns" printed between arrows pointing to his biceps. He might've still had the same haircut on his sandy-blond hair.

All the way to the warm-up ring, Brock walked next to me while Mike walked ahead on Bee to warm her up for me. Brock, in the blue oxford shirt and khakis he reserved for horse shows, kept up a one-sided patter meant to take my mind off my nerves. "There you go, Emma," Brock said. "Looking sharp. Ready to show. Watch your step there; don't want those boots getting muddy. I'll get the step stool so you can get up, don't worry. Got your whip? Okay, then. Good to go." Now, he stood silent, letting Mike give me his last instructions before Bee and I hit the ring.

"Breathe," Mike coached me. I took a shallow inhale. Mike shook his head, then mimed what he meant. In through the nose, chest rising. Out through the mouth, relaxing, shoulders falling. The irony of a gray-haired horse trainer giving a millennial yoga practitioner a lesson in deep breathing was not lost on me. I rolled my shoulders and took my best yogic breath.

"That's better," Mike said. "Let a few of the others trot in first, then we'll take one trip around before going in." We waited. I kept breathing. "Now! Go to the rail. Lower your hands. Good, Emma. Perfect. Just like that." Mike ushered me along the rail as if I were a three-year-old filly.

In seconds, Bee was trotting me through the in-gate. I'd been prepared for her hesitation at the gate and applied leg pressure to squeeze her through, but I hadn't been prepared for the way she rose out of the bridle, stepping high, almost out of control. The organist played "The House of the Rising Sun," the beat bopping along with the rhythm of our trot.

Keep breathing, I told myself, relaxing my lower legs. When the photographer's flash popped, Bee pricked her ears forward and strained against the bridle, but we didn't break.

"Slow down!" Mike called from the rail. "You're going too fast. You don't need to be passing all these people."

I tried to lower and slow my post, rising only inches out of the saddle, using my body to slow Bee's body. Six other horses trotted in the ring with us, and Mike was right. We were trotting faster than all of them. On the far rail, Bee broke into a canter, but the announcer called for a walk, the transition hiding our bobble. At the walk, I kept up a stream of calming talk. For Bee's sake, ostensibly, but really, for me. "It's okay, girl. We're walking now. Just walking. Easy, walk. Nice and easy." Asking a wound-tight show horse to walk is harder than it sounds, especially when the rider is wound tighter than her horse.

At the canter, Bee braced against the bridle and shook her head. The imbalance caused her to switch leads, and Mike waved his hands like an air traffic controller, telling me to stop and start again. Once again, the announcer's call saved us. Back to a walk. Throughout the class, Mike kept us from making egregious mistakes. Nervous as I was, that was a miracle. Until the lineup. When it came time to back, Bee balked, and instead of asking again, my hands lowered and scratched her withers.

In one of my first shows as an adult, riding with a different barn and trainer, my horse had refused to back in the lineup. When I asked again, I did it too harshly, and the horse reacted by standing on his hind legs. Up, up, up he rose, his front hooves pawing the sky. The audience gasped. By some miracle, I stayed on. If he'd risen another inch, he would have flipped, crushing me beneath him. When his four feet hit the ground again, the crowd applauded. We left the ring without a ribbon, but we were alive. Still, I would have preferred applause for a victory pass, not for trick riding.

That experience had stuck with me. So when the judge stayed in front of Bee and me, her eyes asking if we wanted to try again to back, I shook my head, even though I knew that we'd be marked down for my decision.

"Well, your horse parks out very pretty," the judge said, smiling. I thanked her and noticed that her belly swelled. She was pregnant yet spending hours on her feet judging a horse show. Horsewomen are incredible.

Even with our backing gaffe, Bee and I earned a fifth-place ribbon, beating two other horses.

"If you had backed," Mike said as he led us back to the stalls, "you might have gotten second or third." I dismounted, smiling as big as if we'd won. "We'll work on that more at home."

"What did you think?" I asked Ben once I'd changed myself out of show clothes and rubbed the sweat from Bee's flanks. She stood, gnawing on the crossties and pawing. She wouldn't stop until the carrot emerged from my pocket.

"Nice work, sweetie," Ben said, hugging me. "You looked strong out there."

"Just wait," I told him. "We'll get you a pony and some racing silks. It can be your turn next."

When we got home from the show, according to my fertility tracker app, ovulation was just around the corner. It had been a month since Ben's operation.

"Should we give it a go?" I asked him. "I know the doctor said not to expect results too soon, but it can't hurt to try." Seeing that pregnant judge at the Dayton Horse Show had given me courage. After the show, I'd followed her on Instagram. The baby in her belly wasn't her first. Pictures showed her and a toddler together at a barn, the mom training horses, the daughter reaching for them with a grin. Soon, she'd be bringing another baby to the barn. If this judge could work horses with one little girl on the ground and another on the way, surely I could keep riding.

"Sure," Ben said, and he started walking back to the bedroom, eager as a stud being led to the breeding shed.

"Not yet!" I called after him. "I meant in another day or two."

I heard Ben's belt buckle hit the floor. "I'm up for a practice round if you are."

"Okay," I said, following him, "but we'll have to do this a lot over the next week."

"No complaints here," Ben called back to me. "Let's find out just how tight Dr. Wilson and God are, after all. That was one heck of a prayer."

"It was," I agreed, closing the bedroom door behind me.

10

The Duel

In the weeks before the 1983 World's Grand Championship Horse Show, Sky Watch's lameness turned out to be a small infection in the ankle. Even with the excellent care the stallion received, he'd beaten up his body enough that he'd found a way to hurt himself. As Mitch said, "He doesn't rest when he's supposed to, even when he's in his stall. He's in there raising hell." Bacteria had entered the wound and multiplied, tenderizing the area. Luckily, Emiliano had caught it quickly, and the infection hadn't spread to the joint itself or to any of the major structures of the hoof: The coffin bone. The sesamoids. An infection there would have taken Sky Watch out of training for weeks, if not months. Now, with antibiotics on board, he had a chance. Sky Watch might just make it to stake night.

Both Mitch and Don showed their horses conservatively in their qualifying classes during the week, but for different reasons. Don wanted to save as much of his horse's energy for Saturday night as possible. Mitch needed to make sure his mount was sound. Even with cautious rides, they each trotted out with a blue ribbon, Sky Watch beating three other contenders, Imperator six. Small classes, but who could blame trainers for not entering? Showing against either of those horses meant competing for second place.

Maybe that's why all the horses who had competed the previous year didn't show up. French Wine, French Commander, Rare Treasure, and The Rose were nowhere to be seen in the 1983 World's Championship Horse Show program. Rhythm 'n Jazz showed in the amateur division that year. Valley Venture had lost an eye to a virus but hadn't lost his get-up-and-go—he still won classes at smaller shows, but the rules prevented a one-eyed horse from competing in the big leagues. None of the trainers who'd thought they might have had a shot at winning the big one in 1982 attempted it again in 1983.

Through the rest of the week, Mitch hooked Sky Watch to the jog cart. Under a harness, with blinkers wrapped around his head and a neck sweat bundling him from withers to poll, he didn't look like gaited-stake-night material. Pulling the cart, as usual, he trotted with a shuffle, not using any of his natural-born motion.

Two trainers stood at the rail, watching the morning workouts. One nudged the other. "That's Sky Watch," he said, pointing.

"Quit lying." His companion adjusted his baseball cap. "No, it ain't."

"I'll bet you it is. Who else could it be? It's not New York, New York. Has to be Sky Watch."

"You want to put money on it? There's no way. That horse couldn't trot over a Coke can. Maybe it's that sister of Sky Watch's Mitch picked up. Heard he showed her at Devon. But she's supposed to be pretty hot. That horse ain't hot."

"Look between his legs. That's no mare. I've got twenty says that's Sky Watch."

"Sounds like you want to lose twenty dollars. Risky choice with the price of feed being what it is. I'll take you up on that." Mitch and Sky Watch rounded the turn and headed for the pair of railbirds. "Mitch! Who is that?"

"This is Sky Watch, brother," Mitch called as he drove by, chuckling.

"Damn." He reached for his wallet and then shouted after Mitch, "You just lost me twenty bucks!"

Mitch took the lines in one hand and tipped an imaginary hat. "Don't you boys have horses to work? If you need something to do, I've got tack that needs cleaned."

Sky Watch jogged well during the days between the qualifier and the championship, so Mitch hopped onto him on Thursday for a test ride. As always, he tuned in, looking for unevenness, hesitation, heaviness, or any sign that the stud wasn't 100 percent. Just like the previous year, Mitch wouldn't risk his horse at any cost, even if it meant handing the championship to Don Harris. He wondered what Don would say in interviews if Sky Watch didn't show up. Didn't matter. His horse came first. It would be more motivational material for his fridge for the next year. Underneath him, Sky Watch fired evenly on all four cylinders. Mitch dismounted and nodded at Emiliano. The stud would show. He let Bill Munford, show manager, know.

Bill was relieved, but now he faced a dilemma. Word gets around quickly at the World's Championship Horse Show. Faced with showing against Sky Watch and Imperator, no one else had entered the class. No one. Competing for reserve honors was bad enough, but competing for third—that sounded miserable. Bill called an emergency meeting with trainers and exhibitors on Friday afternoon when the show session had ended. Dozens gathered in the ring.

As he always did during the show, Bill wore a tie, constricting his jowls. Bill had been part of the World's Championship Horse Show since the 1960s and had taken over as manager in 1972. He managed the show for twenty-seven years. Under his watch, the total prize money for the show grew from $155,000 to over $1.1 million. "A two-horse show might be good enough for us, but the general public and the media won't watch that. We need more entries for tomorrow night." A dedicated Saddlebred enthusiast, he raised high-stepping colts on his own farm. "For the sake of the breed."

Even though Freedom Hall was sold out for that year's stake night, the breed's decline had already begun. Every year throughout the mid-1980s, the association registered more than 4,300 new Saddlebreds. In 1990, only 3,500 new Saddlebreds entered their records. By the late 1990s, that number had dropped to the upper 2,000s. Now, it sits around 1,300.

Six owners and trainers stepped up to fill in the gap. The Meanors volunteered another one of their horses, Shillelagh, a stallion who'd come in fourth in the stallion stake with Dick Boettcher riding. Bob Irwin with Bi-Mi Superior Attraction. Sultan's Matchmaker, with Johnny Lucas up, who'd come in reserve to Sky Watch in the stallion stake. Ray Pittman and SLS Sportin' Life, an entry who'd competed in the ladies gelding stake and barely trotted out with a ribbon. Maybe the trainer would do better on board the stallion than the owner had. Ring Shot, a competitor from the gelding stake, under the direction of Jim B. Robertson. Roses in Winter, the only mare, trained and ridden by Ann Armstrong Day, the only female entry. There are eight ribbons to hand out on Saturday-night classes in Freedom Hall, and now, the 1983 class had eight entries. Really, though, everyone knew who the audience would be cheering for. The Saddlebred world had been waiting a year for this class. All show season, every trainer, exhibitor, owner, caretaker, and fan had speculated about the outcome of one class: Imperator and Sky Watch's rematch.

I speculated about an outcome of my own: whether the vasectomy reversal would produce a pregnancy. Dr. Google told me that the success rates varied, from as low as 30 percent to as high as 90 percent. A positive pregnancy test on the first try was unlikely but possible. Technically. Still, I'd been preparing. Spreadsheets containing everything from childcare costs to the best time to start a college fund filled the Family folder on my laptop. As if a spreadsheet could prepare anyone for parenting.

In the spring leading up to the vasectomy reversal, knowing there might be a baby in my future, I'd wanted my mom close by, so I'd started a not-so-subtle campaign to move her to Indianapolis. After more than twenty years of teaching in preprofessional high school ballet programs, the last ten in Birmingham's Alabama School of Fine Arts, she would be retiring soon. Retirement. The perfect time to move, right? Indiana's cost of living was low, I argued, and the Midwest would be a good midpoint between my brothers, who now lived on opposite sides of the country, one in Los Angeles and one in West Hartford.

After I sent her dozens of Zillow listings, none of them quite right, my mom found the perfect home on her own. A river cottage just a half mile down the street from me. It needed work, but my mom liked nothing more than remodeling. While packing up her midcentury modern home in Birmingham, she found boxes of her old horse show photos and trophies. "This is Maggie the Cat!" she texted me, accompanied by a cell phone capture of her wearing a top hat and suit astride a big-stepping three-gaited mare, the horse's eye wide and fixed on the camera's flash.

"You know, Mom," I told her over the phone later that day, "Mike has a mare for sale who looks a little bit like Maggie. Hold on. I'll send you a picture of her. Her name is Pyromanium. Isn't that great?" Secretly, I hoped my mom would buy her so I could take a turn on her. Bee's Dayton debut hadn't given me much confidence in her career as a competitive show horse. In the photos from that class, she looks scared, not showy. Stiff. Unsure of herself. Nothing like the screenshot of Pyromanium I sent my mom, the bay mare looking as fiery as her name promised. Small and compact but exploding with energy. Loving the performance. Just like my mom.

"Wow. She's gorgeous," my mom said. "What's her price tag?"

"I have no clue. She's been for sale for a while. You should ask Mike about her."

"Em, I haven't been on a horse in twenty-five years. I can't buy one."

"Your body will remember."

In the Indiana home my mom had just bought, before she moved in, I left a magazine spread open on the counter. An advertisement for Pyromanium took up the entire right-hand page. In it, the bay mare trotted high, with upright ears and wide eyes. The magazines used to call my mom "all grace and talent in the saddle," remarking on "her poise and ability." If she was going to be back in town, she might as well buy herself a Saddlebred. Picturing the two of us traveling to shows together, maybe even with a baby in tow, I couldn't think of a better retirement project for her.

During the years my mom rode as a teen, the crowds had swelled the stands. By stake night in 1983, Freedom Hall was standing room only. More than sixteen thousand filled the arena seats. Sky Watch and Imperator brought the industry to its peak. From then on, the numbers fell. Slowly, at first, then faster and faster. The further the world got from using horses as labor, the further people got from thinking of horses as leisure, as entertainment. On Saturday night at the 2021 World's Championship Horse Show, the stadium was less than 50 percent full.

For over a century, American Saddlebreds had thrilled crowds of couples and families, who traveled to the fairgrounds for the sole purpose of attending the show, treating it no differently than taking the kids to the local baseball game. Kids and parents alike hollered for their favorites, and, between classes, singers and actresses kept them entertained, like a halftime show for the equestrian set. Circus horses like Mr. Rhythm danced, bowed, and reared in the air, pumping up the audience for the horse show to follow. My mom remembers the comedienne Minnie Pearl performing at one of her shows. When her mare caught sight of the actress in her signature big hat, price tag attached, she reared. My mom stayed on and, unfazed, went on to win her class.

Today, American Saddlebred horse shows are tailored for exhibitors, not spectators. No circus horses stand on their hind legs and walk before the show. There are no more Minnie Pearls. Now, horse shows are like ballet recitals, middle school soccer games, or high school musicals. On the opening night of Jackson High's production of *Hamlet*, Hamlet's parents are going to watch, but not many others will. Seeing young amateurs performing something that professionals can do better is not nearly as satisfying. I'd fly to the Oregon Shakespeare Festival to see their *Hamlet*, but I'd rather sit at home and stare at my phone than watch a bunch of sophomores botch the Bard.

The problem isn't just low numbers in the stands. In 2013, almost half of the horses at the top shows in the nation were over ten. At that year's World's Championships, not enough three- and four-year-old horses entered to claim all the ribbons offered in the junior classes, which are limited to horses under four. A look at the number of American Saddlebred foals registered each year paints the same picture. In 1997, more than 3,000 colts and fillies were entered into the ASB registry. In 2008, there were 2,000. In 2012, fewer than 1,500. Since less than half of all Saddlebred youngsters have the natural talent to become show horses, the amount of new blood is getting diluted. Now, all those ten-year-old and older horses from 2013 are aging out of their show careers, and there are fewer and fewer horses to replace them.

To be fair, as early as October 1983, when Imperator and Sky Watch packed Freedom Hall from floor to rafters, *Saddle and Bridle* printed an article describing the same concerns I'm writing about now. Is there a solution? Maybe not, but maybe that's okay. Mike McIntosh thinks people are choosing different options for recreation, but he doesn't think Saddlebreds will disappear. "They've been saying the breed's in trouble since you were showing as a kid," he told me. "And look—we're still here, still doing the same thing. Maybe it'll keep getting smaller, but it'll never disappear entirely."

The 2020 pandemic might have been good for the horse industry. With malls, restaurants, and movie theaters closed, all recreation moved outside. My horsey friends started sharing memes on Facebook: *Trail Riding: The Original Form of Social Distancing; Mares: Keeping Everyone Six Feet Away since Forever; What's Social Distancing? I've Been at the Barn as Usual.* Many barns closed their doors for lessons, and horse shows shut down, but somehow, people were still finding ways to ride their horses. Other outdoor recreation flourished too. The trails around our house, usually empty except for me, Ben, and our dogs, filled. People who had never watered so much as a ficus plant had installed raised beds and were growing their own cucumbers. Bread baking became a fad. Drying one's own herbs became de rigueur. Suddenly, Americans were turning back to the land. As horse shows reopened, they did so to record numbers, welcoming more exhibitors than they had in years.

Maybe Saddlebreds won't disappear. Our shows might stay small, and maybe they'll keep shrinking. Or, perhaps, they'll ride the excitement of the postpandemic reopening and thrive. Either way, I'll still be in the stands at Louisville this year, and I won't be alone. Even so, unless some trainer somewhere has a prodigy they've been hiding, I'm not going to see anything like the drama that unfolded in 1983.

Come Saturday night, stake night at the 1983 Kentucky State Fair, fairgoers couldn't park within a league of Freedom Hall. By 7:00 p.m., as they made their way across the sea of asphalt parking lots around the stadium, the temperatures still hovered around ninety-eight degrees, approaching the record for that day. The entire fairgrounds sizzled. The midway workers wilted, calling in customers from the meager shade of their rides and games. Pigs dug in their stalls and heaved themselves onto their sides in the holes they'd created, groaning. Horses stood in front of the fans corded onto their stalls, eyes half-closed. No breeze cooled the air. Women bared their arms in sleeveless dresses, their hair teased and swept up from their necks. Men took their jackets off and hung them from their arms. The shade and coolness of Freedom Hall were welcome distractions. The crowd settled into their seats, programs in hand. On the cover was Sky Watch at the trot.

The bugle rang out, and the organ played "My Old Kentucky Home." Imperator entered second, his trot bigger than anyone had ever seen it—so big, he nearly came off his feet at the end of the first straightaway. The cheers started before he'd even made it all the way down the chute. Sky Watch followed, and the stadium thundered its approval. The crowd couldn't hear themselves talk, but who wanted to have a conversation when America's greatest show horse was about to be crowned?

The six other horses faded into the background as Imperator and Sky Watch dominated the arena. Don's work on Imperator's trot had paid off. With ears glued forward and legs popping, the gelding marched, commanding the crowd's attention, even when he jumped off his feet again. Clearly, the former world champion was fresh. Don had kept his promise and hadn't overworked his horse between the gelding stake and the championship. As perfectly as Imperator moved, though, the raw power of Sky Watch's trot made the gelding look like an oil painting—stunning but not alive. Sky Watch, on the other hand, was vitalized. His ears swiveled, sometimes pointing back toward Mitch as if the stallion were listening. His stride seemed somehow longer than before. Could he have grown? Or had he matured and learned how best to make use of those long legs?

The entire first direction, the two rival horsemen played it safe. When the announcer called for the walk, they walked. They suspected the judges would call another two-horse workout, and they wanted to save their mounts for when it would really count. At the rack, Mitch made his first play, pistoling out of the turn to catch up with Imperator. That extra gear Mitch had found—he made good use of it. As he passed, the young trainer turned his head to catch Don Harris's eye. The audience boomed, loving the audacity of

Mitch's taunt. Don Harris, not to be outdone, racked the next rail one-handed, touching his hand to the brim of his fedora.

Don Harris reversed to the rail, but Mitch aimed Sky Watch between the red-coated ringmaster and the photographer and cut straight through the center. Now, the stud's ears were pinned forward. Mitch gunned him for Imperator, working off the rail. When the announcer called the walk, Mitch checked Sky Watch's speed at first and then—what the hell, why not?—pushed him down the straightaway for one more pass. When he did stop at last, green shavings sprayed from the ground under Sky Watch's hooves.

Lather coated Imperator's neck. The former champ wanted his crown back and didn't mind working for it. He squatted down and slow-gaited the moment Don asked. Horses know when they're performing well, especially horses with as much show in them as Imperator had. In the stands, husbands looked at their wives, who clapped furiously and shouted for their favorite. These men hoped their women's fervor was for the horses and not the handsome elder statesman trainer or his younger rival. Overtired children bounced in their seats, electrified by the spectacle in front of them. Mothers tried to soothe them, one hand rubbing circles between their shoulder blades, the other clenched in their own laps, eyes locked on what unfolded in the arena.

At the rail, the crowd stood four deep, the lucky ones closest to the ring hanging their elbows over, as if they wanted their own bodies to be part of the action. Some left with bruised arms, their flesh dinged by the legs of passing horsemen. At home, they'd brandish their badges of honor. "See how close I was? Mitch Clark kicked me at the slow gait!"

Mitch rode smart, but hard. His gloves were off—literally and figuratively. Mitch always rode without gloves, a cardinal sin in the horse show world. The only other horseman known for riding gloveless was none other than Granddaddy Garland Bradshaw. For anyone else, gloves were nonnegotiable parts of the horse show outfit. Everyone else wore black gloves to cover their fingers. Brown, if they wore a brown suit. White, for the equitation riders being judged on how quiet and well-mannered they could keep their hands. Mitch's hands did not stay quiet. He moved them where he needed to, sometimes spreading them wide, sometimes cradling the reins close to his horse's neck, sometimes holding them unevenly, one hand higher than the other. Normally, uneven hands constitute a fault, but Sky Watch demanded unconventional riding. Everything about him defied convention. At the rack, he flew by Imperator again, moving so fast that no one would notice whether his rider wore gloves or not. For all it mattered, Mitch could have been in a clown suit.

When the announcer called for the lineup, Don tugged Imperator out of the canter and into a bounce walk for a few steps before taking off at the rack, showing off his own impressive speed. Don's legs hung loose on either side of the horse, his seat even, his face calm. Mitch touched his hand to Sky Watch's neck, and the stud stepped straight into his trot, cutting across the arena the wrong way, aiming for Imperator. For a full thirty seconds, the two trainers traded passes. When they finally angled their horses for the lineup, both Imperator and Sky Watch steamed, their skin hot to the touch. They'd already worked harder than anyone else in the ring, and their performance had only just reached halftime. Riders down, saddles off.

The three judges, all in tuxedos, walked the line of unsaddled horses. Gorgeous specimens, all, but Don Harris presented Imperator with the flair of a magician introducing his lovely assistant. Imperator loved posing. Long gone was the ugly duckling from Peacock Farm. In a beauty contest, Imperator could beat any horse alive. At the other end of the three-hundred-foot ring stood Sky Watch, a little smaller than Perry, with a thick neck and a sculpted face. The two horses couldn't have been more different.

No one should have been shocked when the announcer called two horses back to the rail for a second workout, but the noise level in Freedom Hall rose more than a few decibels when he announced Mitch's and Don's back numbers. Both trainers arrowed for the rail. The conformation judging had only been a brief break in their feud.

Imperator trotted down the rail with his chin tucked and legs flying, Sky Watch moving in behind him and aiming for a pass, but Don kept the gas pedal down, and Imperator stayed in front. The two horses chased each other around the white-fenced oval. When the announcer called the second-direction rack, Mitch blazed by Imperator. Don responded with his signature one-handed rack, this time removing his hat for emphasis. When the announcer called for the lineup, the two horses declined to answer, instead zipping by each other. Imperator slow-gaited down one end of the ring. Sky Watch parroted him, powering along the rail as the audience clapped and whooped. Then he trotted, the biggest trot yet, his stride longer than any 15.2-hand horse's stride should be. Imperator volleyed back with another slow gait. At last, the two trainers pulled their horses up, letting them cease their furious work.

The announcer asked, "Ladies and gentlemen, have you had your money's worth tonight?" He shut his mouth, letting the noise from the stands take over his narration. A baby wailed—maybe Sean, Mitch's son, now almost a year old. "Our choice is unanimous, and it does mark a tied score in the halls of annals. We're at two and two, now." He paused before making it official. "Two twenty-four," he said, calling the number on Sky Watch's back, and the stadium exploded. Women jumped and clapped. Men stomped and pumped their fists. Children shrieked, drunk on excitement. No one could hear the rest of the announcement, but they didn't need to. Sky Watch had defended his title. Imperator had failed to take it from him. Even after a year of preparation, the People's Horse couldn't take down the stallion so freakishly good that either God or the devil himself must have made him.

The stadium darkened, the only light coming from the twin spotlights trained on Sky Watch. In them, Sky Watch flew, his hocks pistons and his front legs springs. As he approached the exit, he saw a crowd blocking the chute. Mitch checked Sky Watch back as if to leave, but the crowd stood their ground, a human wall. They gave Mitch no choice but to take a second victory lap. Sky Watch kept on, moving forward in his circle of light, the darkness always just in front of him.

The 1983 duel has passed before my eyes dozens, maybe even hundreds, of times, but it will always leave me breathless. Two of the best horses in history at the top of their form competing against each other—nothing beats it. Nothing. In the forty years since that duel, no one has produced another horse like Sky Watch or Imperator.

In these old videos, Michele Macfarlane doesn't appear. Even though she owned the world's greatest show horse, in the 1982 and 1983 Five-Gaited World's Grand Championship she only showed up as a name in the program. Sky Watch, owned by Michele Macfarlane. Even when Bill Carrington announced her name as he unveiled the winner, the noise from the crowd drowned him out. Michele, a great horsewoman, has been half erased from her best horse's best performance. She headed home with an extra $7,500 in her pocket, but goodness knows she didn't need the money.

As rumor has it, Michele hadn't meant to buy Mitch Clark a stake horse. She'd ridden the stud and won with him before, on the West Coast, without Imperator as competition. In the early 1980s, Michele put Mitch on the horse because Mitch knew him best and had the best chance of winning. Above all else, Michele loved to win. Watching her horse dominate in his rematch with Imperator brought her plenty of satisfaction, but I'll bet she wondered what it would have been like to be on Sky Watch's back in that victory pass.

I checked the time in the corner of my laptop screen. An hour until the next session at the All American Horse Classic, one of our hometown shows, held at the fairgrounds just fifteen minutes from my house. My finger hovered over the fertility tracker app. Technically, I was late. Not for the horse show. For my period.

Ben returned from the drugstore with three different types of pregnancy tests. "Hope you haven't gone to the bathroom recently," he said.

"It feels kind of silly to test already," I said. "I'm only a day late."

"That's why I bought extras," he said, thrusting the bag in my direction. "Go ahead. It doesn't hurt to try."

After taking the test, I was too nervous to stand around and watch for pluses or minuses to appear, so I headed out to our raised bed to weed around the tomatoes and basil. Like all those other families during the COVID-19 pandemic, we'd started a garden.

"We're pregnant!" Ben shouted from my office window. As if we were stars in a rom-com, I ran inside and jumped into his arms. We held each other and then pressed our palms against my belly.

"Hello, little bundle of cells," I whispered. "Welcome."

I was scheduled to show Bee the next day. "Are you still going to show?" Ben asked.

"Yes," I responded. I'd already rehearsed this moment. "If I wasn't already a seasoned rider, or if I was riding a new horse, this might be dangerous, but Bee and I know each other. She's safe."

"She'd better be." Ben's mouth tightened.

On our way to the fairgrounds the next day, my mom yipped as if I were trotting into Freedom Hall. "I knew it!" she crowed, referring to my pregnancy. "When you and Ben came over for dinner last weekend, I had this sneaking suspicion."

"Mom." I shushed her. "It's early. I might not even have been pregnant last weekend." I paused, wondering on which day the baby could have been conceived. "Okay, so I was technically pregnant then. Still, let's keep it quiet for now. A lot can happen in the early weeks. In nine months, I'll be thirty-five. That's older for a first-time mom. They call it a 'geriatric pregnancy.'"

"You know I was thirty-five when I had you." My mom glanced over at me, her eyes hidden behind red sunglasses. With those movie-star glasses and her curly salt-and-pepper hair cut pixie short, she was going to make one cool grandmother. "It was a piece of cake. You'll do great. Now," she said, getting back to business, "remind me. How far down is your class?" She still hadn't bought Pyromanium, the mare Mike was selling, but she'd started taking riding lessons with me and, just like when I was a kid, styling my hair into the low bun Saddlebred fashion dictated I wear beneath my derby for horse shows. It was only a matter of time until she had a horse of her own. My mom is not a woman who stands on the sidelines for long.

All through my class at All American, it felt as if a light pulsed below my belly button. That day, Bee carried two lives on her back. Our ride was mediocre and distracted, and it resulted in no ribbon, but I didn't tell anyone why my mind might have been elsewhere.

11

Rubble and Smoke

Don Harris had to admit it. He'd been beaten. Always the gentleman, he congratulated Mitch on his win, shaking his hand and looking him square in the eye. This time, the defeat felt different. This time, he had been prepared. Mitch hadn't caught him off guard. Don had ridden his horse conservatively. He'd saved his horse's energy for the workout, making sure the gelding didn't run out of gas. He'd perfected Perry's trot. He'd slimmed the horse down so he could pick up speed. All that effort, and still, a reserve ribbon. He had no choice but to admit it: Sky Watch had trounced Imperator.

His win earlier in the evening, in the Three-Gaited World's Grand Championship with the leggy mare Sultan's Starina, must have soothed the burn of defeat, but still, it had to sting. Standing in my office, still starstruck by the legendary horse trainer on the phone with me, I asked Don how he and Mitch managed to stay cordial with each other.

"We're good friends. We had good, clean competition." I could hear Don's smile in his voice. "In a Q and A session with Bob Ruxer and twelve top horsemen, Bob asked us who was the greatest horse we'd ever seen." I looked at my model of Imperator, ran my finger down his neck. "He went around. Sky Watch. Sky Watch. Sky Watch. Everyone said Sky Watch. Then, it was my turn. I had to say Sky Watch myself." Don chuckled. "Even though it hurt me to say it."

I was stunned. A better interviewer would have asked a smart follow-up question, but nothing came to me. Luckily, Don didn't mind talking.

"I had to wait for my first one," he told me, meaning his first Five-Gaited World's Grand Championship. "Mitch got it right away, but he had a long, long wait to get the next one." Subtle shade thrown on his former rival. "I'm lucky enough to have had four other championships." Even in his midnineties, Don Harris was still a competitor first.

As we wrapped up our interview, I felt the need to say something. What if I never got to talk to him again? The next month, he'd be leaving his Simpsonville home for an assisted living facility. "We'll get room service every day if we want it," he told me with the glee of a nine-year-old boy, not a ninety-year-old man, "and it's a lovely place, but moving is a tough process."

"Sir," I said, "my mom used to watch you show—she had horses with Dale Milligan—and has very fond memories of standing at the rail and seeing you perform. She says there was nothing like it."

"Dale Milligan!" he said. "Oh, yes. He had some nice horses back then."

"Yes, sir. But I wanted to say . . ." I fumbled. "It's been an honor speaking with you. I've been a Saddlebred girl my whole life, so it means a lot that you've taken some time to talk to me."

"It's my pleasure," he said. "I'm glad someone is writing about those days. Tell me—what are you going to call the book?"

I blinked. "*Sky Watch*," I said, feeling uncomfortable about it. "But I'm open to feedback."

"I've got a title for you." I could almost see him leaning back in his chair as he said it. "How about *The Good Old Days*?"

"Those certainly were the good old days, weren't they?"

"Oh, yes." Don's voice quieted. "Yes, they were."

As the Saturday-night barn-aisle parties of the 1983 World's Grand Championship Horse Show hit full swing, a Louisiana attorney named William Dutel and his trainer, John Champagne, walked out of Freedom Hall together. I imagine them ignoring the champagne, cocktails, and discreetly sniffed cocaine—this was 1983, after all—because the two men had a mission. Billy Dutel wanted Imperator. The gelding dominated in the amateur ranks. He believed he had the money to make it happen—and what better time? The two-time champ had just eaten Sky Watch's dirt. Again. Maybe Imperator needed a change.

As in real estate, buying and selling Saddlebreds usually happens with the prospective and current owners' trainers acting as agents. For this, they receive a commission, which can be a major portion of a horse trainer's income. Imperator sold for $350,000, a record price for a gelding, equivalent to almost $1 million in 2022 money. Billy Dutel, a broad man with a large nose and dark hair, had gotten into the Saddlebred business in a big way. He owned his own farm near New Orleans, was maintaining a string of nice show horses, and had started collecting broodmares too. As an attorney, he knew his way around a contract. So did Judge Curtis Meanor, Imperator's owner. The two men might have used their trainers as agents, but I'm sure they themselves wove the sales contract watertight. Together, they submitted a joint statement to the industry magazines, suggesting that all aspects of a sale, including allowances for trainer commissions, should be written into a contract. The business of buying and selling horses—not unlike that of buying and selling used cars—has always had a hint of dirt around it, and these attorneys wanted to scrub the Saddlebred industry clean. They closed their statement with an echo of what the World's Championship Horse Show manager Bill Munford had said during his emergency meeting to fill the 1983 Five-Gaited World's Grand Championship class: "This is essential for the growth we need so badly."

Even in 1983, with Freedom Hall packed to the rafters and horses selling for record prices, Saddlebred enthusiasts were concerned about the breed's future. This gives me hope. If we were worried forty years ago and there are still Saddlebreds around today, the breed isn't going extinct. It's shrinking, but so are most breeds. There might be almost seventy thousand registered Quarter Horses in America today, but that's only half as many as there were twenty years ago. Standardbreds, Paints, Arabians, Morgans—all are diminishing at about the same rate. Saddlebreds are no worse off than the rest of their equine brethren.

Maybe we're landing at what will become the new normal. Every spring, Saddlebred breeders will keep welcoming long-necked colts, nudging them toward their mothers for a lick and a nurse. There will be fewer of them than there were back when seven million American families owned a farm, but they'll still be here. My daughter will be able to show a Saddlebred one day. Yes, a daughter. When a nurse called with the results of the early testing recommended for a "geriatric pregnancy," she asked if we wanted to know the baby's sex. Since I'm the type of person who makes spreadsheets to compare insurance-plan options, I said yes. She revealed that a little girl would be arriving in just over eight months. A May baby.

By October 2020, I was pregnant, but only far enough along that Ben, my pants, and I could tell. While Ben might have been more comfortable with his newly pregnant wife out of the saddle, I wasn't ready to stop. Not yet. There was only one more show left in the season, and even though Sky Watch had had more gameness in one of his tail feathers than Bee has in her whole body, we were going to hit the gate. Bee was turning into a good girl, but she's not made for the show ring the way horses like Sky Watch and Imperator were. She didn't whinny when the horse trailer pulled up to take her to a show. Away from home, she didn't eat well, and Mike started giving her ulcer medication at horse shows. Still, we were going to give it our best shot. She was the closest thing to a show horse I had, and I had no way of knowing what my postpartum riding possibilities would look like.

The gate opened, and the announcer called in our class: park pleasure amateur. Five horses trotted out of the tiny warm-up ring, a glorified bullpen that had felt full with just the five of us warming up. Add in the three-year-old walk-trot horses and the Shatner western horses heading in after us, and it looked like a circus. Bee clicked into it, though. In our warm-up, she took both of her canter leads correctly—our weak spot—and gave to the bridle, making soft contact with the bit without tearing it out of my hands. Like Mitch, I prefer riding gloveless. As a no-name amateur riding in the B leagues, though, showing without gloves on wouldn't have been a statement. It would have looked like I couldn't afford gloves.

We trotted through the gate, and Bee's ears swiveled forward. The Springfield, Ohio, arena boasts generous turns, but the straightaways are short, which meant I needed to make the most of each pass. Through the turns, I wiggled the bit, giving and taking, opening and closing my fingers. Then I looked through Bee's ears and pushed her to the end of the arena, my eyes focused on a spot on the far wall that marked the end of my line. A horse like Bee, who doesn't have much motion, needs to be parallel to the rail as she passes in front of the judge—who, this time, happened to be Debbie Foley, one of the first female trainers to make it big. Trotting at an angle will decrease the perception of whatever motion she's got, and little Bee needed all the help she could get. So I kept my lines as straight as possible. If it looked like we needed to pass another horse, better to pull the whole line five feet toward center ring instead of making a semicircle around the horse we needed to pass.

It might have looked like we were just trotting, walking, and cantering in circles, but we weren't. Navigating a ring with other horses takes finesse. All too often, I botch it. Nerves overtake me, and, when passing a group of horses, I yank my horse around instead of thinking ahead and adjusting my line. Riding a horse is a constant balancing act. Literally, of course, but also temporally and emotionally. Staying in the present moment is vital. Think too much, and my rear winds up in the dirt. But at the same time, not paying attention to whatever is happening in front of me could be lethal. With an extra life inside me, my awareness had heightened. It wasn't just my own butt that would land in the dirt anymore. Now, a tiny, inch-and-a-half-long little girl would get bounced along with me.

Even as a four-year-old, Bee behaved herself. Most of the time. Ben might have been more comfortable if I'd forsworn horses as soon as the plus sign popped up on that pregnancy test, but I trusted myself as a rider. Of course, horses are unpredictable. Anything can happen. Even the twenty-year-old lesson mare can wheel around when a bush outside whips in the breeze. Riding pregnant meant taking a risk, but the benefits outweighed it. Climbing onto a horse made me breathe deeper and let go of everything beyond the barn doors. Deadline struggles disappeared. The stress of trying to find a new house for our growing family—gone. On a horse's back, the world shrinks to the muscles beneath me, the sound of hooves pounding in an arena.

When saddle seat amateurs show in pleasure classes, we're supposed to smile. It is a pleasure class, after all. For the first half of that October Ohio class, I forced the smile. But when we reversed, it became genuine. The class had been going well. Bee's ears stayed up. She moved smoothly—maybe not powerfully, but consistently. At the reverse, I turned Bee toward the middle and aimed for an open spot on the opposite rail, our trajectory bringing us right past the judge, a move out of Mitch Clark's playbook. It worked. The judge watched us trot by, and she marked her card. When the announcer called for the lineup, we trotted right in. Bee was no Sky Watch. We weren't going to win over the thirty-person crowd by making extra passes. Better to line up quickly so the show could go on. The judge liked that too. As we trotted in, she made another mark on her card.

When the announcer called my number for second place, my mouth dropped open, and a squeal escaped. I patted Bee on the neck and scratched her poll. "We did it," I whispered to her. "Good girl." We hadn't won, but there was no beating that first-place horse, all chromed out and churning his feet high. Taking reserve meant we'd ridden a smart class, smart enough to beat a few horses who, talent-wise, should have beaten us.

Bee and I walked back to her stall, Mike striding next to us.

"You did good, you know," Mike said.

"It felt good!" I agreed, beaming.

"You weren't going to beat the horse that won. No one in there was. But coming in second—that was an honest second."

"She really gave to the bridle. She didn't grab the bit and try to run away with me."

"No, she didn't." Mike smiled, holding Bee's bridle while we stopped to let another horse cross our path. "Like I said, you did good. That's about the best we can hope to do."

"Are you growing up, Bee?" I asked, my hand on her shoulder. I felt her body relax under me, the best way she knew to say yes.

After the class, unsaddled and standing in the stall, Bee craned her neck and wiggled her top lip while I toweled the sweat from her neck. *That's the spot.* I lingered, combing her mane and brushing her flanks until the saddle marks disappeared. As usual, she stepped from side to side and flicked her ears back when she saw the brush, pretending that she didn't enjoy every minute of being fussed over. Bee had earned her carrot that day, but she would have gotten one anyway. She took it from my hand, rubbery lips brushing the flesh of my palm. As she crunched, she bobbed her head, ears forward. She knew she'd done her job well.

No fans awaited me in the barn aisle—other than my mom, of course. No crowd hemmed me into the stall. No one asked for my autograph. I didn't win $24,000, like the winner of the Five-Gaited World's Grand Championship did in 2020. These, my only rewards: the blessing of warm horsehide, the satisfaction of a good ride.

A rider like me won't win the big one, won't hop on a stallion and wow the crowd at Louisville. That's okay. That's not what this is about. If my daughter chooses to ride, this is what I hope she'll appreciate: The connection with a being so much larger than herself. Those otherworldly moments when time slows and every muscle fiber moves in time with the horse. A push here, a relax there, giving and taking to get the horse where she needs to be.

Bee and I might not have a better ride than what we'd just had—ever. With show season ending and me due to give birth smack in the middle of next year's season, ending on a high note was exactly what we'd needed. Who knew when, or if, Bee and I would show again?

As my riding career slowed, my mom's restarted. After that horse show, my mom bought Pyromanium, the three-gaited mare of Mike's who still hadn't sold. With a new owner, the firecracker mare softened. In the arena, she still boomed, switching her tail and snorting while she worked, but in the stall, she turned sweet. She nuzzled my mom's hair, ruffling the graying curls. As my mom stood in her stall, face-to-face with her new horse, stroking her nose with all the reverence and joy of a young girl, Mike proclaimed it "meant to be." His wife agreed. "I think that mare was just waiting for her," she said. "As soon as she bought her, her whole personality changed. She used to be a pistol in the stall. I guess all she needed was a person to call her own."

My belly grew, my once-tight core giving way to a foreign roundness. My riding pants no longer buttoned, so I switched to a pair with an elastic waistband. My old bras, all underwire and lace, started to pinch, so those had to be relegated to the back of a drawer, replaced with soft-cupped things as shapeless and comfortable as an old T-shirt. Girls ten years younger than me had been embracing the free-the-nipple lifestyle for years, but I'd grown up in the era of the Wonderbra. Breasts were meant to be lifted, molded into mounds beneath a V-neck, all anatomy undetectable behind foam lining. With pregnancy, a world of comfort enfolded me.

"I might never go back to real pants again," I confessed to Ben, modeling my stretchy jodhpurs, really just yoga pants with suede patches down the knee and calf to protect my lower legs from the saddle and stirrup leathers.

"You're beautiful, no matter what. Doesn't matter what you're wearing." That line had once been frustrating. Ben didn't care whether I wore a little black dress or baggy pajamas. On date nights, after spending twenty minutes attempting to de-frizz my hair and trying on five different dresses before settling on one, that rankled. Now, it resonated.

"Thanks, love." I dug in the pantry for a granola bar. Scratch that. Two. Pregnancy also gave me the appetite of a horse—and the blessing to eat my fill. "I'm off to the barn."

"Are you riding?"

"Yes." I stared at Ben with an eyebrow raised. I knew why he was asking but pretended not to.

"How much longer are you planning on keeping that up?" Ben shook a mason jar full of some pre-workout concoction, then chugged it. Full of vitamin B, caffeine, and amino acids. Probably not that different from the cocktails trainers used to give their stake horses. Nothing illegal, nothing that wouldn't pass the urine screen all horses could be subject to, but just enough to give the steeds some extra oomph in the straightaways.

"Until it's no longer comfortable," I replied. "Until my belly gets in the way. My body will tell me when to stop." According to WhatToExpect.com and the *Mama Natural* blog, "when to stop" would have been at the positive pregnancy test. Along with skiing and rock climbing, horseback riding is a high-risk activity. Luckily, my doctor was a horsewoman herself. "The real risk is falling," I said, quoting her to Ben. "It's not the riding itself. The doctor said not to ride anything too hot or hop on horses I don't know, but on horses like Bee, or the lesson horses, I'll be fine."

"Look," Ben said, "I'm never going to tell you what you can and can't do with your body. But I am going to remind you that riding makes me nervous. Please be safe."

"Thank you for trusting me through something that makes you uncomfortable." I snatched my keys from the countertop. "I've got to go."

"Give me a kiss," he said, and I offered my cheek. "Now, let me kiss that baby." He lifted my shirt and bent down to kiss the roundness beneath it.

A few months later, my belly swelled to the point that mounting a horse seemed laughable. I cornered Mike while he buckled a driving harness around Bee. Since I couldn't ride anymore, he'd taught me to drive, using Bee to teach me. Pulling a jog cart, she looked about as fancy as an Amish horse headed to Walmart, but she was safe. On my first drive, when I banged the cart shaft into the wall, she stiffened but didn't spook at the clang of fiberglass on metal. On my next drive, a chipmunk jumped down from the wall right in front of her face and then scurried back up it. She didn't even flinch.

Ever since our second-place ride in Ohio, an idea had been circling. I wanted to win. If not win, at least be in the running. The show ring and I had unfinished business, but Bee might have peaked, competition-wise. She was a Saddlebred, but she struggled to compete with her cousins in the show ring. I knew that. Mike knew that. Everyone at the barn knew that. Bee wasn't a show horse, at least not the one I'd been seeking.

A show horse should love showing. My mom's mare, for example, cleaned up her feed and asked for more at every show. She spent her show afternoons napping and preparing for a night of performance. When she left her stall, she jigged with excitement. Her ears pricked forward and stayed there. Bee, on the other hand, didn't eat well at shows. She chewed her stall instead of resting. She walked to the show ring willingly, but she didn't brighten when she heard the organ music and saw the stands. If anything, they made her nervy, more likely to grab the bit and stick her chin in the air than flex her neck and strut.

The kindest horse owners find the right job for their horse. If the horse doesn't like jumping, they try trail riding, instead. If trails aren't right, they try dressage. They buy a horse and, as with a pet, consider it a bond for life. My Labrador retriever is terrible at retrieving, but I would never consider trading her in for a dog with a better fetch. Yet, when I looked at my relationship with horses, I had to face the ugly fact of my ambition.

I wanted a show horse. I wanted to win.

Because I couldn't afford more than one horse, owning a show horse would mean selling Bee. This didn't make me feel very good about myself. I loved Bee, loved the way she let me press my forehead against hers, loved how she snuffled her top lip in my hair, loved how she grabbed my jacket zipper between her teeth and jerked her chin up and down. We'd bonded. How could the chance at a ribbon make me throw that away? Throw her away? It wasn't an easy issue to reckon with.

After weeks of journaling and crying, I made up my mind to talk to Mike about her. No decisions yet. Just a conversation about her future. Bee had been wonderful with me as a learning driver. Maybe she'd do well as a lesson horse. Lesson horses usually spend their mornings turned out in a pasture, then come in for an afternoon of teaching kids how to ride. They need to be safe but should still offer some challenge for a beginning rider. They need to be fit enough to be ridden every day, sometimes by multiple riders. They need to be patient enough to adapt to different riders. Ideally, they're bright enough to travel to horse shows and show, but they're not expected to perform at the level I was seeking. Mike would know if Bee fit that bill. Perhaps being a lesson horse would be a kinder existence for her. Or maybe I was trying to make myself feel better about my thoughts of selling her.

"Mike," I said, "I think we need to talk about next steps for Bee." This was code. He knew that I meant "Mike, I'm thinking about selling this horse. What do you recommend?"

"Since you're asking, I'll be honest with you," he responded, looking me in the eye. "I wouldn't spend your money on showing this one once you're"— he paused, glancing at my watermelon-sized belly—"ready to show again." Always following the horse trainer's gentlemanly code. He let his eyes rest on Bee. "I'd save your money and put it towards your next horse. She's done everything she's capable of doing. Her best place is going to be in somebody's lesson program. Now, she's not quite there yet, but she could get there. Probably."

Mike had confirmed what I'd suspected. Bee would be better off as a lesson horse than a show horse, but, unfortunately, she wasn't quite ready to let little kids hang from her. She needed a little more finishing first. On my way home from the barn that day, I cried. Talking to Mike had turned my pondering about Bee into something more solid. It marked a shift.

Where did that leave me, exactly? Even if I sold Bee, another show horse was out of my budget. Was my amateur show career over, along with hers? Were my Saddlebred dreams already done? If so, at least I could rest comfortably, knowing that my daughter had already made her show ring debut, riding along with me that last October and earning a reserve ribbon.

After the 1983 win, Mitch Clark hit his prime. The barn on Hustonville Road now held a string of twenty-four horses, good ones, and all under the banner of Mitchell Clark Stables. A few Mitch owned, but most belonged to outside owners who trusted the World's Championship winner with their own stake-night dreams. On January 20, 1984, Mitch left the barn at lunchtime to drive to town and pay bills. It felt good to have enough paying clients to be able to cut checks without worrying if there'd be enough left over to pay for feed the next month. After a morning of working horses in two-degree weather, he could barely feel his toes in his boots, but still, Mitch wouldn't have chosen any other life.

When Mitch headed back from town, he saw smoke billowing from Hustonville Road and honked his way through the traffic stalling the bypass. His heart dropped to his gut. The twenty-six-stall barn had caught fire. Sky Watch was inside.

Mitch flew up the driveway and jumped out of the car. Barn fires are every horseman's nightmare. Built of old wood, footed with dirt, stacked with hay, and strung with cobwebs, barns are more flammable than charcoal. In minutes, a single spark can spread, tearing through stall walls as if they were paper.

Eight fire trucks surrounded the stable, and forty firefighters swarmed the property. Some wielded hoses, delivering water at 275 pounds per square inch. The hoses were as thick as a man's leg, but they might as well have been trickling against the flames. Other firefighters dashed inside to save the horses. Twenty-four equine souls inside a burning building, terrified by the smoke and flames—and trapped in their stalls.

Mitch saw Warren Nash and David Cleveland, his veterinarians, and didn't even pause to ask why they were there. They hadn't scheduled a visit. How had they known to be there? Mitch could figure that out later. "Where is he?" Mitch called.

Warren knew who he meant. Sky Watch. "He's safe," he said, before running back into the barn.

Mitch closed his eyes for a moment, then dashed in after him. Inside, the smoke rose to the rafters. To breathe, he had to crawl. On either side of him, horses screamed. The fire in the center of the barn roared, loud as the crowd in Freedom Hall. Mitch reached a closed stall, fumbled for the halter hanging on the door, and then tripped the latch. He flung the stall open, sprang to his feet, and slung his arm around the horse's neck. The gelding tossed his head, but Mitch kept his grip and managed to slide the halter over his face. "I know this is scary, friend, but you've got to come with me."

He led the shaking, sweating horse out by the halter, but as soon as they made it out of the barn, the gelding tore out of Mitch's grasp. Blinded by daylight on the snow-covered ground, he wheeled on his hind legs and ran back into the burning building. His stall, now so full of smoke he could barely breathe, felt safer than the cold open air.

Mitch's arms hung at his sides. Around him, similar scenes unfolded. Firefighters tried to drag horses out of the flames, but the ones they managed to get away from their stalls flung their heads, ripped away, and ran back into the barn. Crazed with panic, the horses chose certain death over the uncertainty of the bright, frigid day. Mitch ran to the wide-open barn doors, ready to keep trying. He had to save them. Those horses trusted him with their lives. On some of them, he'd hung big dreams. One of the volunteer firefighters called to him: "Mitch! Don't go back in there. The barn's going to come down."

Mitch heard a crack but couldn't move from where he stood. The horses inside keened. Around him, the smoke billowed, thick and black. The fireman pulled him back. "Get out of here! It's done, Mitch. They're done for."

He was right. Even if Mitch could have saved any of the fifteen horses left pawing and screeching in their stalls, their lung damage would be extensive. They'd never compete again, never even run through a pasture again without coughing. If they survived the fire and smoke unscathed, the stress of the event would undo them. Mentally, they'd never be the same.

Mitch coughed and backed away. With a crack and a boom, the barn shivered and then collapsed on itself, smoke pouring from the doors and windows.

The veterinarians had saved nine horses before the smoke got too thick, but they hadn't saved them all. Equine vets do most of their work on-site, at the barns and pastures where their patients live. Dr. Nash and Dr. Cleveland weren't scheduled to be on the farm, but they'd had a light day and were in the neighborhood. They'd decided to stop by over lunch and check in on a mare they were treating—a lucky break in an otherwise unlucky day. They discovered the fire and acted fast, moving Sky Watch first, before the smoke had even reached him, and stuck him in the barn down the hill. Then, they followed with whatever other horses they could save.

Without the veterinarians' surprise visit, Sky Watch might not have survived. It took less than thirty minutes from the moment the two vets discovered the fire for the barn to collapse. By the time Mitch arrived, the scene was hopeless. After days of investigation, police and firefighters couldn't determine the fire's cause. They didn't suspect arson. The whole thing had happened too fast to track. The fire started in the barn's center, then spread to the hayloft above the stalls. Hay is, quite literally, dried grass, so flames consumed the loft like a prairie fire. From there, it spread to the rafters, eating away at the support beams holding up the roof. Then, down to the stalls.

While he watched, Mitch's dreams turned to rubble and smoke. The horses' screams faded as they succumbed to the smoke or were knocked unconscious by falling debris. The air grew acrid with singed flesh. In the frigid weather, the heat rolled from the burning barn in waves.

When he couldn't stand watching anymore, Mitch turned for the lower barn, where the nine survivors stood, Sky Watch among them. They whinnied, pausing and pricking their ears, waiting for their friends' responses from the upper barn. All they heard were shouting men, rushing water, and the low crackling of flames.

Mitch stopped in each of the horses' stalls. He spoke in low, soothing tones and ran his hands over their bodies, checking for injury. One by one, they calmed. He opened Sky Watch's door last. The red stud stood at the back of the stall, nostrils wide, neck arched.

"You're all right," Mitch told him. "You're all right. You made it."

Sky Watch pawed, and Mitch checked his legs for cuts and bruises, feeling for heat along the long cannon bones. Other than an eye injury, which likely happened from throwing himself around the stall in an effort to escape, the stallion had escaped whole. Alive. Sound.

The cost of all the horses lost that day was immeasurable. Some had promise but hadn't yet been shown, so their value remains unknown. Some, like Sky Watch's sister Sky Blue, were already on the market for upward of $200,000, with interested buyers. Some, like Sky Watch, were not for sale, not even for half a million dollars. Along with the horses, hundreds of thousands of dollars' worth of tack and equipment burned. Mitch's entire business stood in that two-hundred-foot barn, uninsured.

Money could never soothe the pain of seeing fifteen horses die in a fire, but it could have helped Mitch rebuild. Instead, he'd have to start over from the beginning. Mitch lingered in the stall door, eyes on his world's champion stallion. The stallion stood square, his eyes locked on Mitch.

Once again, Mitch had nothing but Sky Watch and his reputation.

The barn fire made the front page of the *Kentucky Advocate* on Sunday, with a follow-up on Monday. Sky Watch, they reported, was safe. By then, the stallion had become a local celebrity. Mitch borrowed equipment, the bare minimum, from trainer friends in the area. A set of long lines. Bits and a work headstall. A saddle and girth. The horse community is always quick to help one of their own, especially in the face of tragedy. Don Harris might have even donated some tack to the cause. The lower barn on Mitch's grandfather's property wasn't meant for working show horses, so he moved the nine survivors to a nearby farm with empty stalls. Garland Bradshaw's work ethic permeated his entire being. Even after tragedy, he needed to work.

"He's probably working horses today," Cyndy Clark told the *Advocate*, just three days after the fire. When asked if he would rebuild, she replied, "Definitely."

Mitch kept on almost as if nothing had happened. Sure, he was working in a different arena out of leased stalls, but he still had horses that needed to work. Michele's five-gaited superpower New York, New York was among the nine saved. Thank goodness for Dr. Nash and Dr. Cleveland, but by God, Mitch wished they could have saved more. Even so, the survivors were working well. Good thing too. In just a few short weeks, he'd be shipping horses to Phoenix for the first show of the season. Michele wouldn't want to miss debuting her string that year, and naturally, she wanted her star stallion among them.

Just like Mitch, Sky Watch responded to the trauma of surviving a fire by turning to his work ethic. After the fire, even in an unfamiliar arena and a rented stall, he worked as furiously as if Louisville were the next week, not six months away. As always, Mitch found himself walking a fine line with the stallion: just enough work to stay mentally sound but not so much that Mitch risked his horse's physical soundness. With a horse like Sky Watch, that's not easy. He'd rather work through pain than stay on stall rest.

At Phoenix, no one in the crowd would have guessed that Sky Watch had survived a barn fire. He won with ease. So did Michele on Naranda, her bay pleasure mare, and with her four-in-hand pleasure driving team. Next on the agenda, as usual, was Devon. Sky Watch's annual show schedule meant the stallion traveled more than twenty-four hundred miles across the United States, covering the Northeast, the Southwest, and Kentucky, the Saddlebred capital of the world. In February, he shipped west, past St. Louis and its arch, the Missouri Ozarks, the cattle towns of Oklahoma and West Texas, and the mesas of Albuquerque. In late May, from a trailer window, he watched the hills of Danville deepen into the Blue Ridge Mountains of West Virginia, then the endless green of rural Pennsylvania, stopping just before the country air gave way to Philadelphia's city stink. Mitch said that even with his high energy and tender tendons, Sky Watch shipped well. Keeping him sound at work was the hard part.

Like clockwork, leading up to Louisville, Sky Watch came up with a limp. I can picture Mitch feeling his legs, shaking his head, and saying, "Figures. Right on time. Okay, stud. We're going to have to take it easy. You're seven now. A grown-up. Think you can handle it?"

After a few days off, Sky Watch was banging around his stall again. A rented stall. In someone else's barn. Not great behavior for a guest. "Fine," Mitch said to Sky Watch, standing in front of his stall while the stallion pawed and gnashed his teeth. "Back to work it is. But now your brain's gone to pot, and I'm going to have a hell of a time getting you to take any instruction from me."

When Sky Watch didn't have his brain screwed on right, he grabbed the bit and took charge. The sensitive mouth Mitch had worked so hard for disappeared and became jaws of iron, fighting Mitch's every move. Mitch would dismount and feel like a boxer punching above his weight.

"Tomorrow, let's give you something else to beat up on." Mitch had an idea. If Sky Watch was going to be hell on his rider, might as well give him something else on his back. Not another person, no. Even though he'd reached the seasoned age of seven, Mitch didn't trust another rider on Sky Watch.

Enter the dumb jockey. Dumb jockeys are metal or, if they're old-school, wood constructions that make a V or T on a horse's back. They attach to a surcingle around the horse's middle, and the trainer can attach reins from the dumb jockey to the bridle and turn the horse loose. The device mimics a rider on the horse's back, providing weight and resistance in the reins, but without the dynamic intelligence of a human rider. Hence, "dumb" jockey. The trainer gets to watch the horse from the ground, driving him forward with her voice and a drop-lash whip—not striking the horse with it, just holding it in the air so the horse sees it. If the horse tries to drop or roll, he could injure himself, so it's important to keep him moving forward.

As usual, Sky Watch needed more than the norm. On the ground, Mitch found he didn't have much impact on the headstrong stallion. So he took to mounting up on another horse, strapping a pair of blinkers on that horse so he couldn't see what was behind him, and riding with a drop-lash whip. He used one horse to drive the other forward. Sky Watch could tear around the ring and get the exercise he needed, and Mitch, on horseback, could keep up. The dumb jockey shuddered and shimmied on the stallion's back, working his mouth with even resistance. If Sky Watch pulled, the dumb jockey held fast. If Sky Watch gave, the resistance faded. It's a self-limiting system.

After a session with the dumb jockey, Mitch hopped back on. He bounce-walked the stallion through the arena's turn, giving and taking with the reins. "You've got a mouth again, don't you? Let's see what you can do." Mitch relaxed his fingers and squeezed with his legs, adding a hair's pressure on either side. Sky Watch took off at a trot, his head high and sucked back, his legs striding long and stepping big. He'd be ready, but with Imperator in the amateur leagues, there wasn't much competition.

As if he hadn't lost everything in a fire at the beginning of the year, Mitch hauled seven horses to Louisville in 1984, Sky Watch among them. In the stallion class, he won, but only because his talent couldn't be ignored. In the class, Mitch thought he was downright rank. He would have been better with a second workout, but no other horse came close enough to touching Sky Watch to merit a workout. Even raunchy from too much time off, Sky Watch walked away with the blue.

Meanwhile, Billy Dutel worked to get along with Imperator. He could ride the gelding but didn't possess the flair or polish that Don Harris had. How could he? Don represented the best of the best, the breed's master showman. With Don, Imperator didn't take a single wrong step. With Billy on board, he'd break his gait or jut his chin. Even though he spent his free time at the barn, Billy spent most of his hours arguing corporate law cases, not working American Saddlebreds. Still, the deep-brown gelding looked good enough to win the amateur stallion-gelding stake, beating the speedster Stutz Bearcat, who'd been showing with amateur Bev Pendleton in the irons for three years.

I wonder if Imperator could smell Sky Watch on the grounds. I can picture him lifting his exquisite head and dilating his nostrils, testing the air for the special tang that meant he'd meet his rival. When he found himself getting brushed and saddled on Friday night instead of Saturday night, he might have cocked his head, curious at the change in plans. The energy at Louisville on Friday night would have been high, but it wouldn't have reached the fever pitch of Freedom Hall on Saturday night in the 1980s. Imperator was a smart horse. He knew enough to tell the difference, to tell that he wouldn't, in fact, face his rival that night.

Billy Dutel legged onto his world's champion. Time to see if Imperator would earn a title in the amateur ranks. Billy must have known that all of Freedom Hall would be watching him—Imperator's former owners, the Meanors, especially. Back then, world's champion stake horses didn't get handed to an amateur. Billy, though, had the confidence of a Louisiana lawyer. Trotting into Freedom Hall, he overshot, and Imperator broke his trot. The crowd didn't mind, giving Perry the ovation the gelding needed to pull himself together and keep going.

Throughout the class, Bev Pendleton and Stutz Bearcat rode at Imperator. She knew he was the horse to beat. Bev's white-legged gelding had the speed to do it, his legs fast as a sewing machine's needle as he racked up to the stake-night favorite. Billy looked over his shoulder and asked Perry for more speed. The request worked, but Imperator lost some of his collection. Even so, after the lineup, Imperator found himself in another two-horse workout.

"Would you like to see a little more?" announcer Bill Carrington called, his voice dipping. The crowd cheered their assent. "Me too. Everybody stay parked in there but these two." Before he could even call them onto the rail,

Bev and the Bearcat zoomed onto the rail at a rack. To everyone's shock, Bill Carrington called the pair back to the pack, preventing a false start. Then, he ordered them back out, but by then, the team had lost focus and momentum. Billy Dutel waited his turn, then gunned Imperator to the opposite rail in a full-on rack.

"On the rail at a *trot*, please," Bill pleaded. "On the rail at a trot." The two amateurs adjusted their gaits, dropping their horses to a trot, but didn't adjust their trajectories. Billy took Imperator counterclockwise, the traditional first direction of the ring, while Bev angled Stutz Bearcat clockwise. The two headed straight for each other as if in a game of chicken, neither one giving ground. This workout was turning into a *Looney Tunes* episode, with the Bearcat as the Road Runner and Imperator as Wile E. Coyote.

"Let's all go the same way, okay?" Bill Carrington asked with a tinge of desperation. The amateur leagues were giving everyone in center ring a few extra gray hairs that night. "The first way of the ring, please."

Throughout the rest of the workout, both Bev Pendleton and Billy Dutel ignored the announcer. They slow-gaited their horses when they were supposed to be trotting. Billy did his best Don Harris impression, with his elbows wide, but his body bounced in the saddle like a sack of crawdads. The crowd ate up the display. This might not have been the clash of champions they'd paid to see when Imperator and Sky Watch faced off, but it was a clash of something. Even in amateur hands, Imperator won, his quality and brilliance overtaking the speed of Stutz Bearcat, a horse with plenty of quality of his own. Perry had earned one more victory pass around Freedom Hall.

Trainers left the fairgrounds for their hotels that night shaking their heads. The amateurs seemed to be taking over. No one talked about the big stake the next night—everyone knew Sky Watch would win. Instead, it was the year of the amateur and lady, at least according to *Saddle and Bridle*. "Of the three World's Grand Champion divisions, one championship stake was won by a horse out of the amateur ranks, and the reserve champion of another division was ridden by an amateur. Two qualifying stakes were won by lady amateur riders, going against the top professionals in the business. Most hearteningly, the percentage of male amateurs, in the five-gaited division at least, now approaches fifty, a startling increase from just a few years ago. The old rigid distinction of stake horses for men and amateur horses for women has collapsed completely."

Still, Saturday night at Freedom Hall was devoted to the old-time stake horse. The idea of the stake horse is similar to a Thoroughbred racehorse, except there's money in racing. A stake horse is a Saddlebred too hot and too talented for anything but a professional to handle. In amateur hands, a stake horse might fall apart. In the mid-twentieth century, large, private Saddlebred barns dominated the landscape. Dodge Stables. Longview Farms. Here, a wealthy family employed a trainer to raise, train, and show their string of horses. They might ride some, but mostly, they spectated, watching the trainer bring their charges along.

Eventually, some of those trainers decided to leave the security of a private stable job to enjoy the freedom of owning their own barn. Instead of one client, they took on many, training a horse for someone here, working a small string for someone there, and even buying their own to train, show, and sell. When they sold the horses they owned, instead of just pocketing a commission for a sale, they could cash a check for the entire sale price. These trainers enjoyed the freedom of working for themselves and the potential to make more money in the long run—although paying the bills is always a struggle in the short term. Mitch likens running a farm to riding a tiger. A trainer who owns her own farm has to keep the tiger fed, or he's going to turn around and think the thing on his back is a snack. Some days, the tiger's only fed through lunch. Others, he's satiated until next week.

Trainer-owned barns are the norm today, but many trainers still work stake-quality horses for clients who will never climb on those horses' backs. The stake horse is more about bragging rights than cash. When the winner of the most prestigious American Saddlebred title is only bringing home $24,000, it's not about the money. A quarter of a million is no small prize, but compared to the winner of the Kentucky Derby, who crosses the finish line for $1.86 million, it's not much. It's not hard to spend more than $24,000 a year training, shoeing, and showing a stake-quality horse. At best, the owner might be able to sell their stake winner, maybe for the upper six figures, but really, it's about the excitement of competition. Freedom Hall is still a playground for the rich.

However, the upper-middle class is infiltrating that playground and has been since the mid-1980s. A pastime that used to be available only to the independently wealthy—the Michele Macfarlanes and Della Larges of the world—became available to regular folks with some disposable income. Say a real estate agent sells a $750,000 home and invests her commission. A couple of years later, it's grown, and she has the money to buy a nice-looking two-year-old for $35,000. Over the next two years, she'll spend $15,000–$25,000 a year on training, shoeing, vet bills, and showing. It's a lot of money, but by the time the horse is old enough to compete in the five-gaited stake at Louisville, he's worth $300,000. After the show, she sells him, pays her trainer a commission, and keeps what's left over to do it all again.

Then there are the amateurs like me, the ones who do this for the pleasure of it, who are willing to pay big money for our hobbies even if our husbands turn pale when the training bills arrive. We don't want stake horses. We want horses we can ride and show ourselves. That's an entirely different market, and it's growing. Today, most of the classes on a horse show's schedule are for amateurs and junior exhibitors. If 1984 was the Year of the Amateur at Louisville, it wasn't an anomaly. It was the beginning of a trend. Now, amateurs buy former stake horses all the time. A horse might be a World's Champion of Champions in the open division one year, then an amateur champ the next. Some of us even want horses we can train ourselves, but most of us will pay a professional for board and training. I dream of living on a farm one day and keeping horses at home, but they'd be pets, not show horses. I'll leave the show training to the pros.

In June 1985, after a show season and a half with Billy Dutel, Imperator walked up the loading ramp on a van headed for Kentucky. Billy Dutel was selling Saddlebreds as quickly as he'd bought them. At $250,000, Imperator could command the highest price tag. A loss for Dutel, since he'd paid $100,000 more, but that was the business. After Imperator and some other high-dollar horses sold, Dutel Farms held a dispersal sale to unload even more of the Louisiana lawyer's stock.

Ron and Paula Kirsh, a young California couple who owned a jewelry business, had bought Imperator, seeking a taste of the Saddlebred big leagues. Dressed in pale suits, with her teased blond hair and his square jaw, the couple looked like 1980s Barbie and Ken. Ron had messed around with Thoroughbreds for a while but didn't like the distance between owner and horse. Paula had always loved the action and good looks of Saddlebreds, but she'd never owned a world's champion. Together, they'd bought Perry and sent him back to Don Harris.

The Kirshes and Don Harris agreed that Don would take Perry back in the ring at Louisville that year. The world needed another rematch between Imperator and Sky Watch. In the months leading up to Louisville, Don would prepare Perry to be a stake horse once again. He was eager to get the gelding back in his barn. A travel veteran, Imperator shipped well, lipping hay and swaying as the truck and trailer wound its way to Don Harris Stables in Simpsonville. Even on a trailer, Perry stood up-headed, every bit the show horse. Except for one detail: duct tape covered his leg bandages from knee to fetlock. Perry's only vice. No matter how well-wrapped, he'd tear off any leg wrap that wasn't duct-taped on. From the knee up, at least, Imperator looked as regal as his name, ready to win back his title. The 1985 World's Championship Horse Show would see another rematch between its two star horses.

Part IV

1985–1988

12

Horse Show Baby

May 14, 2021—my due date—came and went. Still no baby. All week, every labor-inducing trick the internet could churn up had disappointed me. Spicy food, including my brother's signature Habanero Hellfire hot sauce. Medjool dates in my smoothies. Acupuncture. A few R-rated acts. Bouncing on a yoga ball while surfing the web, searching for any other options that might urge my baby girl out of my body and into my arms. One discussion board post suggested going for a drive on a bumpy road. BabyBump3 had probably meant a car, but I could do one better than that. I could drive Bee.

That Saturday morning, my belly so big it barely fit behind a steering wheel, I drove to the barn feeling defeated. I should have been squatting on a birthing stool, breathing through contractions, and picturing each shudder as an ocean wave bringing my baby to me. Instead, the weekend had dawned like any other, so off to the barn it was. My barn family goes to the barn on Saturdays like other people go to church on Sundays. It's a sacred time. We book vacations Sunday to Friday so as not to miss Barn Day. Still, that day, my brain felt as if my body was supposed to be elsewhere.

"Good morning," Mike called to me as I walked in. The previous Saturday, with my due date looming, I'd told him not to expect me for a few weeks, but he didn't question my presence. He had three kids, all adults now, so he knew that a birthing due date was more of a suggestion than a definite plan. As I cross-tied Bee and curried the dust from her coat, he approached the stall with a harness and bridle. "Are you up for driving her today, or do you want me to work her?"

"I'll drive her," I said.

Mike led Bee into the arena. She stood while Mike maneuvered the cart shafts around her. I'd been the first one to the barn that morning, as usual, but the rest of the barn family had started to creep in. So had my mom, who was still wearing her movie-star sunglasses in the bright barn.

"Hey, everyone," Linda called down the aisle, "Emma's trying to bounce the baby out."

One by one, a half-dozen women ambled down the barn aisle and into the arena, each wearing boots and riding pants. Most wore horse show T-shirts. River Ridge, with its twin *R*s scripted over a line drawing of a Sad-dlebred. Spring Warm-Up, with a Saddlebred trotting across the state of Indiana. All American Horse Classic, with the silhouette of a Saddlebred head in front of stars and stripes. These women came in all shapes and sizes, and their average age landed just shy of qualifying for Social Security bene-fits. I was the baby of the group. On my birthday that year, my barn family had spoiled me with candles, lotions, jewelry, and at-home spa supplies. They'd even thrown me a barn baby shower catered with a burrito bar and custom cupcakes, gifting me and the life inside me with a plush rocking horse, a set of horse-related board books, and onesies printed with trotting Saddlebreds. During our Saturday practice rides, the barn family stood in the middle of the arena to watch one another. You knew you were having a good ride when the knot of women stopped gossiping and started cheering for you. At that point, Bee and I weren't exciting to watch, but they sup-ported us anyway.

"Bee's probably wondering what all that extra weight is behind her," one woman chuckled.

"Watch Emma going around the turn! She really has to lean into it," another said, joining in.

"If she goes into labor, who's going to catch the baby?" another ribbed.

Bee trotted me around and around, the drive as bumpy as ungraded gravel, but my uterus remained unmoved. When driving a horse, you can see their whole body in front of you. It's a great lesson in equine anatomy. Bee's round haunches punched in front of me, all the muscle from her year in training with Mike rippling under her dark coat.

My mom stood at the edge of the group with her phone up, filming the drive. "I thought you might want to remember your last drive pregnant," she said, showing me the video after Bee and I had finished.

"Let's hope it's my last one." I rubbed my belly. No contractions yet.

"It had better be!" my mom quipped. "Fern needs to make her arrival before I show my mare again." Together we walked to Pyromanium's stall, and she stuck her ears forward when she saw us. "Isn't she the best? Isn't she the prettiest?" my mom gushed. She and Pyromanium had debuted to win both their classes in their first show together. They had another show scheduled for the following week. Then three more before summer's end. My mom might not have hit the ring in twenty-five years, but she was making up for lost time.

"Hear that, Fern? You've got a deadline." Ben and I had decided to name the baby Fern, after my maternal grandmother, after Dearie. Continuing the damline.

The day of Pyromanium's show, my water broke. My mom skipped the horse show, but as it turned out, she didn't need to. Labor took a full two days. Pushing took longer than a Saturday-night session at the World's Championship Horse Show. Finally, I held my newborn against my chest, skin to skin, so we could breathe each other in as horses do in the field. Fern's hands flexed and curled, frond-like. She opened her eyes, a milky gray for now, then closed them again. She cried in hiccup bursts until, like magic, she latched. Luckily, unlike foals, human babies don't need to stand to nurse. Ben knelt next to the hospital bed, one hand on my shoulder, the other on his baby's back, tears streaming down his face. "Hi, little one," I said, my voice dreamy in the postpartum haze. "I love you."

At ten days old, Fern attended her first horse show, sleeping snuggled on my chest while her grandmother trotted Pyromanium into the ring. Even when a whoop escaped my lips as my mom made a high-trotting pass, she slept. A born horse show baby.

Three weeks after Fern's birth, I took my first postpartum ride on Bee. My core felt as if it had been ripped in two, and my legs wobbled as they swung onto my horse. Bee's trots and canters stayed quiet, as if she knew gentleness was necessary. Mike kept the lesson short, and instead of pushing for more time, I accepted the limit. Fern needed a feed, anyway. She accepted the bottles of pumped milk that Ben offered, but she preferred to quaff straight from the tap. The hours spent on the couch, holding her while she ate and dozed, didn't bother me. The stillness felt welcome. Birthing Fern had also meant birthing myself into motherhood.

With Fern in the world, I stepped back from work, and Bee stepped down from training for shows, giving me a full show season off to fall in love with my daughter. All summer long, Bee stayed home while the horses around her loaded on trailers bound for county fairgrounds and equestrian centers throughout the Midwest. That didn't bother her. If anything, she seemed relieved. She enjoyed our new, low-key rides, as Mike geared her toward the steadiness of a lesson horse instead of the flashiness of a show horse.

On barn days, Fern joined me. I'd wear her in a sling and watch horses work while she snoozed or stared at the big beings trotting around her, her eyes soulful, her mouth pursed. In the stalls, she reached for the horses' noses, smiling when they huffed air at her. The horses were curious about the tiny being who patted their necks with her starfish hands. When it came time for me to ride, I passed Fern to my mom, who hefted her onto her narrow hip and marched her down to the hay cart to play, pointing out every barn swallow and stall fan along the way. Fern was likely to learn barn manners before table manners—long before table manners, if her first months with solid foods indicated anything. By the time she turns three, Fern will know not to enter a stall without an adult, to get out of the way when a horse is coming through, and never to pat a horse she doesn't know.

When Fern turned nine months old, Sky Watch started trotting through my mind again. It was time to visit Mitch. He'd never had the chance to tell me about Sky Watch's later years. On a sunny Tuesday morning two years after my first visit to the barn on Hustonville Road, I drove back to Danville, Kentucky. The landscape looked the same, the Kentucky hills still undulating and green beyond the two-lane highway, but much had changed for me.

Mitch was the same Mitch, still working horses and running his farm. It had taken two months' worth of phone calls and rescheduling for us to find time for my visit. One week, he'd lost his stall cleaner and gotten too far behind to make room for anything extra. Another, he'd needed to drive to Tennessee to pick up a horse. Still another, his local feed store hadn't had what he needed, so he'd been forced to drive out of town just to keep his dadgum horses fed. Could I believe it? I could. Finally, we'd set the date. I'd never been separated from my daughter for an entire day. At nine months old, she still spent most of her time with her mommy.

As I walked into Mitchell Clark Stables, the barn's musk enveloped me, the same as the barn's at home. Sawdust, hay, manure, and horse. Perfect. The stress of navigating traffic, the fatigue from a night of tending to a teething Fern—it all fizzled away when my feet hit the barn aisle. In the stalls, a dozen heads lowered, their jaws grinding alfalfa. My presence didn't stir the horses from their meal. A bay filly paused to look at me and then, deciding I wasn't worth more than a look, returned to her food. Beyond her stall, I found the tack room where Sky Watch's bridle still hung. The red browband with white polka dots. The half-moon curb bit wrapped in copper wire. The reins supple from years of use and care.

Mitch ambled over and wrapped me in a hug. "Good to see you again, darlin'. You couldn't have ordered better weather, could you?" He didn't wait for my answer. "No, this is just about perfect."

The whole barn seemed quieter. Anthio wasn't brushing horses or cleaning tack. He'd taken a job down the road, training for Elisabeth Goth, Mitch's second ex-wife. "We're doing the whole thing ourselves," Mitch said, gesturing to his wife Vicky, who walked over to introduce herself, brushing her hands on her jeans. "You can't get good help these days. Not with who's sitting in the White House." I didn't have the heart to tell Mitch I'd voted for Biden.

"We're thinking of diversifying the farm," Mitch said. "We want something to pass on to the boys." Mitch and Vicky had twins, Garland and Mitchell, high schoolers now who rode gaited horses of their own. "Cattle, maybe."

The thought of anything but Saddlebreds at the farm on Hustonville Road saddened me, but I understood. Making a living in the horse business is hard, even for a legend.

Mitch led me up a flight of stairs and into his office, a dark-walled room with an old wooden desk, dusty couches, and huge windows overlooking the arena. In a glass case stood silver bowls, platters, and trophies—some of them Sky Watch's. On the walls hung photos of the farm's best horses. Sky Watch, of course, with one of his horseshoes hanging above it. Memories' Citation, who won both the Three-Gaited and Five-Gaited World's Grand Championships. In the place of honor above the desk, Garland Bradshaw, aboard one fine brown five-gaited horse.

"Your boys ride, don't they? Do they have any interest in the family business?"

"Not so much. They've enjoyed the horses—and mind you, we haven't just bought them the best things out there; they've had to work for it—but I don't think either of them wants to do this for a living, which is fine."

"What about your oldest? Sean Christopher?"

"Oh, I don't have any contact with him at all. His mother made sure of that."

"That's a shame."

"A damn shame."

Eventually, we got around to the reason for my visit. "Mitch," I said, "the 1985 class. What happened? You were over a year out from the barn fire and meeting Imperator for the first time since the 1983 duel. Tell me about it."

Mitch liked nothing better than telling stories. I sat back and let him talk.

Even working out of a borrowed barn all through the 1985 show season, Mitch managed to turn out new champions. Sultan's Shamrock, a three-year-old five-gaited colt, joined Mitch's string in January 1985, a year after the fire. Jerry Vanier, the owner of such legends as Sultan's Starina, owned him. Just the year before, with none other than Don Harris at the helm, the colt had won the five-gaited two-year-old stake. Jerry Vanier was a good client to have. He owned nice horses and sent them to the trainers he thought suited them best.

Mitch worked with the colt and lengthened his stride at the trot—Mitch's trademark, seen on every horse he'd touched from Sky Watch on. With his star, stripe, and four white stockings, Sultan's Shamrock wore plenty of chrome, and he wore it well. As the season trudged along from fairground to fairground, he took a victory pass at Harrodsburg, the Tilt-a-Whirl and Ferris wheel of the Mercer County Fair brightening his already-bright expression.

Miss Marple, a filly Mitch bred and raised himself, won the three-gaited junior horse championship at Devon. After taking third in the two-year-old five-gaited stake at Louisville in 1984, Mitch decided to trim her. With that neck and that head, why not? Later, in the early 1990s, Miss Marple left the show ring and became a mama. She birthed three colts. Sky Watch sired two of them.

To no one's surprise, Sky Watch also dominated Devon's Dixon Oval that year in his one and only horse show before Louisville. At Devon, Mitch visited with Michele and her mother, Brownie. Even in her early seventies, Brownie still traveled from coast to coast. In a photo captured by *Saddle and Bridle*'s Maureen Jenner, the trio look posed, with Mitch behind the two ladies, his long arms dangling at his sides. Michele lays a protective hand on her mother's chair, smiling with her mouth closed. Brownie wears a hat, a flowered dress, and an expression that matches her daughter's.

Back home in Kentucky, Mitch hadn't yet found the capital to rebuild his barn on the family land. With no insurance, he'd received nothing after the January 1984 fire. More than eighteen months later, his finances were still reeling. Sure, he made it from horse show to horse show and maintained some deep-pocketed clients, but sometimes, it felt as if twine held his whole organization together.

When he heard that Imperator would return to Louisville with Don Harris in the irons, the pair aiming once again for the big one, Mitch smiled to himself. Don and Imperator made Mitch work his hardest, perform at his best. He could use a little kick in the pants just then. Maybe he'd need to dig up those old newspaper articles he used to keep on the fridge.

August rolled around, and for once, Sky Watch went into Louisville sound—or as sound as that stallion ever could be. That season especially, Mitch had struggled to find the balance between working him enough to keep him sane and not working him so hard that he became unsound. All summer long, he'd battled inflammation in those front tendons.

Sitting in his office with me, Mitch pointed at Sky Watch's shoe. "You see that bar across the heel?" he asked. I nodded. "That's because he hit the ground so hard he would literally bend the shoe at the ends. That's how much force he used."

By 1985, Sky Watch himself must have known the stalls at Louisville, the same stalls Garland Bradshaw had used decades earlier. He must have smelled Imperator on the grounds and wondered if he'd get another chance to best the beautiful gelding. Most importantly, the stallion knew what the building beyond the stalls meant. Freedom Hall, constructed just for the World's Championship Horse Show, was meant to be the perfect place to show an American Saddlebred, which demonstrates just how important the Saddlebred had been when the stadium was constructed in the 1950s.

In 1984, Freedom Hall received a makeover to be more hospitable to the Cardinals, the University of Louisville's men's basketball team. Priorities were changing. Construction workers lowered the floor to add more seating, which made the ramp to Freedom Hall a downhill charge instead of an uphill climb. This also made the rail hard to access—a tragedy for horse show junkies. Where else but railside at Louisville can you yell out your best "Yeah, boy!" and be christened with green shavings flung up by a Saddlebred's racking hooves? The lower arena also blocked audience views of the ring from the upper seats. Clearly, something needed to change. If Saddlebreds had to make nice with basketball players, the least the Kentucky State Fairgrounds could do was keep the horses comfortable.

For the 1985 World's Championship Horse Show, manager Bill Munford came up with some solutions. He narrowed the arena by five and a half feet and trimmed down the judges' stand to compensate for the lost space. In theory, the adjustment gave the horses just as much room to work. Even narrowed, Freedom Hall's arena was larger than the ring at most shows. Compared to Lexington, the turns were generous. You could park an eight-horse trailer in them with room to spare.

As always, the five-gaited stallion stake headlined Monday night at Louisville in 1985, with Sky Watch entering as the heavy favorite. He didn't disappoint, entering the ring with confidence. At eight years old, he trotted more coolly than usual. He didn't need to burn himself down to dwarf the competition. Spectators said Mitch piloted him with the authority of his grandfather aboard Captain Denmark. The pair were no longer hotshot newcomers. They were the ones to beat, the seasoned campaigners, the home team. Only once did Sky Watch and Mitch falter. As the announcer called the reverse and trot—Sky Watch's signature move—the stallion slipped in the turn. The audience gasped as he went down behind for half a step. He recovered fast, bringing his feet back underneath him, and finished the class unfazed. Mitch didn't even have to ask Sky Watch for his special sixth gear. The pair earned their victory pass with no need for it.

As usual, Mitch switched bits for Saturday night's class. He always gave Sky Watch a special bit for stake nights, not letting him taste it again until the next Saturday-night class. If he worked him in his Saturday-night bit, the stud would outsmart his bridle, using it against Mitch instead of working with his trainer. In a familiar bridle, Sky Watch could lean on the bit and take away its power or clamp down on one side and render one set of reins useless. Those trainer-stallion conversations turned ugly when Sky Watch commanded them. Rather than show against his competition, the stud would prefer to mow them down. Mitch knew better than to give him the chance. Riding against Don Harris and Imperator, who would be returning to challenge him, Mitch needed every advantage.

The organ struck up "My Old Kentucky Home" as announcer Peter Doubleday called in the seven contenders for the 1985 Five-Gaited World's Grand Championship. Sky Watch entered last, and the crowd rallied for the reigning champion. The situation from their first duel three years earlier had shifted. Instead of Sky Watch challenging Imperator, now Imperator challenged Sky Watch. Mitch knew Don would be riding his gelding hard. After welcoming him back to his barn, Don had started jogging Imperator four or five miles a day, building the horse's stamina. Imperator had never been easy to beat, but Mitch would need to be ready for a direct challenge from the old showman and his crowd-pleasing former champion.

After an explosive entrance and first lap around the ring, Mitch checked Sky Watch's speed in the turn. Something felt off, maybe a little soft. He held the stud back more than he usually would, feathering the reins and pulling his legs off the horse's sides. Surely, there would be a workout. Mitch knew he needed to save Sky Watch's energy for a third duel with his rival. Sky Watch, though, didn't understand why Mitch asked for less instead of more. He flicked his ears back as he trotted out of the turn, doing his job but not happy about it. Charlie Smith saw his chance and gunned The Phoenix, the horse who had taken reserve to Imperator in the gelding stake. Could he do it? The previous year, or the year before that, it would have been impossible, but the team passed Mitch and Sky Watch at the trot. As he headed into the turn, Charlie glanced over his shoulder at Mitch as if he too couldn't believe it. Coming out of the turn, Mitch asked Sky Watch for more, and the stud bloomed into his full brilliance, floating between each step of the trot, his legs flying. The crowd boomed their approval. Sky Watch might have just gotten smoked on the rail, but no one could take his trot from him.

Throughout the rest of the class, Mitch maintained his light hold on the reins and took a surprising strategy. He stayed on the rail. Ever since Sky Watch was a green two-year-old new to Freedom Hall, Mitch had shown him off the rail. It was one of his strengths. That night, though, Mitch kept Sky Watch under wraps, close enough to the rail to kick it. On the call for the reverse trot, organist Gene Wright picked up the pace. Sky Watch took another funny step, breaking from his favorite gait for a split second. Then, Mitch felt a presence behind him. He did the unthinkable. Mitch tapped Sky Watch on the shoulder with the whip. Once. Twice. He had to. Don Harris and Imperator were making their move, and Sky Watch wasn't clicking into that sixth gear. Coming out of the far turn, the gelding overtook the stud, passing him at the trot.

At every gait, Sky Watch succumbed to the assault from other horses. The Phoenix. Merrill Murray and the beautiful mare Our Golden Duchess, who had taken reserve to Sky Watch the previous year. And, of course, Imperator.

Even off his game and getting covered up at the rail, Sky Watch still stood leagues above the rest of the horses. Except one. The only other four-legged being in the universe who could touch Sky Watch shared the arena with him that night—and he'd never looked better. Imperator trotted into the lineup last, Don Harris drawing his gelding up into one final pass for the crowd, who realized they might be witnessing the turning of a tide.

Peter Doubleday asked the crowd if they wanted to see more. They whooped their approval. The workout they'd been hoping for, the third showdown between Imperator and Sky Watch, was about to begin. Mitch and Don squeezed their mounts up and headed for the opposite rail while Gene Wright popped his way into an organist's rendition of the Chordettes' 1950s hit "Mr. Sandman." "Yes," Peter narrated, "they're showing them here for us tonight, folks."

In seconds, the show stopped. Mitch had pulled Sky Watch to a full stop in center ring. During a workout. On stake night. Unthinkable. What did Mitch think he was doing? This wasn't an ordinary time-out. This was something more.

Freedom Hall held its breath.

Mitch conferred with the baffled judges and officials. "He's lame," Mitch explained. "I can't ask him to finish the class. Can I still take second?"

Eventually, Bill Munford had to join in and clear the confusion. "No one's ever done this before, Mitch," Bill replied. "Give us a minute."

"I want to make sure we don't end up in last place," Mitch said. "I'm not risking my horse to finish the class, that's for damn sure, but he deserves more than last."

Bill talked to Don Judd, the call judge, along with two of the ringmasters, and together, they came up with a plan.

Meanwhile, Don Harris kept showing Imperator as if the show weren't on pause. Gene Wright's hands lay still on the organ, but Imperator didn't need a show tune to step high. Besides, the crowd made enough noise to make up for the lack of musical accompaniment. Don racked Imperator down the rail one-handed, cool as could be, as if the kerfuffle in center ring weren't happening. The audience thundered. Imperator's rack was more exciting than watching a man sit on top of a stopped horse, waiting for a group of suits to decide his fate.

One minute and thirty seconds later—an eternity in Freedom Hall—Mitch bounce-walked Sky Watch to the gate. This time, no crowd blocked his exit. Mitch wheeled Sky Watch around to face the ring one last time. He removed his hat in salute, just as he had in the past three years of victory passes.

To complete the unorthodox class, the judges decided that Don Harris needed to work Imperator both directions of the workout, even though his competition had folded. Then, because the second-place horse had excused himself, the rest of the class would need to work again, both directions of the ring. The audience cheered for Imperator as always, but they grew quiet as Don pulled him into the center. Peter Doubleday had to rally them for the second workout to determine the second- through seventh-place horses. "Let's make some noise, folks." Everyone had forgotten they were at a horse show. They clapped weakly, but most of the crowd had their heads turned to gossip with their neighbors. What had happened to Sky Watch?

After the second workout of the class, the remaining six horses in the ring lined up. Everyone in the arena knew Imperator had already won, but Freedom Hall still exploded, ecstatic, when Peter announced the 1985 Five-Gaited World's Grand Champion. Imperator had taken back his throne.

As always, the Louisville local station had filmed the evening and captured an interview with the winner. "Thank you, Bill. There's no feeling like this. This one meant more to me than the first one," Don told TV announcer Bill Carrington.

"Kind of an unusual way to win it," Bill said, prompting Don to comment on Sky Watch.

"Yes," Don said. "I don't know what happened to Sky Watch, but I hope he's all right. I would've liked to grind it out with him, but this made it a little easier. I was a little more relaxed and probably had more fun on that workout."

The lights dimmed, calling Don Harris back to his horse for the victory pass. Don mounted up, removed his hat, and rocked Imperator up into his signature gait. The king had returned. Once, twice, they circled the ring, soaking up the hoots and hollers from the stands. Don Harris and Imperator were silhouetted against the ramp as they exited, Imperator's tail flagging behind him, the end of it trailing along the ground like the train of an emperor's robe.

While Don Harris accepted handshakes and claps on the back, his barn aisle clogged with fans, Mitch called the vet. "I think he tore everything in that back leg loose," he said. A full exam led to a diagnosis of torn ligaments. The cure? Total rest. For at least a year.

Michele decided to retire the stallion to stud. Her friend Bob Robinson had just relocated to Kentucky. He could stand him—at a fee of $5,000 per breeding. For 1986? Astronomical. Unheard of. Today, that would be about $12,000. For the second time in his life, Mitch prepared his favorite horse for a journey to a stall on another farm. This time, he couldn't even hope to see him again in the ring. The greatest athlete the show horse world had ever seen was finished.

Mary-Ann Pardieck, formerly Mary-Ann Teater—the woman in charge of the farmhouse at Teater and Sons, where Sky Watch was born—says she would have recommended $1,500 for his first breeding season. "He would've filled his card that way. He could've bred three hundred mares that first year." Mary-Ann would know. She'd managed the breeding career of Flight Time—the stud who'd produced Sky Watch. Instead, the American Saddle-bred Registry only entered sixteen Sky Watch babies in their files the following year. Sky Watch fans scratched their heads. They'd hoped for more from their show-ring favorite.

In that 1985 World's Championship duel, Imperator didn't beat Sky Watch. Sky Watch beat Sky Watch. The injury must have happened when Sky Watch went down in the stallion stake earlier in the week, but the stud was so game, so hardworking, that no one, not even Mitch, could tell. The injury hadn't become apparent until Saturday night, when Mitch called on his horse and asked for his all. For the first time in his life, Sky Watch hadn't been able to give it.

After Sky Watch left, on a cold day almost two years after the barn fire, Mitch did the only thing he knew to do. He tacked up the next horse, hopped on, and got to work.

As he looked to the winter of training and the upcoming show seasons, Mitch felt a heaviness settle on his shoulders. He'd lost everything. His barn. His star stallion. Mitch was still training horses out of rented stalls. He wanted to make good on his promise to rebuild, even if it took him decades to save the money, but things in Kentucky looked grim. Even his family had cracked under the strain of rebuilding the family business. Soon, Cyndy would be nothing more than a name on divorce papers, and little Sean would be nothing but a memory. When Michele offered to bring Mitch to California to train for her, it had only made sense to accept.

In his office in the barn that he did, finally, rebuild, Mitch puffed out his cheeks. "It was an offer I couldn't refuse." The dream he'd held since the fire hadn't come true until the late 1990s. In 1999, he finally saw beams and joists go up where once had been ash. Then, he bought the farm next to his, the land that had once been his grandfather's. In 1986, none of that was anything more than hope. Mitch was facing a decade on the West Coast, but he didn't know that yet. If he had, he might've stayed in Kentucky. Then again, maybe not. A horse trainer follows the horses, and Michele Macfarlane owned the best in the business.

Compared to working out of borrowed stalls, hustling for clients, sweating in the steam of Kentucky summers, and shivering through its winters, working in a luxury barn in San Diego didn't sound so bad. Palm and eucalyptus, blue skies, and 266 days of sunshine made postponing a dream taste a little sweeter.

13

Just the One

With a baby in my arms and a mare who had already peaked as a show horse, I had a dream of my own to postpone. That week, My Queen Bee would leave Mike McIntosh Stables for Roselane Farm, the barn where I took lessons. The couple who owned and ran Roselane had agreed to board her for me. Her papers would stay in my name, but she would no longer be in training. On her last Saturday at Mike's, I turned Bee out after our ride. Ever since Mike had pulled her show shoes, I'd been riding her early in the mornings before the rest of the barn family arrived. Better not to have an audience for a show horse who wasn't destined to show. Bee trotted over to the retired gelding assigned to babysit her and kicked her heels toward him. He lifted his head and snorted, then resumed eating grass. She cantered a circle around him, then trotted to me at the fence, blowing air every step of the way.

"Where's that motion when I'm riding you, girl?" I asked her, scratching the star on her forehead. "You'd rather be out here, playing, wouldn't you?"

As if she'd understood me, Bee wheeled around and high-stepped back to her babysitter, who ignored her. Then she sighed, lowered her head, and nibbled the shoots of late-fall grass poking out of the dirt.

Mike didn't offer lessons at his barn, didn't keep a string of lesson mounts for people to practice on. Clients got to ride their horses in training once, maybe twice a week if they were lucky. Because I needed more than one ride a week to stay in shape, when Bee started training with Mike, he'd suggested Roselane for extra lessons. I didn't know yet if Bee could hack it as a lesson horse, and Roselane would be the perfect place to test her out.

Cameron and Caroline Boyer have run Roselane Farm since Sky Watch retired to stud. While Mike McIntosh Stables only turns out performance-level Saddlebreds, Roselane Farm is more diverse. Caroline teaches lessons and takes young and adult riders to academy-level shows, and she and Cam train horses in all disciplines, including Western and Hunter. Neither of them is much taller than the pitchforks they wield every morning, cleaning their own stalls before starting a day of training and teaching riding lessons.

Roselane's focus is Saddlebreds, but horses of all types move through their barn. Friesians. Hackneys. A rescued Arabian who'll never carry a rider but enjoys turnout with a retired Saddlebred. It's not unusual to see a Haflinger, a Quarter Horse, or a mustachioed Romany horse or two in the Roselane stalls. That's right. Sometimes, horses grow mustaches. Romany horses are wide, short horses with fluffy fetlocks, flashy coloring, and, sometimes, handlebars feathering their upper lips. At Roselane, at six months old, Fern took her first pony ride—my hands gripping her waist, of course. It's that kind of place. Kids. Dogs. Cats. Throughout the whole affair, Fern knitted her brow, unsure of the shaggy, ancient pony beneath her. Ginger was one of those rare ponies who could be trusted with the smallest of hands on her reins. She passed away not long after Fern's ride, and the whole Indianapolis saddle seat community mourned her loss. She might not have been a show pony, but Ginger had given hundreds of children their first experience with horses, so she was loved as deeply as any stake horse.

Cam and Caroline had agreed to keep Bee at Roselane during her entire transition period—however long it lasted. Together, they'd help me figure out the next steps. What those next steps would be depended on Bee. The decision I'd been toying with since before Fern's birth had finally solidified. I was going to sell Bee. The question was no longer "if" but "when."

However, before Bee could go on the market, Cam, Caroline, and I needed to find out what she could do. We knew she didn't want to show, but we didn't yet know if she was bombproof enough to be a lesson horse. For me to sell her responsibly, Bee needed to prove herself useful. There are quick ways to sell a horse, but those didn't interest me. Too many Saddlebreds at Bee's level—not fancy enough for show but not broke enough for lessons—can find themselves in bad situations. Sold from barn to barn. Placed in an unsafe lesson program where both riders and horses end up hurt. Working as a cart horse, both overused and under-cared-for. I couldn't bear that type of future for Bee.

Over the next few months, I drove to Roselane to ride Bee three times a week. It was a test. Could an amateur like me maintain the training Bee had learned with Mike? If so, she could make it as a lesson horse. If not, we had more work to do. Caroline taught me to relax Bee and round through her corners, giving me instructions from her spot on a swivel chair in the middle of the arena. Sometimes, she walked next to us, demonstrating with her body what she wanted my body to do, her voice calm and reassuring. Caroline's once-red hair had faded to pale straw over her decades in the industry, and she could supposedly spark a redhead's temper, but I'd never seen her lose her cool. With her instructor's eyes, she saw what riders needed to do for a horse to be at her best.

"Sit back," Caroline told me. "Drop your shoulders. Open your fingers."

Relax. Let go. When I complied, Bee softened, giving to the bridle and rounding at the poll.

"Use your tummy muscles," she reminded me. "I know you just had a baby, but see if you can find your core again."

"I'm not sure if there's much core left," I called back.

"Just wait until you have a second kid!" She laughed. "You'll get it. Just give it time."

Instead of maintaining the short, high-powered riding sessions of a show horse in training, Bee and I warmed up slowly and ended each lesson with a long walk under saddle, my reins loose, my feet kicked out of the stirrups, one hand scratching her rump while we walked circles through the arena. While I rode, my mom played with Fern, who, at nine months old, had just learned to crawl. They stacked and unstacked the small traffic cones Caroline used to teach new riders to guide. They paraded around the sawdust pile, Fern on my mom's hip. They investigated the jog carts standing upended in center ring. When the lesson ended, my mom held Fern up so I could stroke her cheek from my spot in the saddle.

"You know," I said to Caroline as I dismounted one afternoon, "having a show horse is great, but it's also nice to just come out and—"

"Ride your horse." Caroline finished my sentence for me, smiling. She paused, looking at the right side of Bee's bridle. "Here, look at this."

I blushed. "Oh my God. She really is a saint." In my rush, I'd buckled the cavesson over the cheek strap instead of under it. To a nonrider, a small detail. To a horsewoman, a grievous error. No wonder Bee had been grabbing one side of the bit harder than the other. For the whole lesson, the pressure had been uneven. Poor girl.

Caroline shrugged. Nothing ruffled her. "I should've checked your tack before you got up."

"If she's willing to put up with that, maybe she'll make a good lesson horse, after all!" With a hand on the reins, I started back for Bee's stall, Bee strolling next to me.

"Maybe so," Caroline agreed.

Back in Bee's stall, I took my time, ignoring my watch. Bee deserved it. "Would you like that, girl? Packing around little kids?"

Bee didn't answer. She gazed at me, her eyes blue-brown pools.

In February 1987, Sky Watch trotted into the ring at the Los Angeles Equestrian Center for the CARES (Center Auxiliary for Recruitment, Education, and Services) California National Horse Show. The three-time World's Grand Champion stallion who'd retired from the show ring, thought never to return, was trying to sneak back in. In front of a fraction of the audience he'd drawn at Louisville, Sky Watch took a victory pass with Mitch on board. Mitch rode him easy, never calling on his full potential, but he didn't need to. From the moment Sky Watch hit the gate, the class had belonged to him. Even working under wraps, the stud had outclassed the competition.

Sitting in Mitch's office nearly thirty-five years after that class, I watched Vicky lead a horse to the farrier. All I could see was the blacksmith's equipment cart, filled with metal tools that haven't changed shape in centuries. Rasps. Clinchers. Hammers. The way we use horses has changed over time, but some of the ways we care for them are timeless. "When everyone thought his career was over, Sky Watch wound up winning on the West Coast with you. What was that like?" I asked Mitch. Our time together was running out. Fern needed me home by her eight o'clock bedtime.

Mitch's phone rang. He pulled it from his pocket, then flipped the switch to silent. "That's just going to have to wait." Mitch might have been hard to get in front of, but once I had his attention, he didn't waver. "It was different. We had to be more careful, couldn't work him as hard. Michele called the shots. All the shots." He looked at me sidelong, hinting at tension between the two, but saying nothing about it. "Me, I was tickled just to see him again."

Mitch did more than see him. He won with him. All season long, Mitch and Sky Watch took victory passes up and down the West Coast shows. Rumor had it Sky Watch might head to Louisville, but he didn't show up. Then, toward the 1987 season's end, Michele told Mitch she'd ride him at the

Cow Palace. She didn't ask. She told. After all, Sky Watch belonged to her, not Mitch.

"It was not a discussion," Mitch said in his office, setting his chin. Whatever else Mitch thought about this agreement, and I'm sure he thought plenty, he wouldn't share with me. Michele took Mitch's place in Sky Watch's saddle. She was within her rights, and she was horsewoman enough to do it, but that couldn't have been easy for Mitch.

Since 1941, San Francisco's Cow Palace has been home to the Grand National, an exposition, livestock show, horse show, and rodeo. The Cow Palace itself is an oblong dome with a footprint over six acres large. While Saddlebreds don't show there anymore, they used to join the equestrian events. The bronc riders loved watching the peacocks of the show ring strut, and the Saddlebred folks got a kick out of calf roping.

From the moment Sky Watch and Michele trotted into the Cow Palace, they'd won the crowd. Sky Watch moved like a hurricane. No hint of his old injury. His time off had done him good. Also, he possessed the maturity of a ten-year-old horse. Other than his year off at stud to heal, Sky Watch had been showing for eight years. He knew his job—and he liked it. His pricked ears and wide eyes proved that fact. In a class of seven, Sky Watch made all the other horses obsolete. When Michele widened her hands and asked her stallion to rack on, he blazed away. The rodeo cowboys took to the rail, jumping on it to wave and holler for the fast-racking team. They'd never seen a horse move like that or a woman who could ride like that. Sky Watch left the Grand National with two more victory passes under his belt. Michele left with a plan.

When I asked Mitch about Michele's decision to show Sky Watch at Louisville the following year, he only repeated his earlier phrase: "It was not a discussion. I didn't make that decision." Forty years later, Mitch still respects his client enough not to air their grievances, whatever they were. "Michele and I have a good relationship now, but things were tense for a while there."

I tilted my head, ready for some gossip. "Oh yeah?"

"Yeah." Then Mitch changed the subject. "I saw her just a few months ago. We hadn't seen each other in years—years!—but we visited for about twenty minutes." Probably more like two hours. Mitch doesn't visit with anyone for just twenty minutes. "Even then, she was shy. Happy to talk to me, but she knows me. If anyone else walked up, she quieted down." Mitch looked me in the eyes. "So don't take it personally," he said. I'd told him how Michele had declined further interviews. "She doesn't like putting herself out there."

"I don't take it personally," I lied. When Michele emailed me to decline, it stung. Months later, my final email to her went unanswered. "It's too bad, though. It would have been great to get more of her perspective."

The CARES California National Horse Show opens the West Coast show season in early March. In 1988, four horses lined up for the five-gaited open stallion/gelding class, Sky Watch among them. Michele guided him to victory and then, in the championship, repeated the feat. Two months later, at the seaside Del Mar National Horse Show in San Diego County, she did the same. Sky Watch was back, and he was winning—with an amateur on board. An amateur who could ride. Michele looked like she belonged on the back of a stake horse, like she'd been waiting her whole life for the chance to do it. She probably had.

Before leaving for Kentucky, I'd revisited my single email interview with Michele. I could picture her sitting down at her computer, her face still wide-eyed and pretty, even in her seventies. After a long day at the barn, answering a stranger's questions must have been the last thing she wanted to do. One of my questions had been about the 1988 Five-Gaited World's Grand Championship—and about any conflict there might have been between her and Mitch around that time. Like Mitch, she'd kept her response vague and respectful: "There's a delicate balance between keeping a horse fit and well trained and keeping him sound. I don't know any trainer who doesn't struggle with this. If you're a knowledgeable horse owner, it's difficult when your 'in training' show horse struggles with soundness issues you think could have been prevented. Mitchell and I always wanted the best for Sky Watch."

I can read between the politeness and tell that Michele thought Mitch had failed to prevent some of Sky Watch's issues with injuries. It couldn't have been easy for her, living in California while her best horse stayed stalled in Kentucky. Between Mitch and Michele, I wasn't going to get to the bottom of that conflict. No matter what had transpired between the two of them, what intense conversations had passed in the Scripps Miramar barn, they each respected the other too much to vent their issues to me. Fair enough. Michele had ended her email interview with me with an ode to Mitchell Clark: "Sky Watch was one of the great ones, exciting to ride and exciting to watch. I'm convinced his greatness was due in large part to Mitchell Clark's phenomenal ability to develop the horse's exceptional athletic ability. I'm so very grateful to have had the opportunity to ride Mitchell Clark–trained horses."

No matter how the decision had been made, Michele entered Sky Watch in the gaited stake at Louisville in 1988. She wrote her name on the lines for owner, exhibitor, and trainer. Because she didn't get paid to train, she was still considered an amateur. No female had ever won the hallowed class, the Five-Gaited World's Grand Championship at the Kentucky State Fair. An amateur hadn't won it since 1924. Michele was both. She didn't know if she would win, but she sure hoped so. Only one horse stood in her way.

After seeing Imperator pass from one amateur to another and struggle under their hands, his former owners decided enough was enough. Judge and Dr. Meanor bought Perry back with every intention of showing him right where he belonged: in the open division, with Don Harris in the irons. Don, of course, was thrilled to have him back. He had all show season to get ready. Rumors stirred that Sky Watch might be back, with his amateur owner-exhibitor aboard.

On August 27, 1988, the Kentucky State Fairgrounds dripped with humidity, as always. The sun set behind the highway surrounding the grounds, the sky giving way from gray to black. In the Scripps Miramar barn aisle, the tack room curtain stirred, and Michele Macfarlane emerged. Turned out in a tailored navy-blue suit and derby, she wore lipstick that matched her tie and the bridle's browband—bright as the red in the red, white, and blue flag hanging from the fairgrounds' flagpole. She dressed conservatively but with class. She wanted her horse to stand out, not her suit. Michele might not have been the only woman headed to the ring, but she was the only woman amateur. Unlike her competition, she wasn't getting paid to train the beast she mounted.

Michele's gloved hands held the reins softly. Every other entry in her class had already trotted, racked, or cantered in the warm-up ring, but she preferred to wait until the last minute, saving her horse's energy for when it really counted. Anyone else would have been racing to the gate, but she stayed cool. Her horse was ready for her. She should know. She'd taken full ownership of his training, making her an amateur in name only. Most amateurs wouldn't last two seconds on Sky Watch, but Michele wasn't most amateurs. As the organist keyed "My Old Kentucky Home," she let Sky Watch groove into his trot.

As the gates closed, announcer Peter Doubleday smiled into his microphone. "We're all set to go, so we can sit down and get revved up as we start with the trot, please." Eleven examples of America's finest horseflesh, all wild-eyed and full of themselves, streamed around Freedom Hall, their knees pumping nearly to their chins with every step, their riders' long coats flapping. The crowd, decked out in summer-light suits or shiny, shoulder-padded dresses, clapped their approval. Late-1980s glitz ruled. Big hair. Teased bangs. You could almost smell the Aqua Net.

Michele knew Sky Watch faced opposition. Unlike the last time Imperator and Sky Watch had faced off, the other trainers thought they had a chance at winning. Imperator was fourteen, after all. Older for a gaited horse. And Mitch wasn't the one on Sky Watch that night. No way could an amateur, a lady amateur, do the job. Callaway's Mr. Republican. Callaway's Caper. Sultan's Matchmaker. The Phoenix. Admiral's Mark. Whirlwind's Golden Trigg. The Concert Master. Covino's Sir Talmage. Lunenburg County. The trainers of these horses thought they had a chance to beat not just one but two kings of the green shavings.

At the trot, Sky Watch flew. Michele posted loosely, sitting a beat or two, then rising up and down in time with each step, conserving her horse's energy. As she entered the far corner, she turned to look down the straightaway, strategizing as best as she could. *Stay slow*, her expression said. *We've got a long way to go.* Sky Watch had his own ideas. He rounded that corner and lengthened his stride, covering swaths of the arena, his hind legs snapping back and under him, his front legs reaching high. The patented Sky Watch trot. Michele hoped he'd pass that trot on to his offspring, but it was still too soon to tell. Not that she would tell anyone much of anything. Even on the biggest night of her life, she kept quiet.

Two big-haired, fair-going sisters ran into Michele in the hotel elevator before the show. A little starstruck, one got up the courage to ask, "So how many horses do you have going tonight?"

Michele replied, simply, "Oh, just the one." No bragging, no show of nerves. Behind the quiet politeness, though, loomed chutzpah. She knew she didn't need to name her horse. Everyone knew Sky Watch.

Imperator impressed as he trotted past the judge, tail trailing behind him. His hindquarters pulsed, one, two, one, two, and his neck flexed. Peter

Doubleday called for the walk, but not a single entry slowed. Each tried to make one more pass, juggling for position. To the audience's delight, when Don hit the end of his straightaway, rather than stop, he turned and cut across the middle of the arena. Audacious, even for Don Harris.

As Imperator finished his extra pass, Don lifted his hat to the stands and glanced at Michele. She didn't ruffle. Don and Imperator might as well have been invisible. Her face stayed unperturbed—the face a woman might make while gardening, not the one expected in a high-stakes sporting event on an animal that, if he'd wanted to, could have dropped his head, kicked his heels to the sky, and tossed her to the rafters. She let Sky Watch bounce in an animated walk to help her horse maintain momentum while still catching his breath. Even at a resting gait, the pair oozed power. Michele's restraint helped the stallion stay quiet—for the time being.

At the rack, Don cut Imperator to the left. He almost slipped, his hind foot skidding, but he caught his balance and picked up speed to reach Bonnie Burn and The Concert Master. For a moment, their silhouettes lined up, Imperator eclipsing The Concert Master, the two horses racking together for what seemed like minutes but lasted only seconds. Imperator pushed ahead, breaking the spell. The crowd boomed, and Bonnie's horse broke into a canter. "Back to the walk," called Peter Doubleday, knowing no one would actually walk yet. "Back to the walk now." Don racked Imperator halfway around the arena once again, which drew more thunder from the stands. Sky Watch stepped down from the rack and minced forward. He was performing, but Imperator was stealing the show. If the judges had called it then, it could have been Imperator's class.

At the reverse, Michele circled Sky Watch in a big teardrop to the rail, totally different from Mitch's usual run-over-the-judge cut across the center. Then, something shifted. Sky Watch brightened. His head sucked even further back into his neck. He soared down the straightaway at the trot, gaining speed and passing the others. Michele must have given him the signal. She sat back, easy, no sweat, and let Sky Watch speed up.

The organist sped up with him, increasing the tempo and intensity. Sky Watch's head stayed set, not a bobble from his neck, and his mane flew. He'd been waiting for this moment. At Peter Doubleday's call to "Walk your horses," instead of backing off, Michele and Sky Watch shot down the straightaway with one more trot, the horse's chest muscles popping. She could show her horse just as well as Don Harris could show his. The crowd gave them an ovation, yelling and clapping. When Michele finally pulled Sky Watch up, shavings sprayed three feet in the air. A sliding stop, like a base runner stealing home. Then, the slow gait. Staccato. Controlled. Imperator's gait, and Don Harris knew it. He peacocked his gelding around the arena, collecting whoops and hollers as he one-two-three-foured down the straightaways.

Then, time to turn them loose. The last rack of the class. "Now rack on! Let 'em rack." The crowd exploded. Sequins on jackets jiggled as women cupped their hands around their mouths and let rip a whoop. Many of these fans owned and rode Saddlebreds themselves, but some had never sat on a horse. They were there just for the buzz of competition. Kentucky moms and dads pointed out the top horses to their kids, the boys jittering in their seats, the girls spellbound and open-mouthed. Most of the spectators sided with Imperator or Sky Watch, of course, but some rooted for an underdog. One candidate was Callaway's Caper, an elegant bay ridden by trainer Jack Nevitt. By 1988, he'd lost the long sideburns he wore in the 1970s while showing the great Belle Elegant but still sported dark curls. Or maybe Sultan's Matchmaker, the one with the flashy white stockings on his hind feet, with the heavyset Johnny Lucas driving him forward with his considerable weight.

At the rack, Michele seemed to do nothing, maybe easing on the reins a hair, but really, she was aiding her stallion with each step, her hips sliding from side to side in the saddle, her fingers interpreting the pulsing tension in the reins and responding to it. Not that she thought about any of this. Just as no one thinks about breathing, she didn't need to think about shifting her weight around the turns to help her horse balance. As Sky Watch took off down the backstretch, the crowd sent him on, clapping and cheering loud enough that, more than thirty years later, one audience member can still pick out her voice among the noise.

When the eleven horses lined up, the audience tensed. They knew a workout was coming. The judges wanted to see seven horses back out on the rail—but not Imperator or Sky Watch. For a moment, in the stands, confusion reigned. Then, collectively, the crowd caught on. The judges were working out the fifth- through eighth-place horses, not the first- through fourth-place contenders. Once they realized what was going on, the audience enjoyed the horse show in front of them. They picked out a favorite and cheered. Really, though, they were waiting to see Imperator and Sky Watch hit the rail. Some even took a bathroom break.

During the first workout, Don dismounted and walked Imperator in circles in center ring. Michele stayed on Sky Watch, who, as *Saddle and Bridle*'s Joan Fry commented, "parked out quiet as a pleasure horse." At eleven years old, the young stud had matured. He knew he'd get his chance. Why waste his energy stomping around now? He'd face his rival soon enough.

The announcer called the seven horses back to center ring. Then, in the moment everyone had been waiting for, he sent out the four remaining contenders: The Phoenix and Callaway's Mr. Republican, but most importantly, Imperator and Sky Watch. The class's third act might as well have been a duel between Sky Watch and Imperator, just as it had been in 1982, 1983, and 1985.

Michele pressed her lips together, glanced around her, and sent Sky Watch flying, the stallion looking as fresh as he had at the beginning of the class. They passed Imperator on the outside rail—moving faster and covering more ground as they zoomed out of the turn. The crowd cheered them on, cheering louder when Imperator couldn't catch up. Lathered under the saddle, even hitting his top gear, Imperator didn't have the speed that Mitch had built into Sky Watch.

Gene Wright bopped into "Hello, Dolly," a horse show classic, and Peter Doubleday called the reverse trot. Again, Michele reversed Sky Watch to the rail, showing just how different her riding style was from Mitch's. Both were calm, collected exhibitors who stayed out of their horses' way, but Michele possessed an aloofness Mitch didn't have. Rather than battle it out in the scrum, she floated above it, choosing her spot on the rail and sticking to it instead of gunning for the horse in front of her. By owning her own space, she made everyone else move around her and Sky Watch.

Near the in-gate, Sky Watch slipped. The audience drew a sharp breath. Then, Sky Watch pulled himself forward as if nothing had happened. Michele's face never changed, never gave any indication that there might be a repeat of the 1985 disaster that had nearly cost the stud his career. With every step, though, it became clearer: Sky Watch was getting better, stepping higher. Even a half hour into the class, he still held reserves of energy.

When the judges finally came to their conclusion, it was unanimous, unlike Sky Watch's first World's Grand Championship win in 1982. At the top of their cards: Sky Watch. Sky Watch. Sky Watch. When she heard the announcement, Michele smiled, switched her whip, and trotted to the winner's circle. As the photographer snapped photos, the announcer trumpeted the news. Michele Macfarlane had just become the first woman to win the most prized jewel in the Saddlebred Triple Crown: the Five-Gaited World's Grand Championship.

At that, Freedom Hall imploded. The women in the stands stood up and pumped their fists, their teased bangs bobbing on their foreheads. Michele patted her stallion on his wet neck. So did the trophy presenters, risking sweat on their sequins for a chance to touch the champ. Throughout the photo session, Sky Watch chomped on the bit but stood statue-still, letting Michele hold him with loose reins.

As reserve champions, Don Harris and Imperator slow-gaited out of the arena to yells and whistles so loud the gelding nearly jumped off his feet. Even at an advanced age, he still had plenty of spunk. His leave-taking was bittersweet. Because of his age, the audience knew he wouldn't be back in Freedom Hall. He might have come in second, but Imperator had earned his standing ovation that night.

TV announcer Bill Carrington stepped into center ring to interview Michele Macfarlane. He took her hand, and Michele stiffened but kept her hand in his.

Bill leaned in. "Michele, were you surprised? When they called your number, everyone in the house stood up. Did you know that?"

"No, I didn't." Nervous laughter. "That's terrific."

"By the way, you beat a great horse."

Michele's voice steadied. She could talk horses. "Yes, he is, a very good one."

"You do all the work on this horse yourself?"

"Yes."

Bill realized he was going to have to ask better questions to get more than one-word answers out of her. "What are you going to do with him now?"

Finally, Michele relaxed. This, she could answer, and happily. "Take him home and raise world champion babies with him!"

During their victory pass, Michele's face cracked into a smile. How could it not? The woman who loved to win had finally done it. She'd won the big one. She would go on to repeat the feat with Memories' Citation in 1996, and then again in 2007 with CCV Casey's Final Countdown. Other women like Dena Lopez, Nancy Leigh Fisher, and Debbie Foley followed in her footsteps, but Michele will always be the first.

14

Let the Horse Lead the Way

In Mitch's office in 2021, thirty-three years after Michele's landmark 1988 class, I asked him what he thought of it. He'd been on the rail, I ventured, or maybe sitting with clients in the stands.

"No," he replied, lifting his chin. "I didn't need to see that."

I blinked. "Really?" Mitch confirmed it. It's hard to believe, but while Michele made history, Mitch stayed back at his stalls, packing up tack trunks. He didn't see a single step of the ride.

If the Mitch Clark who'd herded a two-year-old Sky Watch into a stall in 1979 could have seen the Mitch Clark of 1988, he would have seen success. More than he'd dared to imagine. The former stereo salesman now trained some of the best horses in the country for some of the best clients. Earlier that week, he'd won the three-gaited over-fifteen-two stake with Hocus Pocus Dominocus for owner (and eventually Mitch's second wife) Elisabeth Goth. Elisabeth Goth is the daughter of Bettina Bancroft, one of the then owners of Dow Jones. She's an incredible horsewoman and, like Michele, uses her fortune to further the American Saddlebred. The breed is lucky to have a woman with her clout in its corner. It didn't hurt Mitch to have some Dow Jones cash flowing into his training string along with Scripps Miramar money. If anyone had earned it, Mitch had. He'd put in the time with difficult horses like Sky Watch—and hundreds of others. Whether they went on to World's Championship titles or wound up cruising the B leagues, Mitch gave them the same level of focus and care.

In the end, Mitch had earned his reputation in his own right. He didn't hang off the driving lines of Garland Bradshaw. In the decade since Mitch first launched Mitchell Clark Stables, the trainer had become legendary for his ability to "put a good mouth" on a colt and instill a big-striding trot on any horse with the genetic material to handle it. Mitch learned both of those skills through working with Sky Watch. Mitch made Sky Watch—but also, Sky Watch made Mitch.

Even with Mitch's success, losing his seat on Sky Watch to Michele must have stung. Packing a tack trunk while Sky Watch engaged in his final battle with Imperator couldn't have felt good, although Mitch claimed that it didn't bother him. "It's part of the business." He shrugged. Maybe it is, but the connection between that man and that horse runs deep.

To this day, much of Mitch's brand centers on Sky Watch. On the Facebook page for Mitchell Clark Stables, Sky Watch trots across the profile picture. In Mitch's tack room, Sky Watch's bridle still hangs. In Mitch's office, Sky Watch's horseshoe is nailed next to the door. On Mitch's walls: Sky Watch, Sky Watch, Sky Watch. Even though Michele took him on his final victory pass in Freedom Hall, Sky Watch is still the main success story of Mitchell Clark Stables.

Eventually, Mitch and I stopped talking Sky Watch and moved on to the Saddlebred industry in general. "You know," he said, "I judged a little show in Ohio last fall, near the end of October. I like to help them out when I can." Mitch sat back and smiled fondly, like an uncle thinking about his country nephew. "There couldn't have been more than fifty people on the rail, but they were so loud, you wouldn't have known it."

"End of October?" I asked. "I know that show! Springfield, Ohio, right?" That's where My Queen Bee and I had taken second place in the park pleasure amateur class. "We were there year before last, before I had my daughter."

"That's the one," Mitch said. "At that show, everyone was having a big old time. People were visiting in the aisles, talking shit, right up until the end. Everyone packed up their own tack trunks—no grooms in sight—and half the people rubbed down their own rides. They might not have been on high-dollar horses, but nobody cared. They were laughing. If they won, they walked around bragging, but with a smile. If they lost, they promised their competition they'd be back next year." Mitch pantomimed the competitors at the little show. "You bet I'll be back in there to wipe butt with you next time!" he crowed, pointing. "I'm coming for you."

"It's a fun show," I agreed. Down in Mitch's arena, Vicky stood in front of an open stall door, talking to the farrier, who looked old enough to have shoed for Garland. I worried that his back would give out before the day was done. From decades of shoeing, the farrier's back was arched in a permanent hunch.

Mitch continued. "That's what this industry needs more of. Out here in Kentucky, it's all cutthroat. No one crosses lines and visits someone else's barn aisle. It's a goddamn shark tank."

Then, Mitch confirmed what I'd started to suspect, what Mike McIntosh had predicted. The Saddlebred industry was changing, all right, but parts of it were thriving. Maybe even growing. Saddlebreds weren't disappearing. They might show in different arenas and to a different audience than they did in the 1980s, but ten, twenty, a hundred years from now, I'll bet Saddlebreds will still be trotting to the tune of a tinkling organ.

"I'm a big fan of the grassroots horse show," I said. "You can get the whole family involved. Just last year, I convinced my mom to buy a horse. She's showing a nice walk-trot mare now. I love that my daughter will get to see that."

"Hot damn." Mitch sat up a little straighter. "That's what I mean. Your little girl won't just be going to grandma's house for dinner. She's going to the horse show. She's going to have the coolest grandma around, one who's up there on a horse, getting after it. That's the best."

"Right. And she's promising that mare will be little Fern's first horse, but me? She won't let me anywhere near that mare."

"You bet she won't!" Mitch laughed. "Oh, hell no." In his drawl, hell became a three-syllable word. "That's her horse." He nodded, grinning. "You go ride your own horse. You're the one who wound up with one who doesn't want to show."

I'd told Mitch about My Queen Bee, about how we were trying to find a job for her. He'd assured me that there was a place for all horses and we'd figure hers out eventually.

"I know, I know. It's my own fault, buying a horse off Facebook. Anyway," I said, "that's where I hope the future lies. Small shows, lots of them, with families going together and everyone enjoying themselves. That's what this is supposed to be about."

"Yes, ma'am." Mitch nodded, the lines in his face going somber. "Yes, it is."

Driving home from Danville that night, I pictured Fern's first horse show, her serious face growing even more serious as she entered the ring at a trot and focused on keeping her horse straight. Maybe she'd wear the same navy derby I used to wear, my mom's first show derby, the one sitting on a shelf in my office. *That's it*, I thought. *Fern is the key.* As long as horse-inclined moms like me can pass on an inheritance of horse-love to their daughters, the Saddlebred industry is going to be just fine.

I tried to explain all this to Ben one day while Fern was upstairs napping. "Careful," Ben said. "Saving the entire Saddlebred industry is a lot to saddle Fern with." I mock-glared at him. "Pun intended. But that's too much to lay on our daughter."

He's right, of course. "Logically, I know that. She might not even want to show. And that's fine." I glanced at the baby monitor, at Fern's sleeping form, at her cheek pressed against sheets printed with (what else?) horses. Other than her cheeks, which mirror mine when I was her age, Fern looks like her daddy. Minus the beard. "What I'm trying to say is that Saddlebreds will be okay. They're not going to die out. There will always be horse-crazy kids out there, ones who go to a show with their moms and get hooked, or people like my friend Linda."

Linda didn't ride as a child, but she'd had dreams about Saddlebreds before she even knew Saddlebreds existed. On a whim one day, she attended a horse show at the Indiana State Fairgrounds, and, when the first class of the night trotted in, she couldn't believe it. "For years," she'd said, "I'd been dreaming of horses who looked just like that. With that neck, that tail. I didn't know horses like that existed." Linda had grinned at the memory. "I walked straight to the show manager and asked where I could take lessons."

As long as those of us who love them keep trying to pass it on, the horses will be there.

"Okay," Ben said. "Okay. I just don't want our daughter to have to carry all those expectations."

"She won't," I said. "She'll only have to carry what she wants to." *Or*, I thought, *the horses will carry her, just as they've carried me.*

My oldest friend, Sarah, is a hippie who shaves her head, heats her home with a wood-burning stove, and studies under a Reiki master. She grew up with a mother who trailered her own jumping horses to shows and mucked her own stalls every morning, but the horse gene skipped Sarah. She knows as much about horse care as I do, but she'd rather ferment homegrown pickles than pick a hoof. Sarah has a theory about horsewomen. She thinks horses and the women who love them are made of atoms that all trace back to the same eons-old being. I love that idea. Horses and horsewomen, united as some celestial body in a time before time. That explanation fits better than anything Freud has come up with.

Whether Fern will be like Sarah, who respects her mom's horsiness but has no desire to ride, or like me, who followed in my own mother's stirrups, it's too soon to tell.

After one final horse show at the New York National, where Sky Watch and Michele won with ease, she retired him to stud at Scripps Miramar. By then, Michele said, Mitch had "worked out all the kinks." Other than ripping up blankets, a habit he never outgrew, Sky Watch had turned into a gentleman. I love picturing Sky Watch in the field, nibbling grass. I can imagine him seeing a horse in another pasture, snorting at him, and trotting to the fence with long strides. The show ring might have faded into memory, but the thrill of competition stayed keen.

A decade later, Sky Watch made one last trip from California to Kentucky, but not to show. He joined the Hall of Champions at the Kentucky Horse Park, taking the place of his former rival, Imperator. Until Sky Watch's death at age twenty-four, he represented the American Saddlebred at the country's premier equestrian park while continuing his job as a breeding stud. Only 176 of his foals are entered in the Saddlebred registry. Compared to his father, Flight Time, who sired nearly 700 registered American Saddlebreds, it's not much. Sky Watch's legacy in the breeding shed couldn't match the spectacle of him in the show ring. He was pure show horse, born to perform, not to breed. He wouldn't go on to change the breed forever, like his granddaddy Wing Commander had, but he did set a new bar for American Saddlebreds.

Forty years after Sky Watch's last show, he's still the horse everyone compares their horses to. "Look at that trot. That colt thinks he's Sky Watch," a railbird might whisper as a youngster enters the ring. "She sets her head like Sky Watch," a trainer will say, nodding toward a promising mare. In four decades, there hasn't been another Sky Watch since Sky Watch. That's a different kind of legacy, one that can't be measured in the number of a stallion's get.

Even with only 176 foals, many of Sky Watch's babies went on to produce their own babies. His bloodline lives.

A few weeks after my last visit to Kentucky to see Mitch, Bee walked onto a trailer, headed for a lesson barn forty-five minutes west of my house. There, if things worked out, she'd get to play outside every morning and then go inside for little girls to brush her mane, braid her tail, and ride her in an airy arena. This barn hosted camps all summer long, including Fairy Horse Camp, in which the girls painted the horses in glitter, braided ribbons into their manes, dressed in princess dresses, and then rode their mounts in a Fairy Parade. If Bee couldn't be the show horse I wanted, this was exactly where I'd hoped she would land. While saying goodbye to her the day before, tears had welled in my eyes.

"Bee, you're going to a new farm tomorrow. I won't be there to help you settle in, but it's a good place. Be on your best behavior, okay?" I told her while buckling her blankets. My hands worked automatically, crisscrossing the leg straps and clipping them to their rings. "This could be the perfect spot for you." She turned her head and rested her muzzle on my shoulder. Its weight steadied me. "Thank you for all you've taught me." The importance of a clear canter signal. The need to finish a pass, to never, ever pull down to a walk in front of the judge. More significantly, she'd taught me how to relax, how to let the horse lead the way, even if it meant changing plans.

I stood in front of Bee and pressed my cheek against the star on her forehead. "Here." My hands fumbled in my pockets. "There's a sweet potato for you." Her favorite treat. "And carrots." A close second. Her lips, soft and whiskered, brushed my palm. As I broke eye contact and walked away from her stall, she watched me. To my shame, my eyes couldn't meet her gaze.

By the following Saturday, Bee had a new home. Mary Lynn, the farm's owner, texted me. "These kids are going to disown me if I don't keep her." She sent me a photo of a little girl standing face-to-face with Bee. Bee's head was lowered so they could look each other in the eye. She stood relaxed, her ears and eyes soft. In her element. Some horses don't need to be show ring greats. Some are meant for a more important task, much less glamorous: teaching the next generation. Bee had found her job, and better yet, she'd found her place.

As it turned out, perfect timing.

Linda texted me a photo. A black horse trotting on the green shavings, his mane flying. As a business owner, she didn't mince words. "Cute horse," she said. "He's for sale." His name was My Boogie Nights. I looked his pedigree up online, my finger following his damline back one generation, then another. My eyes widened.

Sky Watch. He was Sky Watch's great-grandson.

In the photo, he's trotting high, his shoulders popping. The hooked tips of his ears almost touch. In the class in which it was taken, it turned out, he didn't get a ribbon. Talented, but not talented enough to land in the top eight of a twenty-horse class at Louisville. Maybe he'd made a mistake—come off his feet, say, or taken a wrong canter lead. Now, three years after that photo, one of Mike's clients had accepted him as partial payment for a horse she'd sold. In turn, she was willing to sell him cheap if he could sell quickly and stay in the barn. Still, he was out of my price range.

"You should try him," my mom said from her kitchen stove, stirring a skillet of rice and poblano peppers.

"I'd love to," I said, pulling Fern away from my mom's coffee table, where she was swinging a leg up as if mounting a horse. Months still from walking, she was already pulling up on every piece of furniture she could find. "But there's no point. I can't buy him."

My mom stepped away from the stove. "Maybe I can help. We'll go in together."

"Really?" I asked.

"Yes, really. You know, you talked me into moving here, then you talked me into buying my mare, which was the best decision ever, but then you stopped showing." She looked at Fern, who was now trying to clamber onto an ottoman with the determination of an Everest mountaineer. "For a fabulous reason, of course." Fern dropped back to all fours and gaped at her before resuming her climb. "But I wanted this to be something we do together. I can watch Fern while you show," she said. "Think about it. He's so cute! You'd have a lot of fun with him."

I didn't think long. That night, while the tub filled for Fern's bath, I texted Mike. The following Saturday, in the chill of Mike's arena, my breath puffed around me in white clouds. Mike walked My Boogie Nights in, then parked him out by the wall. He tapped it with a whip, and the gelding's ears swiveled and pinned, his nostrils flaring. The swimsuit-model pose, just like in the stake classes.

Mike rode him for me first, then let me climb on. The gelding walked off with his head up and ears forward. I squeezed him into a trot and, right away, felt it. The pump of a Saddlebred ready to show. In center ring stood my mom, along with a half dozen other women. The barn family. They stopped their conversations and started watching.

Mike crouched low and waved his hat, giving the horse something to look at. My Boogie Nights squatted down behind and rose up in front. I kept him moving forward, giving little squeezes with my calves, telling him it was okay. The women in the middle cheered, just as if we were at a horse show. My mom held her cell phone up, capturing the whole thing on camera.

"Get your hands up," Mike yelled. "Ride like he's a show horse."

My hands rose. The buzz in my ears disappeared. Yes, this felt right. I was no Michele Macfarlane, but I could pilot a show horse around an arena. Down one rail we went, then a gentle bump, left to right, on the bridle to build collection. We pointed straight for the opposite wall, heads up, and marched. One, two. One, two. My fingers tingled. My spine crackled. A sun was burning in the center of my chest. Yeah, boy. The women in the center clapped and whooped as Sky Watch's great-grandson churned past them, his knees popping up with every step.

In front of me, an arched neck, a flowing mane, and one perked set of ears, framing everything. I smiled. My kind of horizon.

Epilogue

On one of my Kentucky trips, I stopped at the Kentucky Horse Park. I wandered through the Hall of Champions, where Sky Watch had once stood. In February, on a weekday, the whole park stood deserted. Even the stalls gaped empty. All the horses munched grass in the black-fenced pastures, enjoying the late-winter sun. I wondered which stall had belonged to Sky Watch, to Imperator, but the park employees only shrugged. The brass nameplates on every stall shone. The wooden stall doors gleamed. No twists of hay blew through the aisle. No plugs of manure stuck to the concrete floor. The barn didn't have the dirt and grime of a working show barn—but it still emanated that beautiful barn smell. Leather and dung. Hay and shavings.

The horses stalled here, the ones now turned out to pasture, didn't compete anymore. Their job was to represent their respective breeds. During the park's busy season, they paraded twice daily while an announcer offered a litany of each breed's traits. The Thoroughbred's speed. The Quarter Horse's muscle. The Standardbred's trot and pace. The Saddlebred's showiness. I like to imagine Sky Watch during these parades. Even at twenty-four years old, he'd hear the crackle of the announcer's voice and remember the roar of Freedom Hall in 1982 and 1983. For a moment, his head would lift and set, his whole body ready to break into that famous trot, just as if he wore the bridle Mitch still kept in his tack room.

After four years of studying Sky Watch, of leaning into the question of why Saddlebreds matter, I didn't have any answers. At least, not easy ones. Sky Watch's story doesn't mirror my own. Neither does Mitch's or Michele's. My Queen Bee didn't turn a corner and make her Louisville debut to win a blanket of roses and a victory pass on the green shavings. Keeper of the Stars hasn't come to me in a dream and forgiven me for giving up on horses all those years ago.

Instead, the answer is much more complicated. Do Saddlebreds matter? Not really, no. Not to the rest of the world. Without them, the sun would continue to rise and set. The stock market would tick on. Cities would continue their encroachment on the farmland around them. Most people live their entire lives without knowing American Saddlebreds exist, and they seem to do just fine. To those of us who do know them, though, they're portals to an otherworldly place, to a space outside of time. To ride an American Saddlebred is to trot with God.

Sky Watch represents the best American Saddlebreds have to offer. He is the benchmark against which all other Saddlebreds are measured. Making sense of the Saddlebred means making sense of him. Not his bloodlines. His power, his performance. Watching old Sky Watch videos made me want to climb on a horse, hear the ringmaster's bugle, and answer the announcer's call to show at a trot. One day, I'll share Sky Watch with Fern. He reminds me that magic on horseback exists—and it's better when shared.

Standing in Lexington, Kentucky, and surrounded by pastures dotted with all types of horses, from drafts to ponies and everything in between, I had no trouble picturing a future filled with Saddlebreds. For my daughter. For me.

In October 2022, at a local show in northern Indiana, My Boogie Nights and I stood in the lineup in the center of an arena, coliseum-style seating rising around us. As usual, most of the seats were empty, but Jack, as I called him, had just performed as if he'd been competing in front of a crowd of thousands. He didn't care whether twenty people or twenty thousand watched him. He was doing his job and doing it well, and he knew it. All I had to do was stay out of his way and keep him on his feet. Throughout the ride, my lips kept twitching into a smile.

While we waited for the judge's decision, I made small talk with the woman on the horse next to me. "How was your ride tonight?"

"Not bad," she said. "Better than last time."

"That's all we can hope for." My coat, a new-to-me item bought used that year, fit me perfectly. It buttoned around my postpartum waist easily and flared over my hips. Its pale champagne color stood out against Jack's coat, which I smoothed with one hand. My eyebrows probably needed to be plucked, and my face had never quite grown into my nose, but still, sitting on that horse, after pushing him to a ride that good, I felt beautiful.

In the stands, my mom marched up and down the stairs with Fern, who was finally walking. My barn family sat in a knot at one end of the arena, and I could see them nodding with approval and glancing my way. Linda shot me two thumbs up, her smile spreading.

When the announcer's microphone crackled on, I kept my gaze lowered. "We're ready to announce the winner of the Amateur Show Pleasure Championship." Could it be me? Win or lose, I'd had a good ride. "Congratulations go to number 284, My Boogie Nights, owned and shown by Emma Hudelson and trained at Mike McIntosh Stables in Indiana."

My jaw dropped, my face splitting into a grin as wide as if we'd won at Louisville. I leaned over and patted Jack firmly on the shoulder. Mike's assistant trainer Brock ran into the arena to meet me at the winner's circle.

"Where do I go?" I asked him as he fastened a ribbon around Jack's neck and added one to my coat. "What do I do? I haven't won in twenty years!"

Brock laughed. "Just follow my lead. It'll come back to you."

With my barn family cheering from the stands, my mom jumping up and down while holding Fern in her arms, I took my victory pass, trotting Jack where Brock pointed me to go. Jack trotted big and bold, responding to all the excitement as if he'd been made for this. He had. He's an American Saddlebred. A descendant of Sky Watch. A show horse. My show horse.

I'll never forget my first win on Jack, but that isn't my favorite memory of him. Two months earlier, at the Dayton Horse Show, where I'd shown Bee two years earlier, Jack and I left the show ring with a third-place ribbon in our championship class, beating six other horses for a spot in the top three. It had been a good ride. Unlike Bee, Jack relaxed at the horse show. While the announcer's voice crackled over the PA system and the crowd around the arena whooped, he lowered his head and napped. A true performer.

After I'd rubbed Jack dry, Brock led him out of the stall. With the horse show ruckus in the background, he parked Jack out and asked him to stand. Brock wore the same button-up shirt he'd worn when helping Bee and me into the ring two years earlier. The khakis, though, were probably new. A horse trainer is hard on pants.

"Go ahead," Brock said. "Put her on."

I gripped Fern around the waist and lifted her onto his back.

"Now, Martha," he said, turning to my mom, "you grab the lead."

My mom hopped over and stood at Jack's head. Jack seemed to know he was posing for a photo. He pricked his ears and arched his neck. I kept my grip around Fern's waist, holding her on the horse. She didn't clap her hands with glee, but she didn't seem unhappy either. Fern had always been a serious baby, and she took this new horseback vantage point in stride. Her first time on a show horse.

The picture of that moment hangs next to my desk. My mom, arms cocked to hold the lead rope, grinning as big as she does when she wins on her mare—which she does, often. Me, still in my show bun and makeup, with the type of smile I have in the show ring when I relax, holding my daughter up on my horse. Fern, lips pursed, looking a little puzzled, her eyes focused on the neck rising from the shoulders in front of her, one hand tangled in Jack's mane. Three generations. One horse. A Saddlebred legacy.

Acknowledgments

This book moved from idea to reality through the work, time, and support of many, many people.

Thank you to University Press of Kentucky editor Patrick O'Dowd, who believed in this project as soon as he heard about it and who has supported it through all the twists and turns since. Not all editors give their authors as much freedom as I received while writing this book, and I won't forget that. The University Press of Kentucky was the right press to bring this book through the in-gate, and I'm grateful to the Horses in History series editor, Jamie Nicholson, for creating such a friendly stable of books to join.

To my early readers, who offered so much cheerleading and gentle direction—Angela Hofstetter, Sarah Haak, Toni Judnitch, Yalie Kamara, and the entire workshop group at the University of Cincinnati—this book is better for having your eyes on the earliest versions of the earliest chapters. Sarah, thank you for letting me panic-email you pages as I neared a final draft and giving me the reassurance I needed. My thanks, too, go to the accountability group led by Tessa Fontaine and Annie Hartnett, who helped me find the rhythm I needed to push this project to the end and reminded me that, yes, I am a real writer (whatever that is). *Flying Island Journal*, the literary journal of the Indiana Writers Center, published "Damline," an earlier draft of an excerpt from this manuscript. Thanks for putting my words in print.

I wrote this book in between trips to the barn. Mike McIntosh Stables and Roselane Farm, thank you for existing, for creating such caring homes for Saddlebreds in Indiana.

I'm lucky to have had illuminating mentors and teachers to brighten my writing path and keep me from stumbling into the darkness. Dr. Kristen Iversen, who read multiple full manuscript drafts, you amaze me. I'm a better writer and literary citizen because of you. Thanks to your patience and guidance, my sentences are stronger and my instincts are sharper. You changed the way I write and think about writing. Chris Bachelder, thank you for teaching me that plot is, actually, a thing. Your workshop boot-camped this book into something readable. Dr. Sharrell Luckett, you were brave enough to saddle up for this project, and I'm so grateful for your insights and encouragement. I'll forever be indebted to my Butler University mentors, Dr. Hilene Flanzbaum, Susan Neville, Chris Forhan, and Dr. Andy Levy, who each saw something I didn't yet see in myself. Thank you for pushing me to keep writing, keep reading, and keep trying.

A whole community of horsemen and horsewomen came together to help me write this book. My deep, deep gratitude goes to Mitch Clark. You spent hour after hour of your precious time with me. Thank you for the stories, and thank you for trusting me to tell Sky Watch's story. That trust means everything. To Michele Macfarlane, thank you for giving me the green light. This book couldn't exist without you. Angela Hofstetter, you're important enough that you deserve to be here twice. Thank you for our Fridays. Without you, horses wouldn't be back in my life. There would be neither Saddlebreds nor *Sky Watch*. You changed my life. Kim Skipton, who read the entire manuscript and fact-checked all my American Saddlebred history, you made sure I stayed true to the record. Thank you. To Rain Posner, my research assistant, you were my eyes and hands in Lexington. I couldn't have done this without you. To Saddlebred historians like Brendan Heintz and Becky Damron, I'm so very glad you're doing the hard work of preserving the breed and creating online communities to share your memories and treasures. Your labor made writing this book easier, and your pages gave me access to information and people I never would have found otherwise. To all of you who sent me Sky Watch photos, videos, posts, magazines, and trivia, thank you. Thank you isn't enough to cover all your postage, time, and care, but still. My gratitude is yours. To every trainer, caretaker, exhibitor, enthusiast, and owner who shared your ringside experiences of Sky Watch, thank you. You made this book richer. Don Harris, I still can't believe I have your cell phone number. Thank you for sharing your time and your memories.

Every parent who writes knows the importance of good childcare. I've got a unicorn in Angeli Cauley. Thank you for being Fern's bestie, for being a part of our family, and for working extra hours so I could write.

Mom, I wouldn't be the writer, rider, or woman I am today without you. Thank you for your indomitable energy and lifelong devotion. Thank you for hundreds of show buns—my scalp has the scars to prove it. Thank you for the legacy of Saddlebreds. Thank you for showing me how to be a mother.

To the rest of my amazing family, to Pop, Ellen, Chris, and Dan, thank you for always supporting me in writing, riding, and life. Few horse girls have a family as cool as mine.

Fern, my little wonder. You are the reason. You've shown me my most important life's work. I never knew how much I'd love being a mother.

Ben, you didn't know you were marrying a horse girl, but you've never turned back. No one has been more supportive than you. Without you, I wouldn't be writing. I'm grateful for your belief in me and in my craft. I love you, and I love our life together.

To the horses: Glamour Boy, Keeper, Bee, and Jack. You are my mirrors, showing me my true self, for better or worse.

And finally, Sky Watch. You deserve every victory pass you ever took and more. Thank you for inspiring generations of riders. Now, your story belongs to the world.

Sources Consulted

Prologue

Shepherd, E. Lee. "This Being Court Day." *Virginia Magazine of History and Biography* 103, no. 4 (October 1995): 459–60. https://www.jstor.org/stable/4249539.

1. Seeing Sky Watch

American Saddlebred Horse and Breeders Association. *CH Sky Watch Pedigree*. Lexington, KY: American Saddlebred Horse and Breeders Association Registry Records, 1979.

Around the Arena: Horse Show Nostalgia. "Mrs. Judson ('Della') Large [. . .] in front of Chicago's Ambassador Hotel [. . .]." Facebook, May 8, 2019. https://www.facebook.com/photo/?fbid=730112074981181&set=a.647738059885250.

———. "1985—Receiving the ASHA Breeder's Award." Facebook, July 6, 2020. https://www.facebook.com/SaddlebredMemoirs/photos/a.1533174526967555/2681413748810288/.

Budd, Abraham or Sidney. *Joanne*. 1951. Photograph.

———. *Sponging Off*. 1951. Photograph.

Chicago Sun-Times. *1950 Press Photo Mrs. Judson Large/Horses/Equestrian/Chicago*. June 5, 1950. Photograph. Historic Images Outlet. https://outlet.historicimages.com/products/rsd06055.

"Flight Time Stud Services Ad." 1982. Sky Watch archive, American Saddlebred Museum, Lexington, KY.

Historic Images Outlet. *1954 Press Photo Socialite Mrs. Judson Large Modeling in Key Club Fashion Show*. January 1954. Photograph. https://outlet.historicimages.com/products/rsd05813.

———. *1957 Press Photo Mrs. Judson Large with Spring Straw Cap at Annual Luncheon*. January 5, 1957. Photograph. https://outlet.historicimages.com/products/rsd05811.

Pardieck, Mary-Ann. Phone interview by Emma Hudelson. Indianapolis, March 15, 2022.

Sargent, H. Leon. *Joan Robinson at Pin Oak*. n.d. Photograph.

Taylor, Louis. *Anne Durham*. Photograph. In *The Horse America Made*, 186. Louisville, KY: American Saddle Horse Breeders Association, 1944.

2. Twice a Day

Around the Arena: Horse Show Nostalgia. "Midwest Charity memories 1969 [. . .] 'Aries Golden Gift [. . .].'" Facebook, June 12, 2018. https://www.facebook.com/SaddlebredMemoirs/photos/a.1531596870458654/2031882333763436/.

Clark, Mitchell. Personal interview by Emma Hudelson. Danville, KY, March 11, 2020.

"Fire Kills 32 Horses." *Messenger* (Madison, KY), June 13, 1964.

"Garland Bradshaw Stables' Complete Dispersal Sale." *American Saddlebred* (blog), April 28, 2019. http://theamericansaddlebred.blogspot.com/2019/04/42819-garland-bradshaw-stables-complete.html.

Horse World, January 1979.

"Ridgefields Farm Dispersal." 1953. Garland Bradshaw archive, American Saddlebred Museum, Lexington, KY.

Vaught, Larry. "Legendary Horseman Garland Bradshaw Dies." *Advocate-Messenger* (Danville, KY), March 15, 1982.

———. "Retirement Not for Bradshaw." *Advocate-Messenger* (Danville, KY), August 3, 1979.

3. Sparkle and Sweat

American Saddlebred Respectful Discussions. "Sky Watch [. . .] Two-Year-Old Gaited Stake [. . .]." Facebook, May 28, 2020. https://www.facebook.com/groups/694419460609529/posts/3275948712456578/.

Clark, Mitchell. Personal interview by Emma Hudelson. Danville, KY, March 11, 2020.

Macfarlane, Michele. Email interview by Emma Hudelson. Indianapolis, May 13, 2020.

"Moore Rides Winner." *Advocate-Messenger* (Danville, KY), July 17, 1979.

Phillips, Lance. *The Saddle Horse*. Cranbury, NJ: A. S. Barnes, 1964.

Sky Watch and Mitchell Clark: Two-Year-Old Five Gaited World Champion. 1979. Photograph. Sky Watch archive, American Saddlebred Museum, Lexington, KY.

Vaught, Larry. "Retirement Not for Bradshaw." *Advocate-Messenger* (Danville, KY), August 3, 1979.

Wemlinger, June. Phone interview by Emma Hudelson. Indianapolis, January 22, 2020.

4. Difficult Horses

Bullard, Ann. "People's Choice—Michele Macfarlane." Saddle Horse Report Online, February 25, 2008. https://www.saddlehorsereport.com/news/peoples-choice-michele-macfarlane-ch-ccv-caseys-final-3894.

Conley Family. "The Conley Family: A Uniquely American Story." Conley Trust. http://conleytrust.com/.

Gregory, James. "California Migration History 1850–2017." America's Great Migrations. University of Washington. https://depts.washington.edu/moving1/California.shtml.

"A History of Transporting Horses: Museum of the Horse." Museum of the Horse, January 26, 2022. https://www.museumofthehorse.org/a-history-of-transporting-horses/.

National Horseman. "Body Language Controls a Horse Jim Aikman Bob Ruxer Rob Tanner." YouTube, August 16, 2013. https://www.youtube.com/watch?v=QWyyV9mrRIs.

"Sky Watch and Ken Lawson at Del Mar." 1980. Advertisement. Sky Watch archive, American Saddlebred Museum, Lexington, KY.

Sullivan, Paul. "Custom Stalls and Air-Ride Suspension: How Derby Horses Travel in Style." *New York Times*, May 5, 2017. https://www.nytimes.com/2017/05/05/your-money/06wealth-race-horses-kentucky-derby.html.

"Transport of Horses." Veterian Key, July 8, 2016. https://veteriankey.com/transport-of-horses/.

5. The People's Horse

American Saddlebred Horse and Breeders Association. *CH Imperator Pedigree*. Lexington, KY: American Saddlebred Horse and Breeders Association Registry Records, 1974.

Clark, Mitchell. Interview by Bill Keith. Facebook Live. Stayner, Ontario, February 27, 2021.

"Clark and Dedman Ride Winners." *Advocate-Messenger* (Danville, KY), August 20, 1980.

Donaldson, Jamie. *Imperator at Lexington*. Photograph. Imperator archive, American Saddlebred Museum, Lexington, KY.

"Dr. Josephine L. Earlywine Wilkinson (1920–1988)." Find a Grave. Added October 23, 2006. https://www.findagrave.com/memorial/16298394/josephine-1-wilkinson.

"Hugs and Kisses for Imperator and Don Harris." Magazine clipping. Imperator archive, American Saddlebred Museum, Lexington, KY.

"I'll Have What She's Having: Marion Brown Turns 100." *Barista of Bloomfield Ave* (blog), June 21, 2005. https://baristanet.typepad.com/barista/2005/06/happy_100.html.

"Layman John Cuthbert Wilkinson, 1919–2016." Obituary. *Chicago Tribune*, January 6, 2017. https://www.legacy.com/us/obituaries/chicagotribune/name/layman-wilkinson-obituary?id=2732925.

"Limited Edition Shiflet Run." Advertisement. Imperator archive, American Saddlebred Museum, Lexington, KY.

National Horseman. "Don Harris World Championship Rides." YouTube, August 15, 2013. https://www.youtube.com/watch?v=6or9Bvu0L-U.

"1980 KSF Write-Up." Magazine clipping. Imperator archive, American Saddlebred Museum, Lexington, KY.

Saddle and Bridle, September 1980.

"Saddlebred Sidewalk List 1989–2018." American Saddlebred Museum, 2018. https://uploads-ssl.webflow.com/62d81c90cec53793e2215b1e/649dab72267d 293c10e8af2e_Saddlebred_Sidewalk_List_2023.pdf.

"A Talk with Don Harris." Richfield Video Archive, June 2015. https://richfield videoarchive.vhx.tv/videos/rc15-a-talk-with-don-harris.

"The 2004 Year in Review Is Dedicated to Don Harris." *Saddle Horse Report*, 2004. https://www.saddlehorsereport.com/user_files_1/News/1ED_DonHarris _YIR04.pdf.

"Two Views of the Famous Slow Gait." Magazine clipping. Imperator archive, American Saddlebred Museum, Lexington, KY.

Vaught, Larry. "Staffords Combine Talents to Win at Mercer." *Advocate-Messenger* (Danville, KY), July 27, 1980.

"Wanda Menton." Obituary. Saddle Horse Report Online, February 16, 2004. https://www.saddlehorsereport.com/news/obituary-wanda-menton-1012.

Wasemiller, E. R. *Photo of Wooden Sculpture of CH Imperator*. Imperator archive, American Saddlebred Museum, Lexington, KY.

"WCHS1980—Championship Night Highlights." Richfield Video Archive, 1980. https://richfieldvideoarchive.vhx.tv/videos/wchs1980-championship-night -highlights.

6. The Red Mile

Bouvier, Jeanne. "A Highlight on Strokes." *Interior Journal* (Stanford, KY), March 12, 1981.

"Breed Registration Trends." In *2021 Journal of the American Saddlebred*, 67. Louisville, KY: Innovative, 2021.

"Clark Wins on Sky Watch." *Advocate-Messenger* (Danville, KY), November 27, 1981.

Cole, John R., Jr. "Horse Owners See Grandstand Fire as Great Loss to Industry." *Advocate-Messenger* (Danville, KY), August 14, 1981.

Cole, John R., Jr., and Linda Gordon. "Arson Suspected to Be Cause of Mercer Grandstand Fire." *Advocate-Messenger* (Danville, KY), August 16, 1981.

"Danville Trainer Seeks More Trophies." *Messenger* (Madisonville, KY), September 2, 1981.

"Don Harris Has Two UPHA Horses of the Year." Magazine clipping. Imperator archive, American Saddlebred Museum, Lexington, KY.

Harris, John. "Imperator Coasts to 5-Gaited Title." *Lexington Herald*, July 19, 1981.

"Local Squad Answers Calls." *Advocate-Messenger* (Danville, KY), March 24, 1981.

"Muhammed Ali Meets Imperator." *National Horseman*. Magazine clipping. Imperator archive, American Saddlebred Museum, Lexington, KY.

Saddle and Bridle, July 1981.

Saddle and Bridle, August 1981.

Saddle and Bridle, October 1981.

"Shaman Surprises His Rider." *Advocate-Messenger* (Danville, KY), August 21, 1981.

"Sky Watch American Royal advertisement 1981." Magazine clipping. Sky Watch archive, American Saddlebred Museum, Lexington, KY.

"Sky Watch at Lexington." Magazine clipping. Sky Watch archive, American Saddlebred Museum, Lexington, KY.

"Squad Transports Three." *Advocate-Messenger* (Danville, KY), March 5, 1981.

Ulack, Richard B., et al. *Lexington and Kentucky's Inner Bluegrass Region*. Indiana, PA: National Council for Geographic Education, Indiana University of Pennsylvania, 1994, p. 14. https://files.eric.ed.gov/fulltext/ED383629.pdf.

Vaught, Larry. "Area Horsemen Ready for Louisville." *Advocate-Messenger* (Danville, KY), August 16, 1981.

Wall, Maryjean. "Clark Feels Pressure with Sky Watch." *Lexington Herald*, July 14, 1981.

———. "Pressure on Clark, Sky Watch at Junior League Horse Show." *Lexington Herald*, July 14, 1981.

Wallace, John Hankins. *The Horse of America*. Wilmington, DE: Scholarly Resources, 1973.

"World's Largest Hog." Weakley County History, January 28, 2019. https://weakleycountyhistory.com/martin-tn-worlds-largest-hog/.

7. No Other Horses Will Do

American Saddlebred Museum. "Horse Soldiers." Wall text. American Saddlebred Museum, Lexington, KY.

———. "Out of the Shadows: Black Horsemen in Saddlebred History." YouTube, March 9, 2018. https://www.youtube.com/watch?v=fXH6ByafBf8.

Burke, Jane B. "Horse Shows." *Louisville Courier-Journal*, July 4, 1982.

"Garland Bradshaw Was Noted Horseman." *Lexington Herald-Leader*, March 16, 1982.

"Hickey, Clark Win Stakes." *Advocate-Messenger* (Danville, KY), June 9, 1982.

Indiana Historical Bureau. "Morgan's Raid." Indiana State Government. https://www.in.gov/history/3993.htm.

Saddle and Bridle, July 1982.

"Sky Watch Wins at AZ." Magazine clipping. Sky Watch archive, American Saddlebred Museum, Lexington, KY.

"Sky Watch at Devon Ad." Magazine clipping. Sky Watch archive, American Saddlebred Museum, Lexington, KY.

Vaught, Larry. "Imperator Will Not Show at Mercer Co." *Advocate-Messenger* (Danville, KY), July 21, 1982.

8. A Dance of Sensation

"About Our Cover." Magazine clipping, Sky Watch archive, American Saddlebred Museum, Lexington, KY.

"Article about Sky Watch Painting." Magazine clipping. Sky Watch archive, American Saddlebred Museum, Lexington, KY.

"Clarks Have First Child." *Advocate-Messenger* (Danville, KY), September 15, 1982.

"Home Town Hero Wins." *Advocate-Messenger* (Danville, KY), August 19, 1982.

"Louisville Program Cover." Photograph. Imperator archive, American Saddlebred Museum, Lexington, KY.

Rees, Jennie. "Dazzling Sky Watch Surprises Imperator." *Louisville Courier-Journal*, August 23, 1982.

Saddle and Bridle, October 1982.

"Sky Watch 1982 KSF Victory Pass Ad." 1982. Magazine clipping. Sky Watch archive, American Saddlebred Museum, Lexington, KY.

Vaught, Larry. "Clark, Sky Watch Write Happy Ending with Five-Gaited Victory." *Advocate-Messenger* (Danville, KY), August 23, 1982.

———. "Clark Won't Risk Sky Watch's Care for Title." *Advocate-Messenger* (Danville, KY), August 15, 1982.

"World's Championship Horse Show 1982—Stake Night." Richfield Video Archive, 1982. https://richfieldvideoarchive.vhx.tv/world-s-championship-horse-show/season:40.

9. The Horse He'd Wanted to Beat

Clark, Mitchell. Interview by Bill Keith. Facebook Live. Stayner, Ontario, February 27, 2021.

———. Personal interview by Emma Hudelson. Shelbyville, KY, June 21, 2020.

Dauner, John T. "Five-Gaited Mare Walks Off with Classics Grand Championship Trophy." *Kansas City (MO) Times*, November 10, 1982.

"Devon Photo Clippings." Magazine clippings. Sky Watch archive, American Saddlebred Museum, Lexington, KY.

Harris, Don. Phone interview by Emma Hudelson. Indianapolis, October 29, 2022.

National Horseman, October 1983.

"On the Cover." Kentucky State Fair program clipping. Sky Watch archive, American Saddlebred Museum, Lexington, KY.

"Our History." American Royal, May 19, 2021. https://www.americanroyal.com/about/our-history/.

Rees, Jennie. "A Relaxed Imperator Takes Title in 5-Gaited." *Louisville Courier-Journal*, June 19, 1983.

Saddle and Bridle, July 1983.

Simmons, Jane E. "Lee Shipman: Kentucky Hall of Fame Trainer." Art by Crane. https://www.artbycrane.com/americansaddlebredhorses/leeshipman.html.

"Sky Watch Wins Again." *Advocate Messenger* (Danville, KY), February 24, 1983.

Sutter, Ashley. "Harris: Legendary Trainer Returns to Simpsonville." *Sentinel-News* (Shelbyville, KY), August 9, 2015. https://www.sentinelnews.com/content /harris-legendary-trainer-returns-simpsonville.

"The 2004 Year in Review Is Dedicated to Don Harris." Saddle Horse Report Online, 2004. https://www.saddlehorsereport.com/user_files_1/News/1ED _DonHarris_YIR04.pdf.

"2006 Audrey Pugh Gutridge Award." Saddle Horse Report Online, 2006. https:// www.saddlehorsereport.com/news/audrey-pugh-gutridge-award-2528.

Vaught, Larry. "Harris Eager to Test Clark, Sky Watch Again." *Advocate-Messenger* (Danville, KY), July 21, 1983.

———. "When Moore Heals Hero Will Be Ready." *Advocate-Messenger* (Danville, KY), June 5, 1983.

Girdler, Avis. "WC New York New York and Richard Clouse, 1981: American Saddlebred Horses, American Saddlebred, Saddlebred." Pinterest. https://www .pinterest.com/pin/445082375653292527/.

10. The Duel

Bennett, Scott. Phone interview by Emma Hudelson. Indianapolis, April 7, 2019.

Mattsen, Scarlett. Phone interview by Emma Hudelson. Indianapolis, March 2022.

McLellan, Dennis. "The Recession Is Forcing Some Horse Owners to Sell Their Stock: Many Animals Are Sent to Slaughter; End of the Trail." *Los Angeles Times*, April 23, 1991. https://www.latimes.com/archives/la-xpm-1991-04-23 -vw-564-story.html.

"1983 WCHS—Five Gaited Stake Imperator & Sky Watch." Richfield Video Archive, 1983. https://richfieldvideoarchive.vhx.tv/videos/1983-wchs-five-gaited -stake-imperator-skywatch.

"1983 WCHS—Imperator Class 130." Richfield Video Archive, 1983. https://rich fieldvideoarchive.vhx.tv/world-s-championship-horse-show/season:39/videos /1983-wchs-five-gaited-stake-imperator-Sky Watch.

"1983 WCHS—Sky Watch Stallion Stake." Richfield Video Archive, 1983. https:// richfieldvideoarchive.vhx.tv/world-s-championship-horse-show/season:39/videos /1983-wchs-five-gaited-stake-imperator-Sky Watch.

Rees, Jennie. "Sky Watch Sparks Warm Welcome in His Winning Return." *Louisville Courier-Journal*, August 16, 1983.

———. "Suspense, Mystery: The Show Goes On." *Louisville Courier-Journal*, August 14, 1983.

"Remembering a State Fair Icon." *American Saddlebred Daily*, August 26, 2010. https://www.yumpu.com/en/document/read/26970218/saddlebred-american -saddlebred-horse-association.

Renau, Lynn. "Horse Shows and Competitions." In *The Encyclopedia of Louisville*, edited by John L. Kleber, 400–401. Lexington, KY: University Press of Kentucky, 2001.

Saddle and Bridle, September 1983.

11. Rubble and Smoke

American Saddlebred Horse and Breeders Association. *CH Northern Aire Pedigree*. Lexington, KY: American Saddlebred Horse and Breeders Association Registry Records, 1973.

Around the Arena: Horse Show Nostalgia. "Ron and Paula Kirsh [. . .] Shown with Meg Scuffle." Facebook, October 18, 2020. https://www.facebook.com /SaddlebredMemoirs/photos/a.1533174526967555/2770950299856632/? type=3.

"A to Z Horse Show." *Arizona Republic* (Phoenix), February 16, 1984.

"A to Z Horse Show." *Arizona Republic* (Phoenix), February 20, 1984.

"Cause of Barn Fire Uncertain." *Advocate-Messenger* (Danville, KY), January 23, 1984.

Cushing, Rick. "Even in the Amateur Division, Dutel's Imperator Is All Pro." *Louisville Courier-Journal*, August 15, 1984.

Edwards, Brenda S. "294 Sheep Destroyed in Barn Fire." *Advocate-Messenger* (Danville, KY), January 27, 1984.

"Fire Kills 15 Horses." *Messenger-Inquirer* (Owensboro, KY), January 21, 1984.

"1984 WCHS—Class 43 Amateur Five Gaited Stallion-Gelding—Imperator and William Dutel, Up." Richfield Video Archive, 1984. https://richfieldvideo archive.vhx.tv/videos/1984-wchs-class-43-amateur-five-gaited-stallion-gelding -imperator-and-william-dutel-up.

"1984 WCHS—Class 116 Amateur Five gaited Championship—Scan." Richfield Video Archive, 1984. https://richfieldvideoarchive.vhx.tv/videos/1984-wchs-class -116-amateur-five-gaited-championship-scan.

"1984 World's Championship Horse Show—Stake Night." Richfield Video Archive, 1984. https://richfieldvideoarchive.vhx.tv/videos/1984-world-s-championship -horse-show-stake-night.

Rees, Jennie. "Sky Watch Hooves Blaze Trail back from Tragic Fire." *Louisville Courier-Journal*, August 12, 1984.

———. "Sky Watch Steps Out to Win Third Crown in Five-Gaited Class." *Louisville Courier-Journal*, August 19, 1984.

Saddle and Bridle, September 1984.

Vaught, Bill. "Clark, Sky Watch Ready to Try for Third Title." *Advocate-Messenger* (Danville, KY), August 12, 1984.

Vaught, Larry. "Clark Feels Lucky World Champion Saddle Horse Survived Barn Fire." *The Advocate-Messenger* (Danville, KY), January 24, 1984.

———. "Clark, Sky Watch Win Title Again." *Advocate-Messenger* (Danville, KY), August 20, 1984.

———. "Rebuilding Not Easy but Clark Optimistic." *Advocate-Messenger* (Danville, KY), July 27, 1984.

12. Horse Show Baby

American Saddlebred Horse and Breeders Association. *CH Sultan's Shamrock Pedigree.* Lexington, KY: American Saddlebred Horse and Breeders Association Registry Records, 1982.

Clark, Mitchell. Interview by Bill Keith. Facebook Live. Stayner, Ontario, February 27, 2021.

———. Personal interview by Emma Hudelson. Danville, KY, February 15, 2022.

Ello, Chris. "Horse Showing Is Garden of Delight." *Los Angeles Times*, June 22, 1985.

Saddle and Bridle, July 1985.

Saddle and Bridle, September 1985.

Vaught, Bill. "First Time Charm for Clark." *Advocate-Messenger* (Danville, KY), July 26, 1985.

Vaught, Larry. "Injury Costs Clark, Sky Watch Chance to Win Fourth Title." *Advocate-Messenger* (Danville, KY), August 26, 1985.

———. "Sky Watch, Imperator Will Meet Again." *Advocate-Messenger* (Danville, KY), July 26, 1985.

13. Just the One

"Central Reinstates Lovely as Coach; World Champion Sky Watch Retired." *Louisville Courier-Journal*, January 10, 1986.

Clark, Mitchell. Personal interview by Emma Hudelson. Danville, KY, February 15, 2022.

Koerner, Dave. "Imperator Is 'Sitting on Ready,' but Will Sky Watch Show Up?" *Louisville Courier-Journal*, August 21, 1988.

———. "Sky Watch Wows Crowd in His Return." *Louisville Courier-Journal*, August 23, 1988.

Macfarlane, Michele. Email interview by Emma Hudelson. Indianapolis, May 13, 2020.

"1988 WCHS—Class 157 Five Gaited Grand Championship." Richfield Video Archive, 1988. https://richfieldvideoarchive.vhx.tv/videos/1988-world-s-five-gaited-grand-championship.

"1988 WGC Five-Gaited Championship Part 1." Richfield Video Archive, 1988. https://richfieldvideoarchive.vhx.tv/videos/1988-wgc-five-gaited-champ-part-1.

"1988 WGC Five-Gaited Championship Part 2." Richfield Video Archive, 1988. https://richfieldvideoarchive.vhx.tv/videos/1988-wgc-five-gaited-champ-part-2.

"1988 World's Championship Horse Show Championship Night Highlights." Richfield Video Archive, 1988. https://richfieldvideoarchive.vhx.tv/videos/1988-world-s-championship-horse-show-championship-night-highlights.

"Rock Creek Results." *Louisville Courier-Journal*, June 10, 1986.

Saddle and Bridle, September 1986.

Saddle and Bridle, April 1987.

Saddle and Bridle, June 1987.

Saddle and Bridle, August 1987.

Saddle and Bridle, October 1987.

Saddle and Bridle, October 1988.

14. Let the Horse Lead the Way

Clark, Mitchell. Personal interview by Emma Hudelson. Danville, KY, February 15, 2022.

"Hall of Champions." Kentucky Horse Park, Lexington, KY, February 2019.

Index

Horses in History

Series Editor: James C. Nicholson

For thousands of years, humans have utilized horses for transportation, recreation, war, agriculture, and sport. Arguably, no animal has had a greater influence on human history. Horses in History explores this special human-equine relationship, encompassing a broad range of topics, from ancient Chinese polo to modern Thoroughbred racing. From biographies of influential equestrians to studies of horses in literature, television, and film, this series profiles racehorses, warhorses, sport horses, and plow horses in novel and compelling ways.

About the Author

Emma Hudelson is a nonfiction writer from Indiana. *Sky Watch: Chasing an American Saddlebred Story* is her debut book. Her work appears in the *Cincinnati Review*, the *Chattahoochee Review*, the *Rumpus*, and *Saddle and Bridle*. Emma teaches writing in Indianapolis, where she lives with her husband and daughter. She is a graduate of the University of Cincinnati's PhD program in creative writing. She is always planning her next horse show.

www.ingramcontent.com/pod-product-compliance
Lightning Source LLC
Chambersburg PA
CBHW031537260326
41914CB00032B/1840/J